A

Hunawihr, with its fortified church, nestling among the vines at the foot of the Vosges

ALSACE

The Complete Guide

Vivienne Menkes-Ivry

photographs by Christophe Meyer

SIMON & SCHUSTER

LONDON·SYDNEY·NEW YORK·TOKYO·SINGAPORE·TORONTO

By the same author
Buying a House in France (Simon & Schuster 1990)
Paris (Christopher Helm 1991)

Although great care was taken in the preparation of this book, it is impossible, in an era of rapid change, to ensure that the information given in it remains accurate and up to date. The author and publishers cannot accept responsibility for inaccuracies, but they welcome suggestions from readers for amendments.

The author and publishers wish to thank
the Comité régional de tourisme Alsace
for their support.

Cover photograph of Niedermorschwihr by Christophe Meyer

First published in Great Britain by
Simon & Schuster Ltd in 1991
A Paramount Communications Company

Copyright © Vivienne Menkes-Ivry

This book is copyright under the Berne Convention.
No reproduction without permission.
All rights reserved. The author has asserted her moral rights.

Simon & Schuster Ltd
West Garden Place
Kendal Street
London W2 2AQ

Simon & Schuster of Australia Pty Ltd
Sydney

A CIP catalogue record for this book is
available from the British Library
ISBN 0-671-65312-1

Typeset in 9/11 Galliard by Ace Filmsetting Ltd, Frome

Printed and bound in Great Britain by
Butler & Tanner Ltd, Frome

Contents

Acknowledgements	*page*	vii
Introduction		1
Practical information		17
Access		17
Travelling in Alsace		17
Climate and seasons		21
Information sources		22
Hotels		23
Restaurants		23
Opening times		28
Museums and places of interest		29
Other cultural facilities		30
Sports and leisure activities		30
1 A little history		34
2 Alsace cuisine		51
3 Alsace wines *by Charlotte Fleming*		67
4 In and around Strasbourg		72
5 In and around the Northern Vosges		92
6 On and around the Wine Road		110
7 On and around the Mountain road		138
8 In and around Mulhouse and the Sundgau		150
9 Days out from Alsace		164
Hotels and restaurants		177
Index		198

To my mother, for her constant interest and support

Acknowledgements

Of the many people who helped me in the preparation of this book, my biggest debt of gratitude must go to Gilbert Hadey, a tireless promoter of Strasbourg and Alsace, who encouraged me to write it in the first place and provided assistance and support throughout. Jean Klinkert and Bernadette Elchinger of the Association départementale du Tourisme du Haut-Rhin were most generous with their time and, again, provided both assistance and encouragement. Without the three of them, this book could never have been written.

Many thanks too to Pamela Swinglehurst, an excellent companion on a strenuous fact-finding trip; to Claudine Lecq-Löliger, director of the tourist office in Mulhouse; to Cathy Spielmann at the Palais des Congrès in Strasbourg; to Renaud Jautzy and Christian Fleith of the Office départemental du Tourisme du Bas-Rhin; to Jacqueline Rau, Marie-Christine Périllon and Pierre Ianarelli in Strasbourg; to Martine Becker of J. Becker in Zellenberg and David Ling of Hugel & Fils in Riquewihr; to Thierry Messer at the tourist office and Claude Schwoerer-Rentz at the Grand Hôtel in Niederbronn-les-Bains; to Aimée Pensa of the Parc naturel régional des Vosges du Nord; to M. Schiler at the tourist office in La Petite-Pierre; to Dan Weinryd and his wife at the Val Saint-Grégoire in Munster; to M. and Mme Florence in Orbey; to Peter Saur in Baden-Baden, Joëlle Kieffer in Metz and Christiane Drouin in Nancy; to the Litzler family at the Auberge Paysanne in Lutter; and – for typifying the kindness and helpfulness I met everywhere in Alsace – to the postmistress in Ferrette.

Vivienne Menkes-Ivry is a British journalist and travel writer who lived in France for many years. She has been French area editor for Fodor's Guides and has recently published a book on Paris and another on buying property in France. She writes for a number of British, French and American magazines.

Charlotte Fleming started her wine career with Oddbins and now runs her own retail business in Cambridgeshire. She was a recent runner-up in the Pol Roger/Decanter Magazine Young Wine Merchant of the Year Awards.

Christophe Meyer lives in Niedermorschwihr in Alsace and has contributed to many publications on the region.

How to use this book

The **Practical information** section, following the **general introduction**, covers access and transport, climate, information sources, general tips on hotels and restaurants, opening times, cultural, sports and leisure opportunities. Chapters 1-3 introduce you to Alsace's **history**, **cuisine** and **wines**. The **regional chapters** (4-8) each end with a **key data** section consisting of information on access and itineraries, followed by an alphabetical list of main centres with their postcode; address and telephone number of tourist office (TO) if they have one – often the *mairie* (town hall); distance from main town(s) and, where relevant, a local centre; public transport; and main sights, with opening days/periods. **Days out from Alsace** suggests five excursions, with brief notes on restaurants. **Hotels and restaurants** in Alsace are grouped together at the end of the book for easy reference, in a single alphabetical list of towns and villages, with closing days/periods where relevant (though these should always be double-checked locally).

Introduction

'*Alsace – France's best-kept secret.*' So ran the slogan for a recent publicity campaign. It was an astute one, or perhaps a resigned one. The local tourist authorities have grown used to the idea that in spite of its many attractions, their region – admittedly the smallest in France, but probably the most varied – is surprisingly little known to the country's foreign visitors. Even the *Français de l'Intérieur*, as the people of Alsace refer to their compatriots beyond the Vosges, are often unaware that it is part of France. When exchange controls were introduced some time ago, Alsace's *viticulteurs* were amazed to receive letters from their clients elsewhere in the country regretting that they would have to stop buying their wine in Alsace, as their foreign currency allowance would not run to it.

I have an interesting little book called *A Wayfarer in Alsace* by B. S. Townroe, published in 1926. In his introduction the Earl of Derby, a former British ambassador to France, comments: 'Many Englishmen travel through Strasbourg and Colmar on their way to Switzerland in complete ignorance of the treasures of history, architecture and landscape that they are missing.' Well over half a century later, little has changed. The delights of the region are still unknown to the great majority of English-speaking holiday makers who pour into France in their hundreds of thousands every year.

Hence this book. Although one part of me rather likes the idea of keeping the secret to myself, my enthusiasm for both the place and its people prompts me to be unselfish. I feel so strongly that Alsace does not deserve this neglect that I want to do my bit to reveal the treasures H.M. Ambassador referred to all those years ago – and add quite a few more too. The superb cuisine, for a start, is worth the detour all by itself. And so are the delectable Alsace wines, now starting to become very popular in both Britain and the United States. They may even be the key to breaking down the mysterious resistance of the English-speaking world to a region that has so much to offer.

Another key may be improved communications. Not only do many people think Strasbourg is in Germany – they persist in thinking of it as far away and inaccessible. Yet Alsace is much nearer Britain than the Dordogne, to which intrepid travellers trek in droves. With the new motorway from Calais it takes only about six hours to drive from the Channel Coast to Alsace. A direct train from Calais to

Strasbourg takes about the same time. There are now frequent direct flights from London, as well as to the airport that Mulhouse shares with Basel in Switzerland. Strasbourg now has a direct link with New York too, as Mulhouse/Basel has long had. And anyone connecting via Paris can reach Alsace rapidly by plane, motorway or train.

As it is such a small region – only about 200 kilometres/125 miles from north to south and 50 kilometres/31 miles wide – getting about is easy, whether or not you have a car. So it is well-suited to short breaks as well as more leisurely holidays, perhaps combined with a brief trip across the border into Germany or Switzerland. And although the pretty villages on the Wine Road are liable to be crowded during the summer and autumn tourist seasons, the rest of the region is pleasantly peaceful, its character and traditions still intact.

A region with a difference

Character and traditions play an important part in Alsace's appeal. You soon become aware that it has a distinct personality, reflected in its people, its buildings, its customs and many local festivals. It somehow feels different. It is like nowhere else, in France or any other country – a rare attribute in the late twentieth century. And the character of the people, tempered by the tribulations of a particularly tragic history, is such that creeping conformity seems the least likely fate to overtake this narrow strip of land squeezed between the Vosges Mountains and the River Rhine, right in the heart of Europe.

Yet a region with a strong personality is in some ways at a disadvantage. Only too frequently it will become trapped in a series of stereotypes. To the French living beyond the Vosges, the picture of Alsace is made up of clichés: quaint half-timbered houses festooned with geraniums and topped by storks' nests; little girls dressed in embroidered skirts and aprons, with outsize black bows perched on the back of their heads; sturdy peasants tucking into huge mounds of *choucroute*. It certainly has all of these, but it has so much more to offer too – major museums, fine Romanesque and Gothic churches, ancient castles, a rich cultural life, a beautiful and varied landscape, and a wealth of sports opportunities. And those who can see beyond the folksy, picture-postcard prettiness displayed in the tourist brochures discover a hard-working region whose prosperity is based not only on agriculture but also on industry and commerce.

Another cliché sees Alsace – its language, its people, its cuisine – as a hybrid, a mixture of French and German. The region's many German visitors, on the other hand, often insist on thinking that it is really German, with nothing French in its make-up.

The truth is that Alsace is Alsace. It may have elements of both French and German, but essentially it is a region apart, with a distinct culture of its own, and should be enjoyed as such.

Fountains and wells festooned with geraniums are a common sight in Alsace; this one is in Eguisheim on the Wine Road

Winstubs and caveaux

Winstubs, cheerful and convivial places where you can eat and drink to your heart's content without spending a fortune, play an important part in the life of the Strasbourgeois, and to a lesser extent of all the people of Alsace. They sometimes seem like a cross between an English pub and a German *Bierkeller*, but the food is better than in either, and they have a definite atmosphere of their own, one that should be savoured by anyone wanting to get to know the region and its people.

Typically found in narrow side streets, with heavy oak doors, thick bottle glass in the windows and cottagey curtains, they still operate on the *Stammtisch* principle – you don't eat at individual tables but join a cheerful throng grouped round long tables on wooden benches worn smooth as glass by decades or even centuries of use. Even if you speak little French, let alone *alsacien*, you'll soon find yourself striking up a conversation as you rub shoulders – literally – with locals and visitors, maybe even the odd Euro-MP making the most of the monthly sojourn in Strasbourg.

The menu virtually always features such classics as *presskopf* (see p.61 for a glossary of Alsace specialities), plus a selection of popular regional dishes. You will probably find *schiffala* with potato salad, *salade de cervelas*, *spätzele* with a meat dish, perhaps *baeckeoffa* or *choucroute* (but you may have to order these in advance), followed by a generous portion of pungent munster cheese and an open fruit tart, or perhaps a *kougelhopf glacé*. Follow the locals by ordering wine in a *pichet* (jug or pitcher, in various sizes) rather than a bottle, and once you've reached the end of your meal, settle down companionably with a little glass of one of the region's delectable *alcools blancs* distilled from local fruit ripened in the sun.

In the southern half of Alsace the 'n' disappears and the name becomes *wistub*. But more common in the Haut-Rhin is a slightly different institution, the *caveau* or wine cellar (not necessarily below ground level). *Caveaux* are particularly lively in the villages and small towns on the Wine Road (chapter 6). Here the menu may be more varied, with dishes like kidneys cooked in vinegar (*sueri nierli*) with *spätzele*, and individual tables are more common, but the convivial atmosphere is similar.

Introduction

Kaysersberg on the Wine Road is particularly rich in half-timbered houses

Landscapes – the Sun King's 'lovely garden'

After crossing into Alsace via a mountain pass near Saverne, Louis XIV famously caught his breath in wonder at the riches laid out before him and exclaimed ecstatically: *'Quel beau jardin!'*, 'What a lovely garden!' Byron was equally enthusiastic, referring to 'a blending of beauties'. These beauties range from the thickly forested western Vosges, quite high in places, but with gradients gentle enough for easy walking, to the sunny vineyards at their foot, and the lush meadows in the south near the Swiss border. And as Alsace is so small, these very different landscapes can all be enjoyed within a single day.

Since the French Revolution the region has been officially divided into two *départements*, called **Bas-Rhin** and **Haut-Rhin**. Like most people, you will probably find it confusing that Bas-Rhin, with Strasbourg as its main town, covers the northern half, and is therefore at the top when you study the map, while Haut-Rhin, administered from Colmar, is at the bottom.

On the western border, the tall **western Vosges** running parallel with the Rhine have grass-covered rounded tops above the tree line, known in French as *ballons*, with high pastures grazed by the cattle whose milk produces the region's pungent munster cheese. From a distance the blueish-green of the pine forests, interspersed with beech and oak, and the gently undulating silhouette create an impression familiar to French schoolchildren as the *ligne bleue des Vosges*. The **Route des Crêtes**, built along the ridge of the

The undulating silhouette of the western Vosges, clothed with pine forests, creates the famous 'ligne bleue des Vosges'

mountains for strategic purposes, is now a spectacular tourist route, affording magnificent views over deep mountain lakes and forests, and used in the depths of winter as a cross-country skiing trail. The mountains are cleft by long valleys, the widest the **Vallée de Munster**, where most of the eponymous cheese is made nowadays, rather than in the low stone farmhouses on the high pastures. In these valleys too, tucked out of sight of ramblers and skiers, are prosperous industries.

As the mountains descend rapidly to the **plaine d'Alsace**, the fertile central plain, their lower slopes are clothed with the sun-drenched vineyards that have produced deliciously fruity wines since the Roman era. The **Route du Vin** or **Wine Road**, Alsace's most popular tourist route, threads its way among the vineyards, meandering from one picturesque village to another and offering opportunities for wine tasting and buying at every turn. Overlooking many of the villages, the ruined castles of feudal counts and barons perch precariously on rocky spurs.

Ruined castles are also a feature of the **Northern Vosges**, an area of game-rich forests in the north of Alsace. Built to protect the border with Germany, they now seem to blend in with the rocky crags of mountains that are lower than in the west, and of sandstone, rather than crystalline as in the higher Vosges peaks. Much of this area is now a nature park, the **Parc naturel régional des Vosges du Nord**.

The **central plain**, its soil enriched by a thick layer of loess, a yellow loam deposited by the winds of the Ice Age, is a chequerboard of neat fields, replete with fat white cabbages, hops, maize, beet, tobacco and, in the lush **Kochersberg** to the west of Strasbourg, known as 'Alsace's granary', wheat, rye and barley. In this long strip lie the main towns: Strasbourg, the lively capital of Alsace and the seat of several European institutions, with a major river port; Colmar, small and delightful, its centre a maze of narrow medieval streets; and Mulhouse, a busy industrial town famous for its museums.

To the east, the marshy territory right beside the Rhine, known as the **Ried**, is still the habitat of some rare plants and birds, though much of the wetlands has now been reclaimed by draining and planted with crops. The **Ried du Nord**, north of Strasbourg, separates the Rhine from **l'Outre-Forêt**, a gently hilly area famous for centuries for its pottery, with pretty, rather sedate villages between the **Forêt de Haguenau** (Haguenau Forest) and the north-eastern corner of Alsace.

On the other side, jutting out westwards into Lorraine, the area known as **l'Alsace bossue** seems to have been tacked on as an afterthought, its hilly landscape closely resembling that over the regional border.

The landscape is hilly, too, in the **Sundgau**, a peaceful area of orchards and meadows stretching south from Mulhouse to the Swiss border. Essentially a continuation of the Swiss Jura mountain range, with the same chalky soil and a harsh winter climate, it is a prosperous area of neat villages. Its meres and ponds are well stocked with fish, including the carp that have given rise to the **Routes de la Carpe frite** (Fried Carp Roads), another of the signposted itineraries dreamed up by the local tourist authorities.

Hansi

You can't go far in Colmar without seeing postcards and greetings cards adorned with charming scenes of children in Alsace costume, with heavy clogs and big black bonnets for the girls and pointed caps for the boys, the whole enclosed in a decorative border with flowers and birds. In one corner is the word HANSI. This was the pen name of Jean-Jacques Waltz, a writer and artist born in Colmar in 1873, two years after the annexation of Alsace-Lorraine. He was curator of the Unterlinden Museum but is remembered chiefly for his ardent patriotism and brilliant draughtsmanship, which combined to produce grotesque caricatures of German soldiers and officials.

'Uncle Hansi' never gave up his virulent opposition to the occupying forces. His *Mon village: images et commentaires par l'Oncle Hansi*, published in 1914 and containing delightful descriptions of village life and customs, illustrated with his own watercolours, included sly digs at the enemy which earned him a year's prison sentence. But he managed to escape and fought in the French army. Even an apparently innocuous poster for the railways of Alsace and Lorraine, painted in 1921 and complete with stork and a crocodile of children in Alsace costume led by a nun, depicts in the background a restaurant called 'Au Rendez-vous des Patriotes'. Fortunately he lived to see 'the Tricolour Paradise', the title of a book he published in 1918, returned to France after the Second World War. He died in 1951.

You may be able to find a reprint of one of Hansi's books in the bookshops near the cathedral in Strasbourg or in Colmar specializing in *Alsatiques* (books about Alsace, with particular reference to its customs, costumes and popular art).

East of Mulhouse, the **Forêt domaniale de la Harth**, a broad strip of forest peopled with deer and wild boar, reaches almost to the Rhine. As for the Rhine itself, long a busy commercial waterway that has played a key part in Alsace's history, bringing prosperity through trade, but also exciting jealousy from covetous neighbours, it impinges little on your consciousness as you visit Alsace, except when you gaze down from the heights of the Vosges at the plain stretching across the river to the Black Forest.

★

People – an attachment to tradition

The people of Alsace, the saying goes, are first and foremost 100 per cent *alsacien*. But they are also 100 per cent Germanic or Teutonic (as opposed to German). And, nowadays, 100 per cent European too. On top of all that, runs the punchline, they are 150 per cent French.

A mass of contradictions, you might think. Yet once you have understood their troubled history, the way they were caught up for centuries in the never-ending tug of war between France and Germany, it all starts to make sense. Patriotically French after their harsh experiences under German annexation from 1871 to 1918 and again during the Second World War, they are eager to prove their allegiance to their compatriots in 'the Interior', who tend to see them as foreign. Yet in many ways they are a Teutonic people. Their dialect and customs are Germanic, and so are many of their characteristics. Their spick-and-span houses and villages, for instance, are in marked contrast to other areas of rural France.

Yet they also have a strong streak of the Latin in their make-up. They can be exuberant, even excitable. A late afternoon stroll in the Orangerie Gardens in Strasbourg will make you think of nothing so much as the daily *passegiata* in some Mediterranean town. And although they have a well-deserved reputation for hard work, they are far from dull, putting great zest into their obvious enjoyment of life. The atmosphere in an Alsace *winstub* is essentially joyous and convivial, though rarely as noisy and boisterous as a German *Bierkeller* can be.

It is also hospitable. If you have ever thought the French unhelpful or unfriendly, you will be pleasantly surprised in Alsace. Everywhere you will meet kindness and friendliness. The vicissitudes of their history have made them commendably tolerant, and very willing to extend a helping hand to strangers. You will find hoteliers eager to offer advice on restaurants, local museums and beauty spots, waiters asking with unfeigned interest whether you are enjoying some recommended dish, fellow passengers on trains or buses ready to show you where to get off or to give you a lift to your final destination.

Mosquito Hovel Johnny

'*Hans im Schnockeloch*', or '*Jeannot-du-Nid-aux-Moustiques*' to the French, is the archetypal Alsace grumbler, never content with his lot. A kind of folk hero – or should it be anti-hero? – to the people of Alsace, he is based on a real person: a sixteenth-century farmer and inn-keeper in Schnockeloch ('Mosquito Hovel'), a mosquito-infested hamlet beside the river Ill just outside Strasbourg. This gentleman apparently managed to amass a huge fortune, but this didn't stop him perpetually grumbling. In a famous popular song about him written three hundred years later, he is said to have 'all he could ever want – yet he still doesn't have what he wants, and doesn't want what he has'.

Perhaps it was the mosquitoes that soured Hans's life. At the end of the eighteenth century, Goethe was a student in Strasbourg (see p. 101) and reported that he had to wear two pairs of stockings to protect his legs from mosquito bites! And he shocked the pastor of nearby Sessenheim, whose daughter Friederike he was in love with, by remarking that the existence of mosquitoes caused him to have grave doubts about God's essential wisdom and goodness.

Fermes-auberges

An experience not to be missed in Alsace is a meal in one of the working dairy farms in the Vosges serving local dishes to hungry hikers and less energetic motorized tourists, as well as local families on Sundays and in the school holidays. The Munster Valley and the Western Vosges are a particularly happy hunting ground for these inexpensive and friendly 'farm-inns' where you can enjoy a taste of Alsace life along with rustic dishes, open tarts made with berries growing wild in the mountains and pungent munster cheese made on the premises.

The local name for these farms is *marcairerie*, which comes from *marcaire*, milker, and some of them serve a special *repas marcaire* (see p. 140). You may be able to visit the spotlessly clean outbuildings where the cheese is made and see the round cheeses in their traditional wooden tubs and the copper cauldrons full of the rich milk given by cows grazing all day on the sweet-smelling mountain pastures. Then you can choose a soft and creamy cheese, a *munster frais*, or a firmer, more mature one, depending on your taste, as the basis of tomorrow's picnic lunch.

These farm-inns are usually open only for three or four months in the summer, but some also offer modest rooms. After a long day's hiking you settle convivially round the table with your fellow guests, perhaps join in some cheerful singing when someone gets out an accordion, then sleep soundly to be woken by the sound of cow bells as the farmer drives the cows in for milking.

Many of the farms in the Upper Vosges have been officially approved by the **Association des Fermes-Auberges du Haut-Rhin**. This entitles them to display a sign depicting a trestle table set with two places and a steaming tureen of soup, with a hen pecking at the ground beneath it. Members of the association guarantee to serve traditional local dishes and promise a friendly welcome. They publish a *Fermes-auberges* booklet listing over sixty farm-inns, with full details (in French only) of how to get to them, the type of meals served, walks in the area, angling in mountain streams where relevant, camp-sites and leisure activities near by, plus a map pinpointing all of them. Ask for it at tourist offices (it is called simply *Fermes-auberges*), or write to the Association des Fermes-Auberges du Haut-Rhin et des départements limitrophes, BP 371, 68007 Colmar.

Do make sure to book. The farms are small, and most are remote, so you don't want to drive miles only to find that all the benches round the long tables are already taken. Like most restaurants in Alsace they have a 'rest day' (listed in the booklet).

This helpfulness stems partly from a strong attachment to their region, whose delights they want you to share. And that attachment in turn is rooted in a deep-seated respect for its traditions and customs. Most of the fairs and festivals, parades and processions that take place all over Alsace virtually all year round are genuinely popular events, not artificial 'folklore' laid on for tourists. Many of them are religious celebrations, for the people of Alsace, whether Catholic, Protestant or Jewish, are deeply religious. Theirs is the only region in France where there has never been a separation between Church and State – priests, pastors and rabbis receive a salary from the State, and the local authority is responsible for the upkeep of churches and synagogues.

The survival of the traditional half-timbered house is another example of respect for tradition. Everywhere you go in Alsace, with the exception of the high mountain pastures, you will see in both towns and villages houses built on a frame of neatly interlocking timbers, with an infill made of baked clay softened with water and mixed with animal hairs and straw, plastered on to a lattice of thin branches. Traditional motifs are carved into the thick black timbers or painted on the wattle-and-daub walls, partly as decoration, partly to bring luck or ward off evil spirits. Diamond shapes, representing female sexual organs, are a symbol of fertility; a St Andrew's cross, resembling a pin man with arms and legs extended, symbolizes male strength; a curving X, also described as a curule chair, is said to be a stylized representation of sexual intercourse, two interlaced bodies indicating the life force, guaranteeing the survival of the species. The walls are dyed in pale pastel colours or, more often, bright blues or apricots or brick reds, varying from one village or region to another, sometimes a pointer to religious faith – Catholics traditionally favoured the blue of the Virgin's robe in many parts of Alsace, but in the Sundgau were likely to use red or a pinkish beige.

Many of these houses date from a fifty-year span at the end of the seventeenth century and the beginning of the eighteenth, when towns and villages had to be rebuilt after the ravages of the Thirty Years' War. But they were based on the medieval design, originating with the feudal system of peasants needing to be able to dismantle their homes if they were forced to leave their lord's land. (You can see examples of traditional half-timbered houses grouped together in the Eco-Museum near Mulhouse, see box, p. 158.) And a fair number of the houses are much more recent – dating from the nineteenth century, or even from just a few years ago. For the traditional design is still popular in Alsace, and after a period when it looked as though many a district of old houses might be torn down and replaced by modern dwellings, conservation is now the order of the day. Districts like the Quartier des Tanneurs in Colmar have been restored and new houses on the outskirts of towns and villages often copy the old buildings in the centre.

Another characteristic of Alsace that reflects both the region's history and the character of its people: you never seem to find farmhouses or cottages all alone in the middle of a field, as you do, say, in Normandy. Even in an area of large farms like the Kochersberg, they will be grouped companionably together to form a village. The need to band together as a defence against invaders is clearly one reason – many such villages once had protective walls round them. A taste for the conviviality of village life is another.

Wrought-iron inn and shop signs are an attractive feature of towns and villages throughout Alsace. Here again, the tradition has been preserved. In Colmar, alongside medieval signs, you can see a modern sign almost opposite the Koifhus depicting a rabbit holding a lightbulb, outside an electrical suppliers. Nearby a couple of rotund chefs in white aprons and tall hats hold aloft a boar's

---

Folk art and rural crafts

Popular art through the centuries from all over the region is on show in the **Musée Alsacien** in **Strasbourg**, appropriately housed in three half-timbered buildings very typical of early seventeenth-century architecture in the region. **Haguenau**, too, has its **Musée Alsacien** and the **Musée d'Unterlinden** in **Colmar** and the **Musée Historique** in **Mulhouse** have some rooms devoted to local crafts and traditions. In the Sundgau you can visit the **Musée Sundgauvien** in **Altkirch** and the little **Musée Paysan** in **Oltingue**. In northern Alsace try to get to the **Musée de l'Imagerie peinte et populaire alsacienne** in **Pfaffenhofen**, which has some good examples of painting on glass and carefully decorated *Göttelbriefe* (Christening or confirmation cards in the form of letters wishing the child long life and happiness). Replicas of traditional Christmas biscuits and the moulds for making them are the speciality of the **Musée des Arts et Traditions populaires** in **La Petite-Pierre**, and the little **Maison du Village d'Offwiller** gives a good picture of rural life and crafts. Just outside Alsace, but still in the Northern Vosges Nature Park, you can see traditional clog making at the **Musée du Sabot** in **Soucht**. And in the very interesting **Ecomusée de Haute Alsace** near **Ungersheim** (p. 158), with its fifty odd reconstructed houses, you can often see traditional village crafts being practised by local craftsmen.

If you feel like buying some local craft work to take home, you can find well-designed pieces, many of them bearing the label '*Souvenir de France Alsace authentique*' to show they have been approved by the local authorities, at **La Belle Alsace**, 3 rue des Serruriers in Colmar, and at boutiques and gift shops in a number of villages, especially on the Wine Road.

The best-known pottery workshops are in the villages of **Betschdorf** and **Soufflenheim**, where distinctive tableware has been made for hundreds of years. Also distinctive are the fabrics in traditional Paisley patterns sold in boutiques near the cathedral in Strasbourg and in Ribeauvillé: just outside the village you can buy good-value seconds at the **Manufacture d'impression sur étoffes**.

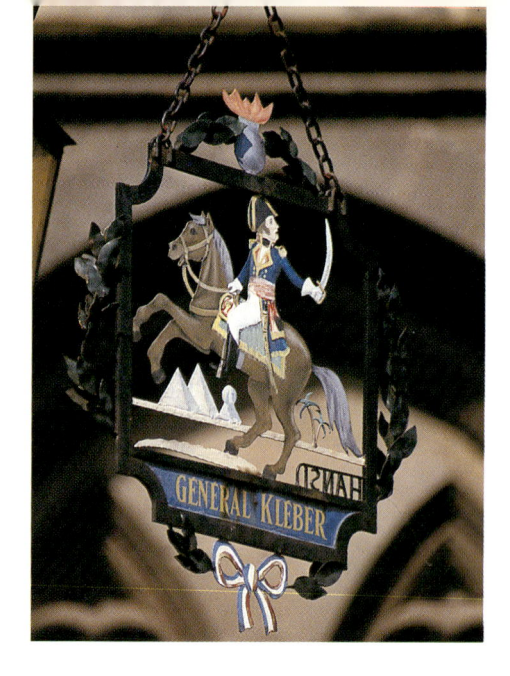

Picturesque signs swing outside many an inn or shop; this one in Colmar celebrates a Napoleonic general born in Strasbourg

head on a platter, to advertise a *charcuterie*. Near the cathedral in Strasbourg, a tailor's is signposted by modern scissors and thimble.

Traditional regional dress, including the *schlupfkapp* – the bat-like headdress worn by women and girls – is still brought out for local festivities, though it has virtually died out for everyday wear. You can see examples in the region's folk art museums (see box, p. 13).

The attachment to tradition that is so strong in Alsace is not a symptom of a nostalgic harking back to a golden age and a rejection of the present. Modern industries and the use of modern farming methods, together with an impressive record on per capita output and exports, illustrate the region's dynamism and adaptability to changing times. Think of it instead as the sign of a region that has managed to keep its character, to be patriotic but not nationalistic.

Language – an enduring dialect

It is easy to think at first that many of the people round you in Alsace, especially in the *winstubs* and in the countryside, are speaking German. The German tourists are of course. But what the local people are using among themselves as their everyday language is one of the Alsace dialects, variants of a High German dialect known to philologists as Alemannic. Technically the dialect spoken close to the Swiss border is called High Alemannic, while in most of the rest of the region the local language is Low Alemannic. To complicate the picture, a Frankish dialect, also spoken in the Rhineland, is used in pockets in the Northern Vosges. And in and around Orbey in the western Vosges the local people speak a Romance dialect called *welche* or *velche*. But the various dialect speakers have no trouble understanding one another and the dialects are commonly grouped together as *alsacien*. Until quite recently *alsacien* was often dismissed by the Français de l'Intérieur as a mere *patois* and the educated classes in Alsace were rather ashamed of it. But with the revival of regionalist sentiment throughout France, along with a widespread sense – not only in France – of the need to return to one's roots and preserve local traditions, the dialect is now thoroughly respectable. As a general rule older people and those living in the country are more likely to speak the dialect at home than younger people and those in towns. But as so often in France, lively young people with a thoroughly urban lifestyle are often only a generation or two away from a modest rural background, and many of the young sophisticates you see in the street, dressed with great French chic, will speak the dialect at home with their parents, and especially with their grandparents.

The dialect is essentially a spoken language, with no official written form. So the spelling of regional dishes varies from place to place. And the *winstub*, that apparently immovable Alsace institution, is so called in and around Strasbourg, but becomes a *wistub* when you travel to Colmar

Born in Strasbourg – a personal selection

- *c.* 1170 Gottfried von Strassburg, poet, author of the lyrical German version of the Tristan and Isolde legend
- 1458 Sebastian Brant, poet, satirist and Humanist
- 1484 Hans Baldung Grien, painter and engraver, probably a pupil of Dürer
- 1678 André Silbermann, organ builder
- 1740 Jean-Frédéric Oberlin, Protestant pastor, philanthropist
- 1753 Jean-Baptiste Kléber, general, assassinated by a Turkish fanatic
- 1833 Gustave Doré, painter and book illustrator
- 1888 Jean/Hans Arp, painter, sculptor and collage maker, co-founder of Dadaism
- 1923 Marcel Marceau, mime artist and creator of Bip
- 1931 Tomi Ungerer, artist, cartoonist and satirist

And born in Colmar

- *c.* 1450 Martin Schongauer, painter and engraver
- 1772 Jean, Comte de Rapp, Napoleonic general
- 1834 Frédéric Auguste Bartholdi, sculptor, creator of the Statue of Liberty
- 1873 Jean-Jaques Waltz ('Hansi'), artist, caricaturist, writer, satirist and patriot

and points south. In the Middle Ages the local language did have not only a written form but its own literature, produced by the great Alsace Humanists like Beatus Rhenanus (see box, p. 126), and the courtly poet Gottfried von Strassburg. But the spread of printing and the enormous influence of Luther's Bible, using a mainly Saxon dialect, paved the way for uniform 'High German' and spelled the end of any chance of Alemannic, or the similar dialects spoken in the neighbouring Rhineland and Switzerland, becoming languages in the true sense of the term.

The survival of this purely spoken means of communication may seem puzzling. But once again it is largely due to the sad fact that the people of Alsace have been forced to undergo so many changes. The first real linguistic pressure came during the French Revolution, when the need to weld the nation together meant that language acquired a new significance as a unifying factor and a deliberate attempt was made to wipe out dialects. This aggressive stance later softened. But French inexorably took over as the language of officialdom, and the one favoured by the upper classes, while ordinary people, especially in rural areas, continued to use the dialect.

Then came the Franco-Prussian War. The German victory and the annexation of Alsace meant that German became the official language. The end of the First World War brought about a new swing of the pendulum towards French – which was reversed in 1940 with the German occupation. Speaking French on the streets was an offence leading to imprisonment, education at all levels had to be conducted in German, names of roads and villages were Germanized. The dialect was frowned on too, dismissed as a 'bastard' version of pure German. Then the German defeat brought French back as the official language and the first language on the school curriculum.

Can you wonder that through all these changes a proud and independent people was determined to keep its dialect along with its traditions?

In recent years *alsacien* has assumed a new cultural importance, with plays and songs specially written to be performed in it. Educated people are usually trilingual – in French, the dialect and German. But so too are many elderly people from humble rural backgrounds. Educated to speak German before 1918, they had to learn French for the first time after the First World War, and since 1945 have had to use it for all their dealings with officialdom. But throughout their lives, they have spoken the dialect at home. They will probably read a German-language newspaper, while their children and grand-children read a French one.

Don't let this linguistic diversity alarm you. With their usual tolerance, the people of Alsace are kind and patient with foreigners and will do their best to help you make yourself understood. In the countryside especially, they will usually be delighted if you show an interest in the dialect – and make it clear that you appreciate that it is not merely German with a peculiar pronunciation, as too many of their visitors are inclined to do.

Practical information

Access

By air
Air France has direct flights from London-Heathrow and London-City to Strasbourg every day but Saturday. Swiss Air and British Airways fly daily from London-Heathrow to Mulhouse-Basel airport.

In 1990 Air France had flights from New York to Strasbourg, with a brief stop to collect passengers in Lyon. Passengers from the United States did not need to leave the plane during this stop.

There are frequent flights from Paris's Orly-Ouest and Roissy/Charles-de-Gaulle airports to Strasbourg and to Mulhouse-Basel, and less frequent ones to Colmar.

Transport from airports Regular bus service between Strasbourg-Entzheim airport and the city centre (15km/8 miles) and between Mulhouse-Basel airport and the rail station in Mulhouse (30km/19 miles); frequent trains from Mulhouse to Colmar and Strasbourg. Colmar's Houssen airport is only 5km from the town centre (taxis available).

By train
Trains from Calais (some involving a change in Metz) take 6-7 hrs to Strasbourg, 7½-8 hrs to Mulhouse. The fastest service from Paris (Gare de l'Est) to Strasbourg takes 3¾ hrs. You must change in Strasbourg for the frequent service to Colmar. Direct trains Paris-Est to Mulhouse via Belfort take 4-4½ hrs; overnight service available.

By car
The A26 motorway from Calais joins the A4 from Paris to Strasbourg at Reims. A good dual carriageway links Strasbourg with Sélestat, Colmar and Mulhouse.

Travelling in Alsace

Driving
Roads in Alsace are relatively uncrowded, with the exception of the main road from Strasbourg to Mulhouse, which can become congested, especially during the evening rush hour. You may be delayed by tourist coaches on the Wine Road, especially in July and August, and by tractors transporting grapes during the grape harvest in the autumn. The valleys leading into the Western Vosges and the Mountain Road may be affected by fog in the autumn. In the winter, when the Mountain Road may be closed, ice and snow can often cause

problems. Road surfaces are in general good throughout Alsace.

Car hire
The major international car hire companies have offices at Strasbourg and Mulhouse-Basel airports and in the towns of Strasbourg, Colmar and Mulhouse.

Public transport
The three main towns all have efficient **bus** networks, which cover both the town centre and the outskirts. Regular bus services connect Colmar with many of the wine villages, Strasbourg with the wine region and with centres in the Outre-Forêt and Northern Vosges, Mulhouse with villages in the Sundgau. Services generally depart either from the station or from the place des Halles in Strasbourg, and from the rail stations in Colmar and Mulhouse. Some of the buses from Colmar to the wine villages can be boarded from near the tourist office and the Musée d'Unterlinden.

Ask at tourist offices for the latest timetables and for the exact point of departure. There is an information kiosk in the place des Halles in Strasbourg, and timetables can be consulted at the various bus stops outside the rail stations in Colmar and Mulhouse. Services tend to be infrequent (or non-existent) on Sundays.

It takes a certain amount of patient effort to find out current times of services, as a number of different bus companies operate in the region. But buses are a good way of seeing something of the life of ordinary people, and on my many bus trips in Alsace I have always found both drivers and passengers very helpful and interested, always ready to tell you what is worth seeing.

You can also travel by **train** for some journeys inside Alsace. The main line linking Strasbourg with Basel makes visiting Colmar from Strasbourg or vice versa very easy: most trains take only half an hour. Strasbourg–Mulhouse takes about an hour, Colmar–Mulhouse about 25 mins. Sélestat is also on this line: 20 mins from Strasbourg, 10–15 mins from Colmar, about 40 mins from Mulhouse.

There is a frequent service from Strasbourg northwards to Haguenau, with some trains continuing to Wissembourg and others to Lauterbourg. Another line runs from Strasbourg to Sélestat via Molsheim, Rosheim, Obernai, Barr and Dambach-la-Ville. By carefully studying current timetables and, if necessary, walking or using a taxi for a few miles, you can visit several places in the same day and be back in Strasbourg for dinner.

Some trains on the Strasbourg–Basel line stop at attractive places like Ribeauvillé and Rouffach. But the station is a good half an hour's walk from Ribeauvillé, so you may like to ring for a taxi from the station (taxi numbers clearly marked on the wall opposite the station) or order a taxi to take you back to your train. It is also quite a long walk from the station to Rosheim, so you may again like to plan to take a taxi one way.

Train tickets in France can be bought in advance but must be date-stamped just before departure: push the ticket into the orange machines at the entrance to platforms. Fines are imposed on those who fail to comply with this regulation.

Maps

The Michelin 1cm:2km map no. 87 covers the whole of Alsace as well as the areas just over the Swiss and German borders and the Vosges beyond Alsace's western border. Large-scale walking maps published by the Club Vosgien can be bought locally. Good clear town plans of Colmar, Mulhouse and Strasbourg, with gazetteers, are published by Plans Guides Blay.

Signposted tourist routes

Alsace has an amazing number of marked tourist routes as well as the well-known Route du Vin (Wine Road) and Route des Crêtes (Mountain Road). You can, for instance, follow the Tobacco Road, the Fried Carp Roads, the Cheese Road, the Castles Road and so on. Tourist offices have leaflets with maps and descriptions of places of interest.

Coach excursions

The SNCF (French Rail) Excursions Service run a large number of whole- or half-day excursions within Alsace. Leaflets, entitled *'Circuits touristiques en Alsace'*, are available from the tourist office in front of the station in Strasbourg and at the information counters at Colmar and Mulhouse stations. You may also find them in tourist offices in towns and villages.

The programme includes the major tourist sights in Alsace. For instance an afternoon trip from Strasbourg takes in the lovely Romanesque church in Rosheim, Boersch, Mont Sainte-Odile convent and a brief visit to Obernai, and also enables you to catch glimpses of Le Hohwald, Barr, Ottrott and Klingenthal. Another meanders through the wine villages, with a wine tasting thrown in, and an opportunity for an hour and a half's walk through the vineyards. Whole-day excursions include Obernai, Sélestat, Haut-Koenigsbourg, Riquewihr and Ebersmunster; the Munster Valley, the Col de la Schlucht, lunch in Gérardmer on the other side of the Vosges, Sainte-Marie-aux-Mines and Ribeauvillé; the Route des Crêtes and the Grand Ballon; Colmar, Les Trois-Epis, the Lac Noir and the Lac Blanc, and Kaysersberg; the Ecomusée (open-air architecture and craft museum near Mulhouse).

Most hotels can take bookings for these excursions. You can also book them in advance at any rail station in France, and at the Maison de l'Alsace in Paris (see Information sources).

The tourist office in Colmar has an excursion programme in July and August only. A half-day trip goes to Riquewihr and Haut-Koenigsbourg Castle and full-day excursions are organized once a week to Strasbourg and the Mont Sainte Odile; Haut-Koenigsbourg, Obernai and the Mont Saint-Odile; Les Trois-Epis, the Lac Noir and Lac Blanc and on to Gérardmer. You can write in advance for the *'Excursions régulières'* leaflet to Office de Tourisme/Syndicat d'Initiative de Colmar, 4 rue des Unterlinden, 68000 Colmar. Bookings can be made at the tourist office.

The tourist office in Mulhouse can supply details of coach excursions run by private companies and it is always worth asking in tourist offices in the Wine Road villages for the names of local coach firms running excursions during the tourist season.

Christmas in Alsace

Unlike the rest of France, where New Year's Eve is the big time for celebrations with family and friends, with a day off to recover afterwards, in Alsace Christmas is the high point of the year for festivities, and it is the only region in France where Boxing Day (26 December, known as *la Saint-Etienne*, St Stephen's Day) is a public holiday. It is also significant that the custom of chopping down a fir tree in the forest and bringing it home to decorate is said to have started in Alsace.

From the Feast of St Nicholas (6 Dec) onwards, Strasbourg's Christmas Market (p. 85) draws huge crowds, streets and shops and private homes are beautifully decorated, and children start opening the windows in their Advent calendars as they count off the days to the Great Day itself. Serious baking gets under way in homes and restaurants, in bakers, confectioners and *pâtisseries*, as the traditional fare is prepared to mark the celebrations that punctuate the calendar at this time of year.

On St Nicholas's Day itself you traditionally eat biscuits in the shape of gingerbread men, with raisins for eyes, called *Maennele* (mannikins). Then throughout December come a good dozen varieties of little cakes and biscuits, called *bröedele* or *bredle*. These used to be hung on the Christmas tree with red ribbons but are now more often served together on Christmas Eve. Among them are *anisbredle* flavoured with aniseed, also known as *wihnachtsbredle* (Christmas biscuits) and *schwowebredle*, made with almonds.

Berewecke is traditionally eaten before leaving for Midnight Mass on Christmas Eve and again for breakfast on Christmas Day. It is a fruit loaf made with dried fruit – figs, raisins, prunes, dried pears and the quetsch plums that make such delicious tarts in Alsace – hazelnuts and almonds, sometimes walnuts too, and flavoured with cinnamon, cloves or aniseed, and liberal quantities of kirsch.

Attendance at Midnight Mass is virtually universal, but whereas elsewhere in France the big *réveillon* dinner on Christmas Eve is often enjoyed in a restaurant, in Alsace shops and restaurants shut early and the big Christmas meal, whether eaten on Christmas Eve or on Christmas Day itself (or both), is held at home, with the traditional crèche much in evidence. Also reminding guests of the true meaning of Christmas, on the sideboard there will be a yeast loaf called a *Christstolle* or *Chrischstolle* in the shape of the Infant Jesus wrapped in swaddling clothes. The meal may start with *foie gras* and is traditionally based on roast goose, with an apple or a chestnut stuffing, mixed with the chopped liver of the bird or with finely diced potato.

Alsace even has a museum devoted to Christmas fare – the Musée des Arts et Traditions populaires in La Petite-Pierre, whose subtitle is '*Les petits gâteaux de Noël en Alsace*' (Christmas biscuits baked in Alsace) (see p. 98).

Climate and seasons

Alsace has a basically continental climate, with cold winters and often very hot summers. It is sunny for much of the year and has relatively little rainfall, thanks to the natural barrier of the Vosges Mountains.

Spring is a good time to see the carpets of wild flowers in the mountains but can be quite cold and rainy. **Summer** storms are common and it can be unpleasantly sultry in the main towns and in all the lowland areas, but the little resorts in the Western and Northern Vosges are generally delightful. The **autumn** is usually an ideal time to visit Alsace, with plenty of sunshine but bearable temperatures, and all sorts of festivals and festivities connected with the grape harvest (see box, p. 24) **Winter** is usually pretty cold but sunny, with enough snow in the mountains for cross-country skiing and some downhill skiing. Lowland areas can be foggy.

Alsace is a popular summer holiday destination for French families and attracts West German visitors throughout the year for weekend breaks, especially during the autumn grape harvest. Strasbourg is a major conference venue, as well as housing the European Parliament, and its hotels can get very booked up at all times of year. The Northern Vosges and the Sundgau are both relatively uncrowded with tourists, though the forests in the north are particularly popular with ramblers and mushroom gatherers in the autumn.

Christmas is a particularly delightful time to visit Alsace, with Christmas markets, beautiful street decorations and a generally festive atmosphere.

Information sources

Alsace's two main tourist offices, to which you should write for advance information, are in Strasbourg and Colmar:

Alsace Tourisme
Office départemental du Tourisme du Bas-Rhin
9 rue du Dôme
BP 53
67061 Strasbourg cedex
tel: 88 22 01 02, fax: 88 75 67 64

Alsace Tourisme
Association départementale du Tourisme du Haut-Rhin
Hôtel du département
68006 Colmar cedex
tel: 89 23 21 11 or 89 22 68 00

In **Britain**, information about Alsace is available from the French Government Tourist Office:
178 Piccadilly
London W1V 0AL
tel: 071 493 65 94

In the **United States**:
French Government Tourist Office
610 Fifth Avenue
New York
NY 10020-2452
tel: 212 757 11 25

In **Australia**:
French Tourist Bureau
Kindersley House
33 Bligh Street
Sydney
NSW 2000
tel: 231 52 44

In **Paris** you can visit the Maison de l'Alsace at 39 av. des Champs-Elysées, 75008 Paris, which has a small boutique selling regional specialities (craft work and some food and drink), and enjoy a first taste of Alsace cuisine and wines in **L'Alsace**, a good restaurant next door, open day and night. Tourist offices for towns and villages are listed at the end of the various regional chapters.

Hotels

Alsace is well endowed with hotels, most of them unpretentious family-run *auberges* (inns) with friendly and helpful staff. Apart from the top hotels in Strasbourg, which are used mainly by business people or Euro-M.P.s and Eurocrats, the region has few luxury hotels. However the recent opening of the charming and very comfortable four-star **A la Cour d'Alsace** in Obernai on the Wine Road may be a pointer to a new style of hotel rather different from the traditional Alsace hotel with firmly regional décor and furnishings. And just south of Colmar the brand-new **Husseren-les-Châteaux** may represent another new trend, with its rooms on two floors and its resolutely modern design, plus pool and sauna. But on the whole you will be staying in well-run traditional hotels, both in the countryside and in towns.

Standards of cleanliness are very high in Alsace. Even in modest inns, bedrooms and bathrooms are virtually always spotless. And friendly personal service is the rule rather than the exception, even in Strasbourg's large hotels. In towns many hotels do not have a restaurant, though a few large ones will offer a limited room service menu, as well as a plentiful breakfast. Hotels in villages usually have their own restaurant. As in most parts of France, you may find it difficult to get a room for a single night if you are not prepared to eat in the hotel's dining room. This will not be a sacrifice, as many such hotels are in fact popular restaurants with rooms: often run as a restaurant by the same family for decades, if not centuries, with rooms added quite recently by a dynamic younger generation. Or it may be that a modest inn has recently opened a much more comfortable annexe, as in the case of the friendly **Auberge Paysanne** in Lutter in the Sundgau, which now boasts a superb annexe in a reconstructed house nearby.

In Strasbourg, rooms are hard to come by when the European Parliament is sitting. Check whether it is a *semaine parlementaire* before planning your trip there. Sittings take place roughly one week in four, but with variations depending on public holidays and other factors.

Outside Strasbourg, the villages on the Wine Road are busy throughout the summer and particularly popular again in September and October, when the grape harvest gets under way and many stage their own wine festivals. Colmar, too, is crowded at this time, as it is used as a base by tourists and by members of the wine trade. Book well in advance throughout the autumn, when the weather and the landscape are often at their loveliest, thus attracting weekend visitors from West Germany and other parts of France too. The Northern Vosges, though no less attractive than the Wine Road, are less inundated with groups travelling by coach, so it may be easier to find accommodation there at peak times. And the Sundgau does not attract many groups either, though Swiss families often keep hotels and restaurants busy at weekends.

Hotel staff usually speak German as well as French and the local dialect. But the people of Alsace have been forced by the vicissitudes of their history to be good linguists, and younger ones especially are increasingly likely to speak some English too. And if you are struggling with inadequate French you will find everyone very willing to make an effort to understand.

If you are planning to spend just one night in a hotel, try to avoid the day or days when its restaurant is closed. During the weekly closure observed by most restaurants in Alsace (see Restaurants, below) the hotel will most probably be shut in the afternoon and evening, though if you have booked for a longer stay there will be someone there to greet you. There will be none of the usual cosy atmosphere and all the guests will have disappeared to another restaurant. Even the pleasantest hotels can seem bleak in such circumstances.

Alternatives to hotels

Alsace offers a number of alternatives to staying in a hotel. Among them is the popular *gîte* formula of self-catering accommodation, generally in a rural building. Write to the following addresses for the official *Gîtes de France* booklets, which also list farms willing to take campers, camp sites, families taking in bed-and-breakfast guests for a night or two, and sometimes offering an evening meal as well, and special *gîtes d'enfants* where children can stay in the countryside during the school holidays.

Bas-Rhin (Northern Alsace)
Relais du Tourisme Rural du
 Bas-Rhin
7 pl. des Meuniers
67000 Strasbourg

Haut-Rhin (Southern Alsace)
Relais départemental des Gîtes
 Ruraux de France et du Haut-Rhin
B.P. 371
68007 Colmar cedex

A certain number of *gîtes* are set aside for the British market. Contact the French Government Tourist Office in London (see Information Sources).

Some local tourist offices keep a card index of families in the area offering bed-and-breakfast. And if you are having trouble finding b-&-b accommodation at a busy time (during the grape harvest along the Wine Road, for instance), it is always a good idea to ask in restaurants and *winstubs*. Many families are willing to take in guests on an informal basis for the odd night.

A speciality in Alsace is the *ferme-auberge* (farm-inn), a working farm offering meals based on regional recipes and, sometimes, modest accommodation (see box, p. 11).

Restaurants

Alsace cuisine, whose delights are described in a separate chapter, has a very high reputation both throughout France and further afield, and the region's restaurants have earned more Michelin rosettes than any other region of France – an impressive accolade. But don't take this to mean that eating out will invariably be expensive. You will find a good choice of

Fairs, festivals and festivities in Alsace

Mid-Lent: Carnivals are staged throughout Alsace, mainly for children; *Grand Marché de la Mi-Carême* in Rosheim
Passion Sunday: Passion Play (in German) at Masevaux (usually also on several other Sundays round this time)
mid-April: *Fête de l'Escargot* (Snail Festival) in Osenbach
1 May: *Foire aux Vins* (Wine Market) in Molsheim, *Fête du Muguet* (Lily-of-the-Valley Festival) in Neuf-Brisach
Ascension Day: annual fair in Orbey
late May: *Foire aux Foins* (Hay Fair) in Durmenach; *Foire aux Vins aux Dominicains* (Wine Fair) in Guebwiller
Whit Sunday and Monday: *Fête du Cochon* in Ungersheim; costume parade in Wissembourg
early June: *Fête du Vin* (Wine Fair) in Riquewihr; *Fête du Kougelhopf* (Kougelhopf Festival) in Ribeauvillé (see p. 60)
on and around 24 June: *Feux de la Saint-Jean* (bonfires and firework displays to celebrate the Feast of John the Baptist and Midsummer Day) throughout Alsace
30 June: *Crémation des Trois Sapins* (ceremonial burning of fir trees), Thann
late June/early July: *Nuit du Vin* (wine festival) in Dambach
early July: *Fête de l'Ami Fritz* in Hunawihr
13/14 July: fireworks, dancing in the street and other celebrations throughout Alsace
14 July: Foire aux Vins (wine fair) in Barr
mid-July: *Streisselhochzeit* (traditional Alsace wedding) in Seebach
late July: *Foire aux Vins* (wine fair) in Ribeauvillé; *Corso fleuri* (procession with garlanded floats) in Oberhaslach
early Aug: wine festivals in several villages on the Wine Road
2nd Sun in Aug: *Corso fleuri* (procession with garlanded floats) in Sélestat
15 Aug: *Le Mariage de l'Ami Fritz* in Marlenheim
late Aug: *Fête du Houblon* (Hop Festival) in Haguenau; *Fête du Tabac* (Tobacco Festival) in Benfeld; *Pfiffertag* (Minstrels' Festival) in Bischwiller; *Grand Corso fleuri* (procession with floats) in Wasselonne; *Journée de la Choucroute* in Colmar
late Aug/early Sept: *Pfifferdai* (Festival of Strolling Players, see box, p. 127) in Ribeauvillé
early Sept: *Fête de la Choucroute* (*Choucroute* Festival) in Geispolsheim; *Fête de la Nativité* in Rosheim
late Sept: *Fête de la Tourte* (Meat Pie Festival) in Munster
October: Traditional grape harvest celebrations along the Wine Road
on and around 6 Dec: *Fête de la Saint-Nicolas* in various places in Alsace
from about 6 to 24 December: *Christkindelmärik* (Christmas Market) in Strasbourg and in Kaysersberg (see box p. 85)

places to eat, including the lively and inexpensive **winstubs** and **caveaux** that are peculiar to Alsace (see box, p. 4), and Alsace's answer to the pizza parlour – restaurants specializing in *flammekueche* or *tarte flambée* (see recipe, p. 65). Even the top gourmet restaurants are reckoned to be among the best value in France in their élite category.

Oddly the **brasserie**, once an Alsace institution, is easier to find in Paris these days, or in a big city like Lyon, than it is in its birthplace. Originally a room in a brewery – *brasserie* is the French word for brewery – where clients were served filling homely dishes to keep their strength up (and keep them sober) while they tasted the beer, it expanded to become a full-scale restaurant, open long hours and specializing in a small repertoire of dishes, accompanied by beer or local wines. A few restaurants in Strasbourg have kept up the *brasserie* tradition. But the once-typical arrangement of cosy little nooks and alcoves surrounded by wooden panelling has often been superseded by a more spacious layout, as in the lively **Au Romain** in Strasbourg (see Restaurant list).

This is a prosperous part of France and the people of Alsace, great enjoyers of food, are not prone to economize in that area. So your first impression may be that there is a shortage of the modest little bistrots and cafés you have come across elsewhere in France. But their place is taken by the *winstubs* and *caveaux* you will soon start spotting in both towns and villages. You will find, however, that many villages off the beaten tourist track, especially in the Sundgau, have nowhere to eat, or even to have a coffee, at all. So you will have to plan ahead in the more remote areas. Or organize picnics at lunchtime: there is certainly no shortage of *charcuteries* and bakeries.

Even if you finish up in a more expensive restaurant than you had originally planned, two factors will help to keep the bill down. Firstly it is quite common in Alsace to order just a main course, without a starter. You certainly won't be treated to the supercilious stares that often greet an attempt to do so in other parts of France. Secondly, the cost of family meals is kept down by the sensible practice, widespread in Alsace but rare elsewhere in France, of serving special children's meals (*repas d'enfants*) at lower prices.

Mealtimes, too, are a bit different from what you may have been used to on your French holidays. Lunch is usually eaten a little later – rarely before 12.30 and often at 1 o'clock – to take account of the hearty breakfast enjoyed in Alsace. It will certainly be less difficult than in many parts of France to find a restaurant willing to take you after 1 o'clock. Dinner, on the other hand, tends to be earlier, with many restaurants, especially those frequented by German tourists, open as early as 6.30 p.m. and filling up fast by 7. Another difference is that Sunday can be a problem in towns. In Strasbourg, for instance, the majority of restaurants are shut for Sunday lunch as well as in the evening. So plan to make Sundays the day you eat out in the country, perhaps in one of the old coaching inns in small towns and villages that seem to have changed little for centuries. Or in a friendly family hotel in the mountains. Another alternative for Sunday is a meal in a **ferme-auberge**, one of the working farms that offer modest meals based on local specialities (see p. 11). If you have to stay in one of the big towns, you may find **tearooms** open: most of them serve light lunches (salads, onion tarts, cheese dishes) as well as huge portions of mouthwatering cakes.

Most restaurants in Alsace have at least one closing day a week, when you will find the door firmly shut and *'jour de repos'* (rest day) writ large on a placard hanging from the door handle or inside a window. The restaurant lists in this book include the closing day(s) in each case. But although they were accurate when the

---

Storks

The legends and folklore of Alsace are peopled by storks, which have been seen for centuries as symbols of the region. They feature in books by illustrators like Hansi (see p. 9), and you will soon spot huge cartwheels or round metal frames fixed to house and church roofs in the hope that a pair of storks will be tempted to use them as a base for their large, untidy nests and so bring luck to the family or local community.

But shooting and predators in Africa, where they migrate in winter, rapidly reduced their numbers. The effect was compounded by draining of the marshes beside the Rhine, depriving them of their natural habitat and the frogs and other creatures on which they feed. By the early eighties a stork census revealed that Alsace's stork population had dwindled to a mere three pairs. It seemed as though visitors would have to make do with the plastic variety that offer a local variant on the garden gnome theme, or the little models perched on ashtrays and a range of kitsch souvenirs. But then a determined attempt was made to reintroduce the birds.

You can now visit several **Centres de réintroduction des cigognes**, fenced-off enclosures where storks hatched from artificially incubated eggs, then reared in incubators and initially fed by hand, are allowed to roam reasonably freely. The experts hope that eventually a new generation of birds will become used to nesting and breeding in Alsace, but will have the migrating instinct bred out of them by having one wing clipped during their first two years of life.

The biggest of these centres is at **Kintzheim** on the Wine Road (see p. 125). **Hunawihr**, a small village between Riquewihr and Ribeauvillé, has its own stork-breeding centre (afternoons only, about mid-Mar to mid-Nov), and so does the peaceful village of **Raedersdorf** near Ferrette in the Sundgau. You can even visit a *parc de cigognes* in the **Orangerie Gardens in Strasbourg**. And there is an enclosure just inside the entrance to the **Ecomusée de Haute Alsace** (see p. 158).

By 1990 Alsace had fifty-odd inhabited nests and there seem reasonable grounds for hoping that by the end of the century a new stork population will have settled in.

Cow bells swinging from the rafters in a farm-inn, a working farm offering meals based on local dishes

book went to press, do make sure to check locally, as they may change without warning. The two departmental tourist offices publish a reasonably comprehensive list of hotels and and restaurants with closing days. Ask for the current edition when you arrive in Alsace, but do double-check if you are making a special trip.

If you know where you will be at lunchtime, booking in advance is a wise precaution on Sundays, and during the whole of the tourist season in the villages on the Wine Road. If you don't trust your French on the telephone, your hotel will certainly do it for you.

Strasbourg's restaurants, like the city's hotels, become very booked up when the European Parliament is sitting. You must always book at the top gourmet restaurants of course, and advance booking is also sensible in restaurants that attract both business people and tourists, like the **Maison Kammerzell** or the **Maison des Tanneurs**. But *winstubs* rarely take bookings. In Colmar, the autumn grape harvest brings both tourists and wine merchants flocking in, so you may have trouble finding a table at short notice.

It would be idle to pretend that vegetarians are well catered for in French restaurants. Alsace is no exception, though I did come across a good vegetarian restaurant in Colmar uncompromisingly called **Rutabaga** (swede). Alas, it had closed on my most recent visit, but is due to reopen in Mulhouse – check locally. The friendly **Munsterspatz**, opposite the cathedral in Strasbourg, serves a couple of vegetarian dishes every day (see Hotels and Restaurants). Otherwise you will have to stick to onion tarts and cream cheese tarts – both local specialities – and acquire a taste for munster cheese with caraway seeds. In early summer you will be in your element, as the whole of Alsace goes on an asparagus diet (see p. 52). If you are not a whole-hogging vegetarian but simply don't eat meat, Alsace cuisine will suit you fine – as well as the traditional pork-based dishes it offers a range of superb fish recipes.

For a guide to prices, see Hotels and Restaurants. Like all French establishments serving food and/or drink, Alsace restaurants, *winstubs*, *caveaux*, tearooms and cafés are obliged by law to include a service charge in your bill. It is up to you whether you want to leave a little extra.

Opening times

Shops are usually open rather shorter hours than you may be used to elsewhere in France. For instance it may be difficult to find food shops open on Sunday, or even on Saturday afternoon in some places. And unlike the rest of the country, you will sometimes come across villages without even a baker's or a café. Evening closing is likely to be 6 or 6.30 rather than 7, but the usual French early start is common (8 or 8.30 for many food shops) and so is the classic two-hour lunch break.

The big exception is Christmas, when shopping becomes an important family occasion, special Christmas markets are staged (see p. 85) and the shops stay open on the two Sundays leading up to Christmas Day. Then when the big day is over everyone has a day off and 26 December, called *'la Saint-Etienne'*, is a public holiday – whereas in the rest of France, shops and offices close only for Christmas Day. Alsace is also different from the rest of the country in observing Good Friday as a public holiday.

Then the region seems to have more local saints' days than there are dates in the calendar, and many of these result in shops and businesses closing for at least part of the day.

Apart from these local celebrations, Alsace's public holidays are: 1 January, Good Friday, Easter Monday, 1 May (Labour Day), 8 May (VE Day), Feast of the Ascension, Whit Monday, 14 July (the main French national holiday to celebrate the storming of the Bastille), 15 August (Feast of the Assumption), 1 November (All Saints), 11 November (Armistice Day), Christmas Day and St Stephen's Day (26 December).

Banks

Banks in small towns or villages are usually shut on Monday but open Tuesday to Saturday. Even if they remain open at lunchtime, the exchange counter is likely to shut between 12 and 2 p.m., even in Strasbourg and the other major towns. Most banks shut at 4 or 4.30 p.m., sometimes earlier on Saturday.

In Strasbourg there are several banks in or near the place Gutenberg, conveniently near the cathedral. And there is an exchange office right in the heart of La Petite France, in the place Benjamin-Zix.

On Sundays and public holidays you can change travellers' cheques or obtain cash with an international credit card and your cheque book in the arrival hall at the main rail station (pl. de la Gare), near the cathedral in the place du Marché-aux-Cochons-de-Lait, and at the Port du Rhin. Look out too for cash-dispensers (*billetteries*) with a sign showing that you can use your Visa card.

In Mulhouse, the currency exchange office at the rail station is open seven days a week, but normally shut for lunch between 12 and 1 p.m. The tourist office in Colmar has a currency exchange counter open Monday–Saturday (with a lunchtime closure) and on Sunday morning; notes and Eurocheques only (no travellers' cheques).

As a general rule it is easier to change Eurocheques (which will also be accepted by some hotels and restaurants, and by many shops serving the tourist trade) than travellers' cheques.

Museums and places of interest

For a small region, Alsace has a remarkable number of museums, ranging from some of the best-known and most-visited in France, like the Musée d'Unterlinden in Colmar with its superb art collections, or the National Motorcar Museum in Mulhouse, equally superb in its own field, to cosy little museums in private houses devoted to local traditions, arts and crafts.

With the honourable exception of Mulhouse (which must surely have more important museums for a town of its size than almost anywhere else in France, perhaps even in Europe), opening hours tend to be irritatingly short. Even in Strasbourg, the main museums were open only half the day for much of the year until very recently, and they still shut at lunchtime even in the height of the summer tourist season. However, as this guide went to press, they were experimenting with once-a-week evening opening (a different evening for each of the major museums), which is definitely a step in the right direction.

But as a general rule, outside the three main towns, you should count on museums being open only in the afternoons, and probably only on Sunday afternoons in the winter months – if then. The opening times given in the lists at the end of each chapter were correct in 1990, but I do urge you to check locally, especially if you are planning a special journey, as times can change, and unexpected closures may occur, perhaps through illness (smaller places are often manned by volunteers) or because a local bigwig is taking some distinguished guest on a guided tour.

However the region's museums do have a big plus point. If you have been put off by the bureaucratic, not to say officious, attitude of museum attendants in many places in France, you will be pleasantly surprised in Alsace, where staff always seem to be friendly, helpful and interested. This is particularly true of the little local folk art and crafts museums, which often owe their existence to dedicated enthusiasts. But I have found that most of the attendants are very willing to answer questions in the bigger places too, and often display impressive knowledge of the collections.

Most museums charge a modest entrance fee. They may waive this on Sundays. And reductions are often available for some categories of visitors:

children below a certain age, students (with a valid student card), the over-sixties, sometimes teachers and journalists, or professional artists. Always take along your passport to prove your age and some professional identity as relevant. Special rates generally apply for groups, but write in advance to warn of your arrival.

Entrance fees are also standard at places of interest like the various Maginot Line fortifications, or in churches with some special exhibit like Schongauer's *Madonna of the Rose Hedge* in the Eglise des Dominicains in Colmar.

Ordinary churches are usually open from about 7.30 to 12.30 or 1 and about 3 to 7. Even in Strasbourg Cathedral, certain areas are shut over lunchtime. In some small villages you may have to collect the key from the priest's house or a local shop or café.

If you go on a guided tour it is standard practice to give a small tip to the guide, even if he or she seems to be a cut above a paid attendant – enthusiastic volunteers need something to cover their expenses after all, and certainly won't spurn your proffered gratuity.

Other cultural facilities

Strasbourg spends a high proportion of its annual budget on the arts. It stages an important international music festival in June, called **Musica** (programme from Société des Amis de la Musique de Strasbourg, 24 rue de la Mésange, 67081 Strasbourg Cedex, or from tourist offices once you reach Alsace). The **Orchestre philharmonique de Strasbourg** performs both in the **Théâtre Municipal** and in the **Palais de la Musique et des Congrès**. Concerts are held in the **Pavillon Joséphine** in the lovely Orangerie Gardens and, at intervals during the summer, in the courtyard of the **Château des Rohan**. The city's opera company, the **Opéra du Rhin**, is well known, and so is the **Théâtre national de Strasbourg**. The season in both cases runs from about October to May or June. **Colmar** has its own international festival in early July.

Occasional concerts are staged in many of the region's churches and abbeys, like the **Vendredis de la Chartreuse** programme in **Molsheim**'s Carthusian monastery, or the **Heures musicales des mardis** in the Collégiale Saint-Martin in **Colmar**. **Mulhouse** has a **Bach Festival** in June, and the little village of **Oltingue** in the nearby Sundgau is well known for its annual September organ concerts – it has a superb listed Callinet organ (programme from the Association du Patrimoine Oltingue-Sundgau, 121 pl. Saint-Martin, 68480 Oltingue). Programme details are available from regional and local tourist offices, and keep an eye open for posters advertising one-off events in towns and villages, mainly during the summer tourist season.

Folk dance performances are staged in the **Château des Rohan** courtyard in **Strasbourg** and outside the Koifhus (place de l'Ancienne-Douane) in **Colmar** on a regular basis from about Easter to October, and from time to time in the villages on the Wine Road.

Sports and leisure activities

Walking

The people of Alsace seem more

Alsace's many lakes and meres, set amid beautiful scenery, offer many opportunities for boating or angling

German than French in their love of hiking and nature rambles, and the region is also popular with German and other tourists for walking holidays. The **Club Vosgien**, the local equivalent of the better-known Club Alpin, has organized over 15,000 kilometres/9000 miles of marked paths. Its walking maps are available in bookshops, newsagents and tourist gift shops all over Alsace. It is also worth asking for them in travel bookshops at home before you set off. The **Parc naturel régional des Vosges du Nord** (Chapter 5) publishes a large number of leaflets about opportunities for nature rambles in the Northern Vosges forests.

The Club Vosgien is at 4 rue de la Douane, 67000 Strasbourg.

Write to the departmental tourist offices (see Information sources) for their *Randonnées pedestres* handbook, which gives details of marked paths and opportunities for joining groups of ramblers. It also includes information about the helpful *Randonnées sans bagages* (Hiking without Luggage) schemes, whereby your luggage is transported to each overnight stopping place on a planned route.

Riding
A number of farms in the Northern Vosges offer riding holidays with self-catering accommodation (usually in *gîtes*, sometimes camping on the farm), or simply riding lessons and accompanied rides in the forest.

Write to the **Parc naturel régional des Vosges du Nord** (Chapter 5) for their **Randonnée, tourisme équestre** information pack, which gives full details of these *fermes-équestres*, as they are known.

Skiing
There are roughly 1000 kilometres/over 600 miles of marked cross-country skiing trails in the Vosges and in a normal year you can count on snow above 900 metres/3000 feet from about mid-December to the end of March, with March often seeing the best snow. Day passes and weekly passes are available, enabling you to use all these trails. Downhill skiing is also practised in some areas, with snow canons topping up as necessary.

The little ski resorts in the Vosges put the accent more on ski than on après-ski and are well equipped, with 150 drag lifts throughout the area. Most of those on skiing holidays stay in the sunny valleys, as the high slopes tend to be windy, but there are a number of *fermes-auberges* (see p. 11) open in the winter, offering modest overnight accommodation. Ski schools are run in all the resorts, and sledge rides and the like are on offer.

Skiing in the Vosges is not as elegant as in the Alps, but the sunny climate, the friendly family atmosphere and the generally low prices make it well worth considering a skiing holiday in Alsace.

Write to tourist offices (see Information sources) for the comprehensive booklet called *Le Ski dans le Massif vosgien*. The hoteliers in the Munster Valley have got together to organize all-in skiing packages under the label *'Forfait Ski "Tonic"'*. Write to the Groupement des Hôteliers de la Vallée de Munster, BP 6, 68140 Munster.

Tourist offices will also provide a small booklet listing cross-country trails called *Ski de fond dans les Hautes Vosges*. It includes details of access and accommodation in each case.

Boating

Alsace's waterways can be explored on board a variety of craft: motorboats, speedboats, catamarans, houseboats and barges ply along the Rhine, the Ill and a 300-kilometre network of canals. Canoeing and kayaking are also practised in Alsace and gourmet cruises are organized.

Write to tourist offices for their **Tourisme fluvial** literature and for *Alsace: Découvertes au fil de l'eau*, a brochure in French, English and German describing the various possibilities.

Angling

Alsace offers many opportunities for angling in mountain streams or in the meres in the Sundgau. Permits are required. Ask at local tourist offices about day permits (usually bought from cafés or nearby camp-sites).

1
A little history

The history of Alsace, right up to recent times, makes the word 'vicissitudes' seem inadequate. Long coveted for its fertile soil and its strategic site tucked between the natural barriers of the Vosges and the Rhine, it has suffered frequent invasions by marauding armies and by rulers great and small bent on using it as a pawn in the power struggles that have so often buffeted central Europe. Yet somehow, as each conqueror withdrew, allowing them a temporary respite, the people have managed to pick up the pieces and rebuild their shattered lives, their towns and villages and the industries and agriculture on which their prosperity depends.

The region has been inhabited since at least the **Neolithic era**, but little is known of its history until the arrival of a **Celtic tribe** shortly before **1000 BC**. The 'Pagan's Wall' circling the long-holy Mont Sainte-Odile (see Chapter 6) remains a mystery, probably built by the Celts' predecessors, who are thought to have come from Illyria. The Celts put up fortresses to protect their trading settlements, but were soon being harassed by various Teutonic tribes based to the east of the Rhine. An era of invasions and incursions came to an end with the arrival of the **Romans** in **58 BC**.

Julius Caesar decreed that the Rhine was to be the eastern boundary of Roman Gaul, and to protect it, built a series of fortifications and military camps. One of the camps, known as Argentoratum, was eventually to develop into Strasbourg.

During the Roman era, Alsace flourished. Vines were planted, roads and large comfortable villas were built, the Rhine became a busy commercial waterway, and the therapeutic properties of the waters in the northern forests were discovered and exploited – the spa town now called Niederbronn-les-Bains was founded by the Romans. But **Barbarian invaders** had to be repelled at frequent intervals – Attila and his Huns were among those who attacked Argentoratum, laying waste the surrounding countryside. They had been preceded by the **Alemanni**, a Teutonic people who were initially soundly beaten in a battle near what is now Colmar, but eventually successfully invaded Alsace in the mid-**fourth century AD** and then gradually drove out the Romans.

The Alemanni, whose language is the root of the dialect still spoken in virtually all of Alsace today, were themselves driven out by the **Franks** in the **fifth century**. Alsace now became part of the Eastern Kingdom or **Austrasia**. Under the Frankish king Clovis, an early form of Christianity was introduced into the region – the first church to be built on the site now occupied by Strasbourg Cathedral dates from this period. Then in the mid-**sixth century** it became a duchy, whose rulers lived in fortified castles perched high up on rocky crags – many of them now the picturesque ruins that overlook the villages on the Wine Road. They included **Duke Eticho**, whose daughter Odilia was to become Alsace's patron saint (see box, p. 130). When the **Carolingian dynasty** came to power, Alsace was divided into North County and South County – Nordgau and, the name still used today for the area south of Mulhouse, Sundgau.

Charlemagne seems to have had a soft spot for Alsace, which benefited fully from what is known as the 'Carolingian Renaissance'. Strasbourg became a flourishing commercial centre – for some time now, the former Argentoratum had been called 'Strateburgum', the 'town of roads' (meaning the town where roads – and especially trading routes – meet). Churches, abbeys and monasteries were built, one of the finest the abbey church of Marmoutier, founded by a disciple of St Columban, who had

The ruined rectangular keeps known as the Eguisheim Towers – witnesses to Alsace's troubled history

brought the Gospel from Ireland to the remote Vosges valleys.

After Charlemagne's death in **814**, his empire was gradually broken up. Alsace initially found itself under the sway of his grandson **Lothaire**. But the great emperor's quarrelsome descendants had neither his ability nor his unifying vision. Lothaire's brother **Louis the German** temporarily snatched Alsace away. Then in 842, Louis and their half-brother **Charles the Bald** ganged up on Lothaire, swearing the **'Oaths of Strasbourg'** just outside the city. In signing this document – historically important as the earliest in which 'vulgar' Romance and Germanic tongues were used – they pledged themselves to an alliance against Lothaire. A year later the **Treaty of Verdun** formally divided up Charlemagne's inheritance. Alsace was back under the rule of Lothaire, as part of the new kingdom of **Lotharingia**, the original name of Lorraine. This represented the 'Middle Kingdom', sandwiched between the territories east of the Rhine presided over by Louis and Charles's western territories, covering much of present-day France.

The next two centuries were a troubled period for Alsace. Still Charlemagne's descendants argued and fought over who was to control it. After the death of Lothaire's son, Charles the Bald attempted to incorporate it into his French kingdom. But it was Louis who won in the end, and in **870** Alsace joined his German kingdom. It was to remain in the German sphere of influence for the next eight hundred years, as a province of what came to be known as the **Holy Roman Empire**. In the early decades of the **tenth century**, **Magyar invasions** wreaked terrible havoc, leaving towns and villages in ruins. Rebuilding took place against a background of fighting and rivalry between local counts, some of them mere robber barons, some of them members of newly powerful families like the **Counts of Eguisheim**, who gave Alsace its one and only Pope, elected as **Leo IX** in **1048**. But power was not all in secular hands: the **Bishop of Strasbourg** was an influential figure, and the region's mighty abbeys had an important role to play.

The arrival of the **Hohenstaufens** as Dukes of Alsace in **1079** ushered in a new era of relative peace and unity.

An etymological puzzle

The experts disagree on the origin of the name Alsace, the French version of Elsass, used both in the dialect and in German. It may, according to one theory, mean simply 'the seat (or land) of the [River] Ill'. But the people were known as the Alesaciones as early as the seventh century, and another derivation is that the name comes from the Celtic word *alis*, meaning 'rock' or 'hill', and *atia*, 'in the land of', giving the plausible 'in the land of rocky hills'. A third theory speaks of Latin *ali*, meaning 'others' or 'different people', plus Teutonic *Saz*, settlement: 'a land settled by strangers'.

Romanesque architecture in Alsace

The Romanesque style reached Alsace almost a century later than the rest of France. The pure and sober lines are still there, but the overall design may be more complex than elsewhere and the decoration is clearly influenced by the many sculptors, architects and painters from all over Europe whose paths crossed in Alsace during the Middle Ages. The use of the local pinkish sandstone also gives a different look to many of the Romanesque churches that have somehow survived the vicissitudes of the region's history, often needing a great deal of restoration.

Among the most interesting churches, described in greater detail in the relevant chapters, are:
Andlau: abbey church with wonderful sculpture on the porch and in a frieze round the outer walls
Guebwiller: Saint-Léger, superb façade
Kaysersberg: Sainte-Croix, late Romanesque porch with tympanum depicting the Coronation of the Virgin Mary
Lautenbach: former collegiate church
Marmoutier: abbey church, with monumental façade
Murbach: abbey church, with only the tall and beautiful choir extant
Rosheim: Saint-Pierre-et-Saint-Paul, remarkable for its human and animal figures perched on the roof
Sélestat: Sainte-Foy, with three towers and richly carved capitals

Ask in tourist offices for a good clear leaflet called *La Route romane d'Alsace* which describes the three separate itineraries, covering Northern, Central and Southern Alsace, that make up the Alsace Romanesque Road devised by the local authorities.

The **Middle Ages** were in many ways Alsace's golden age. When **Frederick Barbarossa** succeeded his uncle as Holy Roman Emperor in **1152**, Haguenau became the *de facto* capital of the empire. In **1167 Herrade of Landsberg**, the abbess of the convent founded by St Odile, wrote her famous *Hortus Deliciarum* or *Garden of Delights*, a learned compendium of knowledge about the history of the world and of the Church, which she herself illuminated with superb miniatures. Alas, it was one of the many thousands of priceless manuscripts and books destroyed during the shelling of Strasbourg in the Franco-Prussian War seven hundred years later. During the second half of this same century Alsace was embellished with many beautiful **Romanesque churches**, slightly different in style from the Romanesque that had reached other regions of France somewhat earlier (see box). In about 1210 the poet **Gottfried von Strassburg** wrote his lyrical German version of the Tristan and Isolde legend.

This artistic flowering took place at a time when Alsace could boast of a number of rapidly expanding towns and cities, each with a wealthy merchant class and powerful guilds and trade associations. In the early years of the **thirteenth century** Strasbourg won the privileged status of 'free imperial city'. Sixty years later, the citizens threw out their young prince-bishop. He had nurtured dreams of taking over the whole region, but his cavalry had been soundly beaten by the bourgeoisie's infantry at the **Battle of Hausbergen**. The city's magnificent Gothic cathedral was built under the direction not of the bishop, but of a body controlled by the town council. Other towns that grew in importance during this period were Sélestat and Colmar, Wissembourg, Obernai and Mulhouse.

Afraid of losing their hard-won privileges, they were only too aware of the need to defend their interests against the lawless robber barons who, taking advantage of the confusion that followed the collapse of the Hohenstaufen dynasty in the mid-thirteenth century, were still inclined to sow terror among the towns and villages in the shadow of their feudal castles. The result, formalized in **1354**, was a federation of ten towns, the **Decapolis** (see box).

The **Hundred Years' War** helped in some ways to increase Alsace's prosperity, as it became a convenient depot and trading post for goods that could not easily be transported through war-torn France. But it also

The Decapolis

The collapse of the Hohenstaufen dynasty with the execution of the last of the line in Naples in 1258 spelled the end of a period of relative peace and prosperity in Alsace, which was once again divided and ruled over by a whole string of feudal lords, perpetually quarrelling among themselves. After nearly a century of something approaching chaos, ten of the region's most powerful towns decided to unite to ensure their continued prosperity and to negotiate privileges from the Holy Roman Empire.

In 1354 they set up the Decapolis, under the protection of the representative of the Emperor Charles IV, whose official residence was in Haguenau. As well as Haguenau itself, the towns that vowed to offer mutual support and assistance were Colmar, Kaysersberg, Mulhouse, Munster, Obernai, Rosheim, Sélestat, Turckheim and Wissembourg. All had strong defensive walls and fortifications, parts of which have survived to this day, and they played an important part in defending Alsace from a series of invaders. Strasbourg had acquired a separate status as a 'free imperial city' with its own special privileges. And Mulhouse subsequently pulled out of the Decapolis to ally itself with the Swiss federation. But during the later Middle Ages the Decapolis was very much a force in the land, and the special status of the ten towns was still recognized in the seventeenth century, when they were treated differently from the rest of the region under the Treaty of Westphalia, under which Alsace was ceded to France at the end of the Thirty Years' War.

Martin Schongauer's beautiful Madonna of the Rose Hedge, *painted in Colmar in about 14/3 and now in the Eglise des Dominicains*

led to attacks from all sides. Bands of English mercenaries had to be repelled several times. So did the **Armagnacs**, the aristocratic party of the Duke of Orléans, whose fierce rivalry with the **Burgundians** tore France apart in the fifteenth century. The damage inflicted on towns and countryside was compounded by the **Black Death**, that terrible scourge of medieval Europe.

By now the **Habsburgs** were on the imperial throne. In **1469** they precipitated a new crisis in Alsace by selling their territories in the northern half of the region to **Charles the Bold, Duke of Burgundy**. For a time it looked as though he would conquer the rest of Alsace. But in **1477** he was killed fighting at the gates of Nancy and the danger of Alsace becoming a Burgundian possession receded.

In spite of the many troubles of this period, the region became a major intellectual and artistic centre. The brilliant team of architects and stone masons working on **Strasbourg's cathedral** drew journeymen from far and wide. The Colmar painter and engraver **Martin Schongauer** influenced artists all over Europe. Strasbourg, the scene of **Gutenberg**'s invention of movable type thirty years earlier, now had many of the leading printing workshops in the German-speaking world. This new vehicle for the rapid dissemination of information helped to spread the ideas and ideals of the **Humanists**, who were well represented in Alsace: the magnificent library built up by the Humanist scholar **Beatus Rhenanus**, friend and biographer of Erasmus, can still be visited in Sélestat.

*

In the early **sixteenth century** the **Reformation** had a considerable impact in Alsace, which still has a fairly large Protestant community to this day, though it is now predominantly Roman Catholic. Several of **Luther**'s tracts were printed in Strasbourg and the great preachers for whom the city was famous included a number of his followers. **Calvin**, too, spent several years in Strasbourg, meeting Luther there. The libertarian ideas that went hand in hand with the Reformation inspired the poorest of Alsace's people, scraping a living on the land or in the towns, to stage a series of uprisings. In **1525** a peasants' revolt known to historians as *la Guerre des Rustauds* (the 'Bumpkins' War') was put down with great brutality by the Duke of Lorraine, responding to an appeal from the panicking local nobility and the Bishop of Strasbourg. About twenty thousand peasants, tricked into laying down their arms, were slaughtered outside Saverne.

After a period of commendable religious tolerance, the rising tide of Protestantism was also stemmed, during the **Wars of Religion** that were the sadly inevitable consequence of the Reformation. But worse was to come. The outbreak of the **Thirty Years' War** in **1618** was a black day for Alsace. Already the previous year the region had been briefly invaded and pillaged by the troops of Philip III of Spain. As the armies of the Holy Roman Emperor, the Swedish king and Louis XIII of France trampled across Europe, along with bands of mercenaries, it became a battlefield. Some towns and villages never recovered (though from the tourist's point of view there is a silver lining in the attractive seventeenth- and eighteenth-century houses that replaced the shattered medieval dwellings).

The war ended in **1648** with the **Treaty of Westphalia**, under which the Habsburgs had to hand over most of Alsace to France. Strasbourg remained a free imperial city for the time being, Mulhouse was still attached to the Swiss federation, and the ten Decapolis towns were in the curious position of being still part of the Holy Roman Empire, yet owing allegiance to the French king. But essentially, eight centuries of German rule were over.

It still took many decades before France gained full control of Alsace. **Louis XIV** took advantage of the war against the Spanish Netherlands to

---

Strasbourg's famous preachers

As you study its superb Late Gothic pulpit, imagine the huge cathedral echoing to the fiery words of Johann Geiler (1445–1510), known as Geiler of Kaysersberg, the greatest orator among Alsace's many famous preachers. From the pulpit, which was specially designed for him by the Strasbourg sculptor Hans Hammer, he thundered against what he claimed were the loose morals of the age, castigating some of the clergy and preaching dozens of sermons on the 'fools' satirized by his friend Sebastian Brant in his *Ship of Fools* (p. 81).

At the height of the Reformation another crowd-pulling preacher also came from Kaysersberg – though Geiler was in fact born in Schaffhausen, and merely brought up there. But Matthäus Zell (1477–1548) was born and bred in the little town, the son of a vine grower. He is said to have attracted as many as three thousand people to his eloquent sermons propagating Luther's doctrines. The bishop disapproved and he was eventually excommunicated, though this did little to affect his support in the city. Like many another Reformation cleric he decided to marry, and started saying mass in German instead of Latin.

In the year that Zell married, 1523, a Dominican monk from Sélestat, Martin Bucer (1491–1551), settled in Strasbourg and followed in his predecessor's footsteps by preaching the doctrines of the Reformation. Known for his reasoned, intellectual discourse rather than for populist oratory, he worked with Calvin, who spent the years 1538 to 1541 in the city. Bucer attracted the hatred of the emperor Charles V, who was fiercely opposed to the Reformation, and after he had spent twenty-five years in Strasbourg, the city's magistrate was forced to expel him. He travelled to England at the invitation of Archbishop Cranmer, where Edward VI appointed him Professor of Divinity at the University of Cambridge and commissioned him to work on *The Book of Common Prayer* and other instruments of the Anglican Church. Five years after his death in 1551, Mary Tudor had his remains ceremonially burnt, but when Elizabeth I became queen, she promptly rehabilitated him.

Gutenberg and early printing in Alsace

Strasbourg was the setting in the 1430s for the first crucial experiments by Johann Gensfleisch, better known as Johann Gutenberg, the man generally honoured as the inventor of movable metal type and thus of printing. He had been born to a patrician family in Mainz just over thirty years earlier, but the whole family moved to Strasbourg in 1430, probably to escape their creditors. He remained there for about fifteen years, possibly earning his living as a goldsmith – many early printers were goldsmiths, since the casting of the type required absolute precision.

His early attempts at printing, carried out with financial help from friends and acquaintances, started in about 1439. But they were a great drain on his own meagre finances and when he returned to Mainz he had to borrow money from a goldsmith and investor called Johannes Fust. The two men went into partnership in about 1450. This guaranteed him enough capital to finance his printing press, but in return he had to hand over a part share in his invention. Fust soon decided to call in the loan and in 1455 took him to court to recover the money. But Gutenberg had spent it all working his embryo press, which had not yet produced any return on the capital invested in it. Fust won the case and promptly seized the press, employing Gutenberg's type designer Peter Schöffer. Early the next year appeared the world's first printed book, always known as the *Gutenberg Bible*, a beautiful volume with two full columns of Gothic type per page, decorated initials left blank for 'rubricators' and set within decorative borders.

Although Gutenberg's name mercifully remains attached to this glorious piece of work, which must have been completed before he was forced out, it was, in the words of the bibliophile Alan G. Thomas, 'a tragic and shameful situation in which Gutenberg was expelled from his own invention and deprived of the fruits of his genius'. He did eventually find another backer and set up another press, on which he printed his *Thirty-six-line Bible* (Fust and Schöffer's had forty-two) in 1457. A large-format Latin dictionary followed three years later. But Gutenberg never achieved financial success and had to be baled out by a pension from the Archbishop of Mainz. He died in 1468, at the age of nearly seventy.

Gutenberg's departure did not bring to an end Strasbourg's role as an early centre of printing. The first Bible to be printed in German was produced there in 1466, and by the end of the Middle Ages the city has a good fifty printers' workshops. Its prominence as a source of printed books helped to foster the Humanist school that played such a prominent part in the intellectual life of Alsace.

The tympanum of Kaysersberg's Romanesque church of Sainte-Croix is surmounted by a vigorous Coronation of the Virgin

remove the risk of an uprising in the ten imperial towns by ordering his troops to tear down their fortifications. In January **1675** French troops under General Turenne scored a famous victory over the Empire at the **Battle of Turckheim**, defeating an army almost three times as large. In **1678** the **Peace of Nijmegen** formally ratified France's new eastern border. Three years later, Strasbourg, too, was forced to yield.

The transition to a new sphere of influence went reasonably smoothly, thanks largely to Louis XIV's wise insistence that 'Alsace's customs are not to be tampered with'. Although French became the official language, there was no real attempt to wipe out the dialect. The Treaty of Westphalia guaranteed protection to the region's Protestants, even though Louis insisted that Roman Catholicism was to be the main religion. They therefore did not suffer persecution as Protestants did elsewhere in France after the revocation of the Edict of Nantes. An unusual situation grew up whereby in mixed communities the Catholics held their worship in the chancel, while the Protestants had the rest of the church. Alsace still has many *églises simultanées* (simultaneous churches), as they are somewhat oddly known. The Jewish population was mainly left in peace.

By the beginning of Louis XV's reign in the mid-**eighteenth century**, most of the ruined towns and villages had been rebuilt. Prosperity had returned, symbolized by the elegant Châteaux des Rohan in Strasbourg and Saverne, and a host of other fine buildings, both domestic and religious, that were mostly much more French in spirit than the region's earlier architecture. This was also the period when powerful family dynasties set up successful industries in Alsace. Mulhouse was starting to become a major industrial city, with particular strength in textiles. In and around Niederbronn in the northeast, the De Dietrich family created important ironworks. The Hannong family in Strasbourg built up a flourishing china-manufacturing business.

Although it had been forced to capitulate, Strasbourg still enjoyed many of its old privileges and its brilliant university attracted major scholars. Goethe was a student there in the 1770s. He wrote some of his loveliest lyric poetry in Alsace, inspired by his love for the pastor's daughter in nearby Sessenheim (see box, p. 101). In 1788 a young Corsican second lieutenant called Napoleone Buonaparte also spent a few months studying in the city, where, or so it is said, he took lessons from the fencing expert who was later to teach another student at the university, one day to become his arch-enemy, Prince Metternich.

By the time the **French Revolution** broke out in **1789**, the people of Alsace felt thoroughly French, even though they were still culturally close to the German-speaking world. Many of the initial ideas of the Revolutionaries were eagerly embraced in Alsace, partly because they were seen as favouring devolution of power to local institutions. Patriotic fervour reached fever pitch when an army captain composed in Strasbourg the stirring battle hymn that was later to become France's national anthem (see box, p. 45). But with their deeply held religious beliefs, the people thoroughly disapproved of the 'nationalization' and destruction of church property. And with their ingrained tolerance, they were sickened by the excesses of the Terror. Any hope of gaining some degree of local autonomy was dashed when the region was arbitrarily divided into the two *départements* that still obtain today, Haut-Rhin in the south and Bas-Rhin in the north. But the Revolution did lead to Mulhouse's decision to become part of France in **1798**, thus creating a fully unified Alsace under the French flag.

The **Napoleonic era**, too, was greeted with enthusiasm. The Little Corporal inspired more volunteers in Alsace than in any other region of France. And many of his most valiant generals were Alsace men. General Kléber came from Strasbourg, where he is still honoured today in the name of the city's main square. So did Marshal Kellermann. General Rapp was from Colmar and Marshal Lefebvre from Rouffach. Napoleon famously stood up for these fearless soldiers when he overhead some of his officers poking fun at their accent or their use of dialect: 'Who cares if they don't speak French? Their sabres do!'

The birth of a national anthem

A plaque on the wall of the Banque de France opposite the town hall in the place Broglie in Strasbourg tells you that *La Marseillaise*, France's emotive national anthem, was first sung in a house on the same site on 26 April 1792.

It always seems peculiarly fitting that this most patriotic of French provinces should have given birth to that most patriotic of national anthems (*'Allons, enfants de la patrie,/Le jour de gloire est arrivé . . .'*). And yet also peculiarly ironic that Strasbourg, whose French identity was twice forcibly removed, should have lost to another large town at the other end of France the glory of giving its name to the hymn sung on all great state occasions.

In fact it was written as a battle hymn for the French Army of the Rhine, and its composer was a thirty-two-year-old captain in the French equivalent of the Royal Engineers, Claude Joseph Rouget de l'Isle. He was born in the Jura, south-east of Alsace, and, a volunteer in the Rhine Army, was stationed in Strasbourg. The mayor at the time was Baron Frédéric de Dietrich, a mineralogist who had been elected a couple of years earlier. He had suggested the subject and it was in his drawing room, just a few days after revolutionary France had declared war on Austria, that the young officer sang his *Chant de Guerre de l'Armée du Rhin*.

A stirring engraving in the Cabinet des Estampes (Print Room) in the Château des Rohan in Strasbourg depicts him with one arm held aloft, the other clutching a sheet of music to his breast, while his audience in the chaotic-looking room lean forward eagerly, hanging on his every word, and the mayor's daughter, neatly coiffed, accompanies him on the piano. A famous print by the later patriot Hansi (see box, p. 9) allows us to glimpse the poet through a window, in exactly the same posture, while a tricolour flag flutters from the elaborate dormer window above him, and a troop of revolutionary infantry in their tricorne hats march valiantly through the sky past the silhouette of the soaring cathedral spire.

The hymn was taken up by the *fédérés* volunteers from Marseille marching up to Paris (it had reached them via guards from Montpellier). As the people of the capital first heard it on their lips, it was soon rechristened *La Marseillaise*, rather than *La Strasbourgeoise*, which would have been so much more appropriate, especially as it is very much a frontier march, designed to instil a spirit of defiance in an army preparing to fight the absolute monarchies who were the declared enemies of the Revolution. 'That battle song has cost us five hundred thousand men,' one of the German commanders is said to have remarked.

During the **ninteenth century** industrialization continued. Mulhouse's textile factories became world leaders in chintzes and other printed fabrics. Canals and railways were built. The fertile soil of the 'Alsace plain' became a major agricultural producer, with tobacco and hops important.

But only too soon that rich soil was once again the theatre of a disastrous war. The **Franco-Prussian War of 1870-1** was largely fought in Alsace and resulted not only in terrible destruction and loss of life, but in the return to the German-speaking world of a people who were by now, with very few exceptions, patriotically French, while still maintaining their individual character and continuing to speak the dialect among themselves.

In the first few days of the war with Prussia, the north-eastern corner of Alsace saw appalling carnage. France's equivalent of the heroic but doomed Charge of the Light Brigade took place at the little spa town of Moosbronn on the edge of the Forêt de Haguenau: a cavalry charge by the Sixth Cuirassiers, virtually all of whom were massacred, could do nothing to affect a situation in which General MacMahon's forty-six thousand French troops were outnumbered by more than three to one. By 12 August, the enemy was laying siege to Strasbourg. For three nights from the 23rd, the city was subjected to heavy shelling. Three hundred people were killed and many more injured, the cathedral was damaged and the superb library of precious manuscripts and early printed books in the former Dominican monastery was destroyed by fire. By the end of September the siege was over. The border town of Neuf-Brisach, fortified by Louis XIV's brilliant military engineer Vauban, was taken soon after.

When 1870 was over, the Prussians had captured the whole of Alsace. The following year France had to sign the **Treaty of Frankfurt**, under which both Alsace and Lorraine were ceded to Germany. **Bismarck** appointed his rich young cousin, the new husband of Paris's best-known courtesan the Marquise de Païva, governor-general of a new 'imperial territory' linking the two regions together as Elsass-Lothringen (Alsace-Lorraine). Many prominent Frenchmen, including Victor Hugo, protested vehemently at this handing over of territory against the will of the inhabitants. The Alsace-born Bishop of Angers wrote a famous letter to the Kaiser expressing his abhorrence at the annexation (see box, p. 127). But to no avail. The Germans were determined to make their new possession a fully German territory. French was banned in schools and all newspapers had to be in German.

In **1872**, as provided for under the Treaty of Frankfurt, the people were given an opportunity to say whether they wished to retain their French nationality and move elsewhere, rather than becoming German. Nearly fifty thousand, many of them teachers, doctors, lawyers and business people, did so. The leaders of those who stayed concentrated – without success – on trying to obtain the status of a separate imperial state.

Bismarck's attempts to win over the people had little success either. Although the period of annexation to Germany brought social benefits not then available in France, there was still lasting resentment at his public comments about the territory having been annexed purely to form a 'glacis' or strategic buffer to protect Germany's western border in the event of another war with France. The Colmar cartoonist **Hansi** mercilessly caricatured the Germans and stimulated fierce patriotism with his books and drawings of children in regional costume (see box, p. 9).

The German era left an architectural legacy in some imposing public buildings in Strasbourg, alongside their version of art nouveau, and, more unexpectedly, the complete reconstruction of the ruined medieval castle of Haut-Koenigsbourg, supervised personally by the Kaiser. Alsace enjoyed considerable industrial development, too, and was soon well ahead of France in the provision of mains water and drainage, and of electricity.

Shortly before the First World War it seemed briefly as though Alsace might achieve the longed-for autonomy when the Reichstag granted her her own parliament. An idea was even mooted locally that she might join some sort of federation with Switzerland and Luxembourg to provide mutual defence against both France and Germany. But nothing came of this. And a celebrated incident in Saverne in **1913** revealed the depth of feeling against the German occupiers. When a young German officer spoke disparagingly of the quality of Alsace recruits, the insult led to a near-riot and he had to be court-martialled to appease local indignation – though he was subsequently acquitted. The **'Saverne Incident'**, as it became known to the world's press, considerably embittered Franco-German relations.

*

The German occupation after the Franco–Prussian War endowed Strasbourg with art nouveau decoration as well as imposing buildings

Just over eight months later, the two countries were at war and, once again, Alsace became a battlefield. Within days of the outbreak of the **First World War** in August **1914**, French troops crossed the border into Alsace and reached Mulhouse, though they were soon forced to retreat. Mulhouse was taken again and a French army under Marshal Joffre managed to gain control of the Western Vosges and reach a number of towns in the valleys. The Route des Crêtes, running along the ridge of the mountains from Cernay to Sainte-Marie-aux-Mines, was built to ensure communications with the valleys on the Vosges front (see Chapter 7).

In an emotional speech to the local people in Thann, Marshal Joffre rashly assured them that from now on Alsace would be French for ever. But there were four years of fierce fighting to be endured before Alsace was returned to France after the 1918 armistice. The endless rows of crosses and stars of David in the military cemeteries near the battlefields of Le Linge or Vieil-Armand, where 30,000 were slain, bear silent witness to Alsace's tragic position, constantly in the line of fire throughout her history. To add to the tragedy, many of her sons, conscripted into the Kaiser's army, had to fight their former French compatriots. The sufferings of the region were compounded when the French authorities decided to intern as enemy aliens anyone normally living in Alsace who happened to be in France or her overseas territories at the outbreak of war. Even the great Albert Schweitzer did not escape this highly insensitive ruling (see box, p. 144). And the immediate postwar period was embittered by a policy of distinguishing between those who had allegedly been 'pro-German' and those who had remained 'pro-French'.

But although there was some local agitation for Alsace to become an autonomous region, the great majority of the people were delighted to be part of France once again. With their usual readiness to knuckle down, they managed to adapt to new markets and rebuild after the damage caused by the war. The economic depression of the **1930s** inevitably had some effect, and Alsace also suffered from France's unwillingness to invest in a region on which Hitler was starting to have designs. This period was also marked by the building of the ill-fated **Maginot Line**, planned as an impregnable defence for France's border with Germany (see box).

The Nazi threat proved only too real. A mere twenty-one years after its return to France, Alsace was being bombed by the Luftwaffe on the outbreak of the **Second World War**. In June **1940** the Maginot Line was easily breached and the region was once again annexed to 'the Fatherland'. Nearly half a million of her people left. Some had been evacuated to other parts of France, others were expelled by the Nazis, others managed to escape.

This time, rigid Germanization was the order of the day. Schoolchildren were imprisoned for speaking French in the street – and wearing a beret (caps were issued instead). They were later forced into joining the local branch of the Hitlerjugend. Place names and street names, even people's first and surnames, were converted into German. The people of Mulhouse still laugh wryly at the bureaucrat who failed to spot the incongruity of changing their rue du Sauvage (Savage Street) into Adolf-Hitler-Strasse. Many were deported, and the only concentration camp on French soil was set up at Le Struthof in the Vosges, where at least ten thousand died.

Many young men were conscripted into the Wehrmacht, some even forced into joining the S.S. Large numbers of them were killed on the Russian front, or had to endure the horrors of the Soviet camps. At home, their compatriots were subjected to bombing and, as the war drew to a close, to heavy fighting on their soil once again. Many of the villages on the Wine Road were virtually flattened in **1944** and Mulhouse suffered severe damage. Fierce fighting in February **1945** eventually enabled French and American troops to deploy a textbook pincer movement to flush out the Germans from what is known to Second World War historians as the 'pocket of Colmar'.

The return of those who had spent the war years elsewhere in France inevitably led to tension during the difficult **post-war years**, with accusations of collaboration, and remarkably little sympathy on the part of the

The Maginot Line

The ill-fated Maginot Line was called after André Maginot, France's War Minister when, in 1930, the decision was taken to build a system of fortifications to protect the country's north-eastern border. It took most of the thirties and vast sums of money to construct what was then considered to be a brilliant technical achievement – a subterranean network of concrete blockhouses, 'pillboxes' and passages, with little visible above ground except a series of rounded reinforced steel observation towers and firing posts.

But the designers and strategists turned out to have been living in a fools' paradise. (France's lack of true preparedness for the Second World War and her military leaders' purely defensive strategy were early denounced by a young officer called Charles de Gaulle – who was promptly branded a Fascist by the military Establishment.) The Maginot Line, the concrete symbol of this defensive thinking, proved totally inadequate in the face of tank warfare and air strikes and was easily breached by the German invaders in June 1940.

The line of fortifications stretched from France's border with Belgium and Luxembourg down to the Swiss border. It crossed through the Northern Vosges, where the **Four à Chaux** fortifications have recently been opened to the public, then ran parallel to the Rhine, via **Marckolsheim**, whose casemate has been turned into a Maginot Line Memorial. Guided tours are also organized at **Schoenenbourg**. Over the border in Lorraine at **Simserhof** near Bitche, where you can visit the **Musée national de la Fortification** (Fortifications Museum).

French authorities for those who had been forced to fight for the Nazis. But hard work and determination once again led to the rebuilding of towns and villages, and of industry and agriculture. And shortly after the end of the war Alsace embarked on its new role as a symbol of European reconciliation and unity.

In **1949** Strasbourg was chosen as the seat of the **Council of Europe**. Thirty years later the **European Parliament** held the first of its regular monthly meetings in the city. The smart modern Palais de l'Europe now houses not only the Council and the Parliament's chamber but also the **European Court of Human Rights**.

Alsace is now a prosperous region, well equipped to benefit – for once in its history – from its strategic site at the heart of Europe, now that European unity is becoming a reality. Few would deny that its people have earned both their prosperity and their symbolic unifying role, after eleven centuries of suffering from the division of Europe that was the outcome of that fateful meeting in Strasbourg in 842 between Charlemagne's grandsons.

The European Parliament holds its monthly plenary sessions in Strasbourg's Palais de l'Europe

2
Alsace cuisine

Choucroute and *kougelhopf*, *bäckeoffe* and *sueri nierli*, *wädele* and *lewerknepfle* – even if you are a connoisseur of French cuisine you are likely to be entering unfamiliar territory when you settle down with a glass of *muscat* or *crémant d'Alsace* to study a menu made up of Alsace's best-known dishes. For like its people, Alsace cuisine has a distinct personality. And like its landscapes, it is remarkably varied.

The people of Alsace have a reputation for being good trenchermen, with what the French like to call a 'solid appetite'. But although comforting, filling dishes served in large portions do indeed feature on the region's menus, as befits a land where winter can be harsh and where long hours are spent in the open air tilling the fields or tending the vines, the gastronomic picture is much more varied than that. The local chefs are as adaptable as the rest of the people, and imaginative variants on regional recipes in *nouvelle cuisine* style are among the most interesting gastronomic experiences you'll enjoy anywhere in France.

The chefs themselves are often remarkable too. Alsace may be the smallest region in France, but – as you will often be told with justified pride – its restaurants have been awarded more Michelin rosettes than any other region. The *Auberge de l'Ill* in Illhaeusern and *Le Crocodile* and *Le Buerehiesel* in Strasbourg are among the handful of France's top restaurants, and slightly lower down the scale are dozens of places serving superb cuisine. There is a pleasing lack of pretentiousness about the great Alsace chefs – Emile Jung at *Le Crocodile* really does sometimes sit down with his clients for a chat and a glass of beer, and the Haeberlins from Illhaeusern are fond of dropping in for a meal of hearty regional fare at the lively *Pifferhüs* in Ribeauvillé.

A well-known saying maintains that whereas French cuisine is good but served in small portions, and German cuisine is served in large portions but is no good, Alsace cuisine is both good and served in generous portions. There is some truth in that, more so than in the other well-worn cliché about its being a hybrid, a cross between French and German cuisine. In fact the region's troubled history means that its cuisine has been subject to a wide range of influences, not least that of its old-established Jewish population – the traditional special occasion dish of *carpe à la juive* is more likely to be found here than elsewhere in France. You will also constantly come across unexpected variants on familiar French themes, like the custom of serving *crudités* with a *pot-au-feu* (called *suppefleisch* in the local dialect).

The refreshing lack of pretentiousness in even the top establishments no doubt stems partly from an obvious delight in sharing the pleasures of the table. The *gemütlich* ambiance of the traditional *winstub* or *caveau* (see p. 4), where customers share tables and soon join in their neighbours' conversation, typifies the convivial attitude to eating and drinking in Alsace. But it is tangible too in virtually all the region's restaurants, making even the gourmet highspots seem rather different from the hushed 'temples of gastronomy' in Paris or Lyon. When a waiter asks if you are enjoying the dish you have ordered, you always feel he genuinely wants to know. And restaurant staff never seem too busy to help you understand menus. Other guests may well join in too, pointing out dishes based on produce typical of that particular area, like the carp recipes in the Sundgau or game from the forests in the Northern Vosges. The particular interest and pride in local specialities, great even by French standards, is just as evident in markets and *charcuteries* and on the upland farms where you can enjoy a modest meal or buy freshly made cheese or fruit tarts. So eating out or choosing the ingredients for a picnic or a meal in your own *gîte* are more than just a gastronomic experience: they are also a way of getting to know the people, their customs and way of life, sometimes even their history.

You will be told how one of the masterpieces of French cuisine, the delectable *pâté de foie gras en croûte*, was invented in the late eighteenth century by one Jean-Pierre Clause, who was employed as a chef by Alsace's military governor, the Maréchal de Contades.

The marshal was born in Anjou, a province known for its wine and its excellent cuisine. Determined to dazzle his master, Clause decided one day to bake a whole goose liver inside a pastry case lined with a mixture of finely chopped veal and fat bacon. The result was so superb that the marshal sent a messenger post haste from Strasbourg to Versailles to present the new dish to his royal master Louis XIV. The Sun King, a great gourmet, pronounced it excellent and Clause's reputation was made. He soon set up his own business, and over two hundred years later the speciality that made his fortune still has pride of place in the windows of Alsace's top *charcuteries* and on the menus of gourmet restaurants, though nowadays the pastry case is usually made from a type of brioche dough made with yeast.

You will learn too how the rigid Protestant régime in Mulhouse, whose citizens eagerly embraced the ideas of the Reformation, forced the city's Jewish community to settle near the Swiss border in the Sundgau, a region with an honourable history of religious tolerance, where they had a lasting impact on the local cuisine. And if you are in Alsace in the early summer, someone is bound to tell you, as you tuck with relish into a *repas d'asperges*, a meal whose main ingredient is an enormous quantity of succulent asparagus, that Alsace's vast asparagus output is due almost entirely to the inspiration of a Protestant pastor who had been a missionary in North Africa (see p. 86).

The interest in food – some would call it an obsession – that you meet everywhere in Alsace is undoubtedly one factor in the region's wealth of culinary delights. Another is the variety of high-quality fresh produce available locally. A land blessed with mountain streams and forests, with high pastures and low-lying meadows and plains, plus a mainly sunny yet not too dry climate, is bound to enjoy a natural bounty in the way of plump freshwater fish and game, wild mushrooms and wild fruit. And – providing its inhabitants are industrious, as the people of Alsace so clearly are – unrivalled opportunities for food production. The rolling meadowland near the Swiss border is dotted with orchards whose fruit soon finds its way into crisp open tarts and fragrant fruit spirits, and with meres where carp secretly glide. The fertile plain beside the Rhine is planted with round white cabbages and potatoes, with wheat and barley and maize. Asparagus and hops flourish just north of Strasbourg. The narrow strip running from the lower slopes of the western Vosges to the plain produces Alsace's superb white wines, and the farms high up in the mountains make pungent munster cheeses and the creamy *fromage blanc* that is so delicious doused in locally produced *kirsch*. And throughout the region, pigs are reared to produce Alsace's extraordinary range of *charcuterie*.

Garlands of sausages, elegantly arranged knuckles of pork, thick white china terrines of pâtés, huge glistening hams, truffled *cervelas* sausage, alternating rows of black puddings and snowy white *boudins blancs* – wherever you go in Alsace displays in *charcuterie* windows will be among your first impressions of the riches that lie in store for you in the region's restaurants and *winstubs*. Pig-rearing is no longer conducted on the same small scale as when virtually every family would fatten its own pig and call in the local butcher to kill the beast on the spot, prepare the chitterling sausages and blood puddings for immediate consumption, then carve the carcass up into chops and hams, shoulder and belly joints ready for salting to keep the household going for the next six months. But *charcuterie* is still the basis of many of the region's specialities.

You will soon come across *schiffala*, a dish of smoked and salted blade of pork with potato salad. *Söymage* or *saumawe* is stuffed belly of pork, stitched up before cooking, then sliced; *wädele*, knuckle of pork with potato salad and horseradish; *presskopf*, brawn or head cheese in aspic; *süri rüewe*, a stew of smoked bladebone and knuckle of pork with turnips, onions and Alsace wine. If you like kidneys, don't miss one of my favourites, *süri nierli*, pigs' kidneys cooked in vinegar. And try to taste some of the many different types of sausages that originated in Alsace: *saucisses de Strasbourg*, for instance, are boiling sausages rather like the familiar frankfurter, but plumper and usually including a little beef as well as pork. *Knack* is a smaller version, traditionally eaten as a snack between meals with a glass of beer. And the suggestively shaped *männerstolz* will always raise a snigger from those who know the name means 'male pride'. *Cervelas*, a lightly cured, spicy sausage, was long ago anglicized as saveloy; it rarely includes brains these days (the name comes from *cervelle*, brains) and

New wine and new walnuts are traditionally enjoyed in the convivial atmosphere of a cosy winstub *or* caveau

is eaten either grilled, or sliced as a popular first course with tomatoes, sliced raw onion and whatever green salad materials are in season, dressed with a mustardy vinaigrette.

Without *charcuterie*, Alsace's best-known winter dish would be no more than pickled cabbage, as indeed its name, *choucroute*, means. The Français de l'Intérieur, unable to get their tongues round the dialect term *sürkrüt* (closely related, of course, to German *Sauerkraut*), sensibly modified it by replacing the first syllable with *chou*, cabbage. The fat, tightly packed white cabbages grown in and round the villages of central Alsace are shredded and preserved in salt and seasonings, particularly the juniper berries that help to give *choucroute* its distinctive flavour. The famous dish referred to as *choucroute garnie*, or *choucroute garnie à l'alsacienne* (see recipe, p. 63) consists of the pickled cabbage, cooked in lard or goose fat with onions and salt and smoked bacon, then piled high on a serving dish with an amazing quantity of sausages and pork chops, little knuckles of ham, black puddings, chunks of smoked ham and much else besides. Pots of grated horseradish mixed with cream, a few drops of olive oil and lemon juice (a far cry from the vinegary concoction you can buy in bottles) and yellow Dijon mustard are the usual accompaniments.

But *choucroute* is not inseparable from *charcuterie*. Chez Yvonne, Strasbourg's most fashionable *winstub*, serves *tarte à la choucroute* as a first course, and you may come across pheasant or preserved goose (*confit d'oie*) served on a bed of pickled cabbage. Guy-Pierre Baumann, a celebrated restaurateur from the Sundgau who runs several of Paris's best-known brasseries, and now presides over the superb medieval *Maison Kammerzell* beside Strasbourg Cathedral, has recently managed to persuade the people of Alsace that *la choucroute aux poissons* is not just a fad taken up by Parisian gourmets but an acceptable alternative to the traditional dish, especially in summer. If you are overwhelmed by the sight of other diners tackling gigantic mounds of pork products with their *choucroute*, then try ordering this interesting variant. Lighter and more delicate in flavour, it usually consists of several freshwater fish – pike, pike-perch and tench, perhaps salmon too – lightly poached and served on a bed of pickled cabbage with a creamy, Riesling-based sauce. In fact according to the historians this 'new' version of a traditional dish is not so new: Alsace cooks used to prepare fish with pickled cabbage centuries ago, just as they once made fish terrines that are not dissimilar to the prettily striped modern versions made fashionable by *nouvelle cuisine* chefs.

Fish from the region's streams and rivers play a large part in Alsace cuisine. *Truite au Riesling* is not so very different from the classic *truite au bleu*: very fresh plump trout lightly simmered in a court bouillon prepared with a generous helping of Riesling. Riesling is the key ingredient, too, in *matelote à l'alsacienne*, also called *matelote au Riesling*, a delicious dish of pieces of eel stewed with trout, pike and pike-perch in a Riesling-based fish stock or court bouillon. *Sandre à la crème* (pike-perch in a creamy sauce served with freshly made ribbon pasta) regularly appears on menus, since pasta with fish is a favourite combination with the local people. Pike (*brochet*) is also served this way. *Délice de sandre* is another variant on the fish-in-a-wine-sauce theme, with fillets of perch poached in Riesling and fish stock with finely chopped shallots and chives, and then double cream and a beaten egg yolk gently added to the reduced juices in the pan. In the Sundgau chunks of carp from the local meres are lightly fried in batter, then served with wedges of lemon, plain boiled potatoes and a little bowl of home-made mayonnaise. *Carpe frite*, which features in much of the region's publicity, can be insipid, but properly prepared, it is a curiosity well worth trying. If you are lucky you may also be able to try *carpe à la juive*, baked carp stuffed with raisins, chopped almonds and various herbs and spices, a dish with a distinctly Central European flavour.

Another creature of ponds and meres dear to the heart of every true son or daughter of Alsace is the frog. The Ried, the marshy plain beside the Rhine, used to be overrun with them, and though they are now much less common, rather than deprive themselves of the joys of a *soupe aux grenouilles* (frog soup) or frog's legs poached in wine and served with pasta, cooks make do with imports from Eastern Europe. In the elegant restaurant of the Château d'Isembourg near Rouffach I had an interesting combination of frogs' legs and snails wrapped in a cabbage leaf and served in a light creamy Riesling-based sauce – a good example of a modern adaptation of a traditional delicacy. For snails, too, are popular in Alsace. Snail breeding was allegedly introduced into the region by monks, who saw snails as a useful standby for meatless Fridays – but legend does not relate whether *escargots à l'alsacienne* were invented in a monastery. They are simmered in a mixture of water and Alsace wine with carrots, shallots and herbs, then served with butter worked with finely chopped garlic and herbs. The snails are usually smaller than the classic *escargots de Bourgogne* and the final taste seems more strongly flavoured, presumably because of the wine used.

The region's distinctive wines enter into the composition of so many dishes that you should not be surprised to find *coq au vin*, that staple of the French household repertoire, transformed into *coq au Riesling*. The use of the delicately grapey Riesling makes this dish taste quite different from the heavy, almost sticky red-wine sauce you may have come across elsewhere in France. Once again double cream is added to the juices left in the casserole to make a sauce and thinly sliced mushrooms are included at this stage, rather than the whole button mushrooms that go into the standard *coq au vin*. Ribbon pasta is usually served with it, and with *poularde au Riesling*, a young pullet prepared in the same way.

Another favourite accompaniment to main courses is *spätzele*, small lengths of pasta, boiled in the usual way, then lightly browned in the oven, or occasionally fried till golden. There are echoes of Italian cuisine too in *knepfle*, little dumplings made with mashed boiled potatoes or semolina mixed with flour and chopped parsley, usually a small amount of chopped leek too, then moistened with egg yolk and cooked like *gnocchi*. *Lewerknepfle*, tasty dumplings made with minced pig's liver, lightly fried onion and minced smoked bacon, are particularly popular.

Spätzele go well with the game that appears on every restaurant menu in northern Alsace in the autumn. The forests of the Northern Vosges are full of succulent pheasant and wild duck, hare and venison and even wild boar. Game is often jugged (*hasepfeffer*, jugged hare, is common) and served with the delectable edible fungi found in the forests, and perhaps a relish made from wild berries. Game pâtés and terrines make a good first course at this time of year, again sometimes served with local fruit, or with pickled beetroot. Instead of *spätzele*, game – and other meat dishes – may be accompanied by *grumbeerekechle*, a type of pancake or omelet made with grated potato, chopped onion and parsley stirred into beaten eggs and fried. You may also spot this on *winstub* menus as a main course, or be served it by itself after the soup course in a *ferme-auberge*.

Miniature versions of another Alsace speciality, *Ziwelküeche* or onion tart, may sometimes be served as an accompaniment too. A full-size onion tart makes a good starter on a cold day, or a main course with salad in summer (see recipe, p. 62). Even more popular these days is Alsace's answer to the ubiquitous pizza, *flammekueche*, oddly known in French as *tarte flambée*, used to be a family dish made from the dough left over from bread making, but is now found all over Strasbourg and some other towns and villages (see p 65).

Tarts make a universal pudding course too, filled with the region's delicious fruit. Of all the cultivated fruit, tiny golden mirabelle plums make perhaps the best tart (*tarte aux mirabelles*), but *tarte aux quetsches*, filled with purple quetsch plums, and apple and rhubarb tarts are also good. These open fruit tarts taste rather different from the standard *tarte aux pommes* and the like that you meet all over France, because they are made with crumbly shortcut pastry. This type of pastry, much the same as that used for onion tart, but with sugar added, is also the basis of another Alsace speciality, *tarte au fromage blanc* (cream cheese tart, see p. 64). *Fromage blanc* is served on its own with a generous sprinkling of *kirsch*, not with thick cream and sugar as in homes and modest restaurants elsewhere in France.

Before pudding, you will be offered cheese – usually munster, the only well-known cheese produced in Alsace. Made on the *marcaireries*, the farms in the Vosges whose cattle graze on the lush mountain pastures, it is a softish cheese with an orangey-yellow crust and a very strong smell. It is undoubtedly an acquired taste, but you should certainly try it, making sure if you are buying it to ask for munster *fermier*, which means that it is guaranteed to be from a farm in or near the Munster Valley (see Chapter 7). Although purists frown on the practice, munster is usually served with a little glass or china bowl of caraway seeds, called *karvi* locally, or *cumin* in French. You may find it in *winstubs* as a main course with potatoes in their jackets.

Caraway seeds are also used to flavour one of the many varieties of bread made in Alsace, and so is aniseed. Both are again ingredients in the little biscuits called *bredle* traditionally made for the Christmas festivities but nowadays often displayed in the region's *boulangeries* and *pâtisseries* at other times of year (see p. 20). Here, too, you will see Alsace's best-known cake, the distinctively shaped *kougelhopf*, an essential component of all celebrations and also eaten by many families with their breakfast coffee (see p. 60). Alsace's pastry cooks are famous throughout France and you should certainly aim to join the ladies in hats tucking in to coffee or tea and cakes in one of Strasbourg's tearooms – but make it a day when you are having only a light supper. The sweet version of knot-shaped *bretzels* (the dialect name for what we call pretzels) are popular with tea or coffee too, though the salted savoury variety familiar outside Alsace may also be served with your *apéritif*. Prettily wrapped and ribboned, sweet *bretzels* and *bredle* make good presents to take home. So too do the decorated gingerbread hearts with a ribboned loop so that you can hang them on the wall of your kitchen for luck.

A week of meals in Alsace

Let us suppose that it is your first day in Alsace. You have read this chapter, you have started to memorize some of the names in the 'Menu Reader' on p. 61, and you have been studying the windows of the food shops near your hotel. You venture into your first Alsace restaurant, not too fancy, and, judging by its menu, offering regional cuisine so that you can start to try out some of the dishes you have heard about. For this first meal you would probably do best to pick something straightforward: perhaps onion tart, followed by *poulet au Riesling* (chicken in a creamy wine sauce with pasta) or *wädele* (knuckle of pork with potato salad), then a green salad to balance the meal, and a fruit tart to finish.

By the next day you are feeling more adventurous and may like to experiment with a *choucroute*. If you do not feel ready to tackle that yet, you may feel more at home with a *bäckeoffe*, a comforting stew that for once includes beef and lamb as well as pork (see recipe, p. 62). You would be wise to skip an *hors d'oeuvre* when you are trying out these filling dishes.

The following day it will be time to enjoy a dose of *winstub* ambiance. Here you must study the Menu Reader again, and don't be afraid to ask your neighbours for help in choosing. *Presskopf* with a green salad and potatoes, followed by *bibelkäs* (*fromage blanc* with shallots or chives) might be a good choice.

On another day you should certainly try a *flammekueche*, choosing a restaurant that specializes in it. Then you will want to visit a *ferme-auberge* to sample the traditional *menu marcaire* (see p. 140). If it is May or June, make sure to plan an 'asparagus meal' of mounds of the succulent spears with various sauces, and, if you have any room left, a plain grilled chicken.

Then a day will come when you splash out on an expensive restaurant, but still want, since you are in Alsace, to keep as far as possible to regional specialities. The obvious choice for a first course must be Alsace's superb *foie gras*. It may be served very cold, the thin, pinky-brown slices carefully arranged on a large plate, perhaps studded with truffles and decorated with little cubes of aspic. Or you might like to try it hot, sautéed gently in butter and probably served with

Knot-shaped sweet bretzels *are a feature of Alsace's traditional Christmas fare*

apples, again sautéed in butter. The main course could be locally caught fish, or game if it is autumn, with a wine-based sauce in either case. And for pudding, a sorbet flavoured with a local fruit spirit like Poire William would be an appropriate prelude to a little glass of the spirit itself, the perfect *digestif*. Needless to say you would be drinking Alsace wine, of which Charlotte Fleming speaks so knowledgeably in the next chapter.

Kougelhopf

All over Alsace, decorating the walls of restaurants and tearooms, and given pride of place in souvenir shops or boutiques specializing in local craft work, you will soon spot deep cylindrical moulds in copper or earthenware or painted china, with twisted fluted sides. These decorative objects make good presents to take home, but you can also buy cheaper ones in aluminium in kitchen shops, for their primary purpose is purely functional. They are used to make Alsace's best-known cake, *kougelhopf*, known to dialect speakers as *koïlopf* and sometimes transposed phonetically into French as *kouglof*.

Legend has it that Marie Antoinette introduced the people of Alsace to this distinctively shaped light yeast cake flavoured with almonds and raisins and, on special occasions, with kirsch. But as both cake and mould were already familiar in the region by the mid eighteenth-century and Marie Antoinette was not born until 1755, this seems far-fetched.

Early recipes suggest that *kougelhopf* then had a biscuit-like consistency and was richer than the versions baked today, with a higher proportion of eggs. Nowadays it is served at any time of day. At breakfast you dip big wedges of it into a steaming bowl of coffee. It may be served as a pudding at lunchtime or in the evening, with a glass of grapey Alsace wine, or with a mid-afternoon cup of coffee. And on festive occasions a richer version will have the place of honour in the centre of a table groaning with goodies.If you're invited to a cocktail party or business reception in Alsace, don't be surprised to see thick wedges of *kougelhopf* being handed round after the savoury cocktail bits.

You may come across unexpected uses of the traditional moulds: at the family-run *Au Cheval Blanc* in Molsheim I much enjoyed the speciality of *kougelhopf de légumes à la crème d'avocat*, a light vegetable terrine baked in the familiar fluted mould, with a creamy purée of avocadoes.

But *kougelhopf* really comes into its own in early June, when the village of Ribeauvillé on the Wine Road, the self-styled '*Kougelhopf* Capital of the World', stages its annual **Fête du Kougelhopf**. Children dress up in the regional costume and local pastry cooks bake giant *kougelhopfs* which are paraded through the streets on stretcher-like stands, decorated with red-white-and-blue ribbons and garlands of leaves and flowers. Large quantities of wine are drunk and great fun is had by all.

Menu reader

Even if you're used to eating in French restaurants, you'll find menus in Alsace a puzzle at first. Try to learn the names of some of the local specialities before you venture into your first *winstub* or brasserie and you'll feel much more at home. Some of these dishes are described in greater detail elsewhere in this chapter.

Bäckeoffe (also spelt **Baekoffa**, **Baeckaoffa**, **Baekenoffe** and in various other similar ways): The name literally means 'baking oven' and this classical regional dish used to be taken to the local baker's to be cooked slowly; a flavoursome stew of various types of meat with onions and potatoes, braised with white wine (see p. 62).
Bibelkäs (or **Bibeleskäs** or even **Bibelass Käs**): *Fromage blanc* with chopped shallots, or sometimes chives, stirred in, served with fried potatoes.
Choucroute (sauerkraut): The Alsace dish *par excellence*, served in huge portions: pickled cabbage with sausages, smoked ham and knuckle of ham (see recipe).
Flammekueche: Also known as **tarte flambée**, the Alsace version of pizza, but larger and thinner (see recipe).
Fleischnecke: Pieces of boiled meat, cooked as for a *pot-au-feu*, then rolled up to look like snails (the name literally means 'meat snails'); may also be made with chicken.
Grumbeerekechle: A type of pancake made with grated potatoes.

Kassler: Smoked fillet of pork, sometimes served in a pastry crust.
Knack: Small boiled sausages, popular as a snack with a glass of beer.
Lewerknepfle: *Quenelles* made with minced calf's liver (or occasionally pig's liver) and cooked in a pan of boiling water.
Presskopf: Brawn in aspic, served with green salad and potatoes.
Schiffala: Smoked and salted bladebone of pork, soaked overnight and boiled; usually served with potato salad.
Spätzele: Short, thick lengths of pasta, cooked in the usual way in boiling water, but popped into the oven for a few minutes before serving, so that they are lightly browned and a little crust has formed on top.
Streusel or **streuselküeche**: A type of cake baked with a layer of flour blended with butter and mixed with sugar and cinnamon spread on top.
Sueri nierli: Veal or pig's kidneys braised in vinegar.
Suppefleisch: Alsace's variant on the traditional French *pot-au-feu*: the boiled beef is served with *crudités* rather than with its own vegetables.
Süri rüewe: A dish traditionally served in Colmar, made from bladebone and cured knuckle of pork stewed with onions and turnips in white wine.
Wädele: Shin of pork served with strong horseradish and potato salad.
Wasserstriwle: Similar to *spätzele*, a speciality of southern Alsace.
Ziwelküeche: Onion tart (see p. 62).

Recipes

Tarte à l'oignon or *Ziwelküeche* (onion tart)
Pastry: 250g plain flour, 125g butter, half a tsp salt, 3–4 tbs water
Filling: 250g onions, 75g lard (or 75g butter and 1tbs oil), 100g smoked lean bacon
White sauce: 50g butter, 60g flour, ½l milk (or ¼l milk plus ¼l double cream), 2 egg yolks, salt, pepper and nutmeg to taste

First make some rather crumbly pastry by rubbing the butter, cut into little pieces, into the sieved flour mixed with the salt. Add enough iced water to moisten the dough so that you can shape it quickly into a ball. Without kneading or rolling it, spread it out quickly in a buttered flat flan tin or fluted china tart dish, using your knuckles to push it into place evenly and thinly.

Now peel the onions and slice very finely. Melt the lard (or use butter and oil if you're not worried about authenticity) in a thick frying pan and sauté the onions very gently until they are a light gold colour. While they are cooking, cut the bacon into thick strips, pour boiling water over them to blanch them, and leave them to dry on kitchen paper.

Make the *béchamel* by melting the butter in a heavy bottomed saucepan, and then sprinkling on the flour, but don't let it go brown as in a classic *roux* before adding the milk, stirring all the time. For a richer mixture, use half milk and half cream, or even all cream. Season with salt, pepper and nutmeg and cook over low heat until it has reduced a little. Beat the egg yolks, remove the *béchamel* from the heat and stir in the eggs. Then add the onions, stir well and check the seasoning. Pour the mixture into the pastry case and sprinkle the little strips of bacon on top.

Bake in the centre of a hot oven (200°C) for about 25 minutes, or until the filling is lightly set. Serve very hot as a first course, or with a green salad for a light meal, and a bottle of Sylvaner.

Baeckaoffa (meat and potato hotpot)
You need a large earthenware or iron casserole for this most famous of all Alsace family dishes. Ingredients are for 5 or 6 hearty appetites, followed by a green or mixed salad.

500g shoulder of pork, 500g shoulder of lamb (mutton, if you can get it, would make the dish more authentic), 500g beef (blade or chuck are the nearest equivalents to the French cut known as *paleron* used for *baeckaoffa*), 1kg potatoes, 2 largish onions, 2 cloves garlic, a bottle of Riesling or Sylvaner, a few sprigs of parsley and thyme, 2 bay leaves, salt and pepper

Cut up the meat into largish chunks, put them into a large bowl and pour over a marinade made with enough of the wine to cover, one onion, thickly sliced, the cloves of garlic, crushed or chopped, and the herbs and seasoning. Leave for 24 hours.

The next day, peel and slice the potatoes and arrange a layer of them on the bottom of the casserole. Lift the pieces of meat from the marinade with a perforated spoon and arrange a layer of each type of meat on top of the potatoes. Then chop the other onion and put a layer of that in the casserole, followed by another layer of potatoes and meat. Season with salt and pepper as you go. Pour over the marinade mixture and add the rest of the wine.

Cover with a sheet of foil, pressing the edges down firmly, then put on the lid. If you want to do as an Alsace housewife would, seal the lid with a flour and water paste instead of using foil, the object of the exercise being to make sure that the fragrant bouquet doesn't escape. Many cooks in Alsace add a split pig's trotter and a pig's tail.

As you won't be able to take your casserole to the baker's, pop it into a medium-hot oven (175°C) for about 2½ hours. Serve piping hot straight from the casserole with the same wine as you have used for the marinade, or a Pinot Blanc or Noir. A perfect filling dish for a family meal or an informal supper party on a cold day.

Choucroute garnie à l'alsacienne (pickled cabbage with pork, ham and sausages)

2kg sauerkraut, 2 medium onions, 200g lard, ½l Alsace wine (preferably Sylvaner), ¼l good stock (or water)

Meat: You can vary the quantities as the mood takes you, but a traditional filling *choucroute* for about 8 people should have all of the following: 1kg smoked shoulder of pork, 4 cured knuckles of pork (*jambonneau*), 500g smoked bacon (in a single piece, not rashers) and another 500g green bacon, again in the piece, 2 black puddings, 8 *saucisses de Strasbourg* (frankfurters will do as a substitute), another 8 pork sausages; if you are self-catering in Alsace, look out for sausages known as *montbéliards*, and add to your shopping list eight *quenelles* made with minced liver (*quenelles de foie*)

Seasoning: salt, freshly milled pepper, a bay leaf, 3 or 4 cloves, 8 juniper berries, 2-3 cloves garlic

If you are using tinned sauerkraut, it is essential to rinse it thoroughly in plenty of water or the finished dish will be far too salty. Fresh sauerkraut bought in a delicatessen merely needs draining.

Chop the onions roughly, melt the lard in a large ovenproof dish or casserole and soften the chopped onion in it gently. Pour over a little of the wine and heated stock, then arrange the various pieces of pork and bacon in the dish or casserole. Add the sauerkraut in a layer on top of the meat and tuck in the cloves of garlic, the bay leaf, cloves and juniper berries. Season with salt and pepper. Pour over the rest of the wine and enough stock to cover (add a little hot water if necessary). Put the lid on and cook over low heat on top of the stove for 1½ hours, or transfer to a medium oven for 2 hours.

Shortly before you are ready to serve, poach the frankfurters and, if you are including them, the *quenelles* in gently simmering water, and grill the black puddings and pork sausages.

Lift the sauerkraut from the casserole with a slotted spoon and arrange it heaped up in the middle of a large warmed serving dish. Lift out the pieces of meat, slice as necessary and arrange them and the sausages, black puddings and *quenelles* round and on top of the sauerkraut. Check the seasoning, adding pepper if necessary.

Serve with plain boiled potatoes and several bottles of Riesling.

Make sure the pudding is something very light and urge your guests to finish with a little glass of one of the Alsace fruit spirits, as a delicious aid to digestion. Some recipes call for the addition of a little glass of kirsch shortly before the end of the cooking time, for the same reason.

Choucroute is also very good with pheasant, either roasted separately or browned all over in butter or pork fat, then added to the sauerkraut for the last half hour. Serve the pheasant carved into neat pieces and arranged on and round the sauerkraut in the same way, with a few rashers of fried or grilled smoked bacon. Or cook a piece of smoked bacon in with the sauerkraut and chop it into cubes or sticks which you can scatter over the top of the finished dish.

Tarte au fromage blanc (cream cheese tart)
Pastry: Make the pastry in the same way as for the onion tart on p. 62, but add 2tbs sugar to the sieved flour and salt before rubbing in the butter. Spread the dough into the buttered tart tin with your knuckles, prick it all over with a fork and bake blind for 5 minutes in a hot oven (205°C).
Filling: 500g *fromage blanc*, 2dl *crème fraîche* (or double cream if you can't get it), 4 eggs, 175g caster sugar, 1tbs flour, ½tsp salt

Pour the *fromage blanc* into a bowl (or sieve ordinary cream cheese), beat in first the sugar, then the salt and flour, followed by the cream and, carefully, the eggs. Beat till smooth. Pour the mixture into the pastry case and bake for 40-45 minutes until the filling is set and lightly browned. Sprinkle with a little sugar and serve warm, with a glass of Gewürztraminer.

Tarte aux fruits à l'alsacienne (open fruit tarts)
Pastry: Again, make the pastry as for the onion tart on p. 62, but adding 2tbs sugar to the sieved flour and salt
Fruit filling: In Alsace the most common fruit used are mirabelle plums, quetsches or apples (sweet eating apples rather than cooking ones), but you may also come across wild bilberry, rhubarb, apricot and pear tarts. For pastry made with 250g flour and 125g butter, you will need almost 1kg of fruit
Custard mixture: 2 eggs, 1tbs sugar, 2dl double cream (or 1dl milk and 1dl double cream)

Prepare the fruit: cut plums or apricots in half and stone, peel and core apples and cut into neat slices, top and tail rhubarb and cut into small chunks. Cook for a few minutes in a very little water, with sugar to taste. Drain and arrange neatly on the pastry case. Sprinkle over a little sugar and bake in a hot oven (200°C) for about 25 minutes or until the fruit is soft. Meanwhile beat the eggs and sugar lightly and stir in the cream. Pour the mixture over the fruit filling and bake for another 5 minutes. Serve hot or warm, sprinkled with a little more sugar.

A Gewürztraminer is the traditional accompaniment to these delicious tarts, which can also be made as individual tartlets.

Flammekueche

A great speciality in Strasbourg and the surrounding area is *Flammekeuche*, misleadingly referred to in French as a *tarte flambée*. It isn't a 'flambéed tart', but a bit like a pizza, only larger, flatter and crisper. It was traditionally made on baking days in country districts, when the dough left over from bread making was rolled out very thin, then covered with a mixture of cream, diced fat bacon and thinly sliced onions. Once baked, it was shared out during a family gathering, with everyone breaking off a piece for him or herself.

You can now find *flammekueche* in cheerful restaurants all over Strasbourg and in some nearby towns and villages. They are particularly good at **L'Horloge astronomique** near the cathedral, at **La Bourse**, a large brasserie in the place de la Bourse, and at **La République**, an inexpensive and very popular Strasbourg institution in the rue du Faubourg-National, where you can sometimes dance to a live band. Outside Strasbourg, **Au Boeuf**, in a seventeenth-century building in Blaesheim (183 rue du Maréchal-Foch, 88 68 81 31) and the half-timbered **Auberge du Pont de la Zorn** in Weyersheim (88 51 36 87), which has a large terrace for summer meals, are both well known for their *flammekueche*. If you feel like baking one yourself, here's the recipe:

1 small onion, 50g butter, 400ml double cream, salt, pepper and nutmeg to taste, 75g smoked bacon, 500g bread dough, 1tbs oil

Chop the onion and soften it gently in the butter until golden and transparent. Stir in the cream and season to taste with salt, freshly milled pepper and grated nutmeg. Dice the bacon into thick little sticks and fry them gently until the fat runs and they start to brown.

Roll out the dough very thin and lay it on a large baking sheet. Spread the cream and onion mixture evenly on to the rolled out dough and pour the oil on top. Dot with the bacon pieces and bake in a very hot oven for 10 minutes

The autumn grape harvest brings both tourists and members of the wine trade flocking to Alsace

3
Alsace wines

by Charlotte Fleming

The wines of Alsace are unusual among those of France in several ways. The grape varieties, bottles and labels are very Germanic. Indeed, many of the varieties are found nowhere else in France, though they are common across the Rhine in Baden. But the wines themselves are French. Dry, quite full-bodied and comparatively high in alcohol, they have little in common with the normal style of German wine making. These are wines made to accompany food, rather than for the drawing room or summer garden. The people of Alsace themselves claim their wines can partner any meal.

Alsace wines are also unusual among French wines in that the Appellation Contrôlée is for the grape variety, not the *commune*. This, though, has been slightly confused over the past few years with the introduction of *Grand Cru* vineyards, which have separate appellations. Only specified varieties, matched to the soil, may be planted on *Grand Cru* sites. Expect to pay a premium for them – but they are worth it.

There are four 'noble' grape varieties. Chief among them, as in Germany, is the **Riesling**, which has been grown in the region since at least 1477. The variety is late-ripening, and needs plenty of sunshine and not too much rain, so the shelter provided to the Alsace vineyards by the Vosges produces near-perfect conditions for it. Here it makes wines of great elegance and subtlety, particularly if grown on limestone. Alsace Riesling goes wonderfully well with *truite au bleu*, most other fish and, of course, *coq au Riesling*. Together with Gewürztraminer, Riesling is probably the best-known and most typical Alsace wine.

Gewürztraminer means 'spicy [vine] from Tramin' and seems to have originated in the eponymous South Tyrolean village. However, it typifies Alsace wine for many people. It easily achieves high levels of alcohol, and is one of the varieties most frequently left for late-picking (*vendange tardive*, a term which may only be used for Riesling, Gewürztraminer and Tokay). Late picking creates very luscious wines, sometimes, but not invariably, with some residual sugar. A characteristic flavour of lychees, lowish acidity and very often a heavily-perfumed 'nose', make this variety easy to spot 'blind'. Indeed, the bouquet is sometimes so overpowering – *pommadé* or, as one eminent British wine writer has described it, 'tart's boudoir' – that it is rather unpleasant. The drinker can soon become tired of it, and go in search of something more restrained. The less overwhelming versions go excellently with munster cheese, curries, and other spicy food, and Gewürztraminer with smoked salmon is a classic combination. The vine does best on rather heavy clay or limestone soil.

Third in the hierarchy, but increasing in popularity, is the **Tokay**, now usually hyphenated '-Pinot Gris' to avoid confusion with the sweet Hungarian Tokaji (no relation, though legends regarding their various origins abound). **Pinot Gris** probably mutated from the Pinot Noir of Burgundy, the *gris* referring to the pinkish colours of the grape skins. It shows itself in the wine only as a rather deeper gold, rather than any reddish hue. It is the least aromatic of the Alsace wines, but one of the most robust – high in alcohol, full and rich, without the obvious varietal character of the other 'noble' grapes.

All the 'noble' varieties have nicknames. Riesling is 'King', Gewürztraminer is 'Emperor', Muscat is 'Crown Prince'. Pinot Gris is 'Sultan' – soft, fat and rich. It can age well, especially in a good vintage or if late-picked. In Alsace it is considered one of the two ideal partners for *foie gras*, the other being Riesling. Pinot Gris also goes well with poultry, white meat and *bäckeoffe*, that huge stew of mutton, pork, beef, potatoes and seasonings plus wine. It even survives *choucroute* – though only Gewürztraminer can really fight back!

Muscat is the last of the 'noble' varieties. This can either be the Muscat *à petits grains* which, further south, produces luscious sweet wines, or the lesser-quality Muscat Ottonel. In Alsace, Muscat is vinified dry, very light and deliciously grapey in flavour – the perfect *apéritif*. The Muscat *à petits grains* is very prone to mildew problems this far north, despite the lowish rainfall, and the Muscat Ottonel only slightly less so. Research is under way to produce a tougher Muscat wine, with the good flavour of the Muscat *à petits grains*, but less prone to rot. Such research, however, takes many years. In a blend of the two, the Muscat *à petits grains* gives fullness and character, the Ottonel finesse. In a good Muscat year, the wines are delicious, and an ideal accompaniment to asparagus and mild fish dishes, or by themselves in a summer garden.

Of the 'lesser' grapes, **Sylvaner** is the most important, in that it covers the largest area of vineyard of any Alsace variety. It is prolific and rot-resistant even in cool climates, and is also a very popular vine in Germany. While not capable of producing wines of great intrinsic quality, the Sylvaner makes very good everyday quaffing wine, and accompanies fish and white meats very successfully. It can be very 'earthy' in flavour, and rather dull, but good examples have some fruit and a zingy freshness that atones for any lack of character. It is also sometimes used as a palate cleanser after a heavy meal. Wines from this variety tend to be very reasonably priced.

Pinot Blanc (also known as **Klevner** or **Clevner**, not to be confused with Klevner de Heiligenstein – see below) can in fact be made from five separate varieties. It is normally made either from the real Pinot Blanc or from Auxerrois, sometimes erroneously called Pinot Auxerrois;

other permitted varieties are Pinot Gris, Pinot Noir and Chardonnay, though these are seldom found under this name. On the whole wines from grapes other than Pinot Blanc itself will be sold as Klevner or Clevner. Given this confusion, it is quite hard to specify taste characteristics, but the wines sold under these three names seem generally to be lightish, softish and attractive, if unmemorable. They are usually good value for money, not being famous – probably about half the price of a decent Riesling.

The **Pinot Noir**, of Burgundy fame, produces Alsace's only red – or more often deep rosé – wine. Most of the wines made from this variety in Alsace are not very exciting: they tend to be disconcertingly full given the light colour, oddly scented and quite fat, while lacking any great character. Just occasionally, however, one can be found with some of the depth and quality associated with great Pinot Noir. Plantings are increasing, so it must be assumed that the people of Alsace see some future for the variety.

Chasselas plantings are, by contrast, decreasing. This is very much a workhorse variety, and normally disappears into **Edelzwicker**, the 'noble blend', with Auxerrois, Pinot Blanc, Knipperlé and other lesser varieties. In Switzerland, Chasselas (often sold as Fendant) has a high reputation, but it seems unable to achieve such quality in Alsace. Plantings are reducing at such a rate that soon there will be no Chasselas left here. Its loss will be unmourned.

The **Klevner de Heiligenstein** probably comes, like the Gewürztraminer, from Northern Italy, in this case from Chiavenna (Cleven in German). This is a pink grape, no relation to any of the other grapes also known as Klevner in Alsace. Its proper name is Savagnin Rosé, and it is thought to be an ancestor of the Gewürztraminer. While less aromatic than Gewürztraminer, Klevner de Heiligenstein wines have some spiciness and are quite full-bodied. There is very little acreage of the vine, but the small quantities of the wine produced are usually much admired.

Crémant d'Alsace is made by the same method as Champagne – second fermentation in bottle. It comes from any of the three Pinots, Auxerrois, Riesling and/or Chardonnay, but mostly from Pinot Blanc and Auxerrois. While not of a comparable standard to Champagne, Crémant d'Alsace makes a good celebration wine, at a very reasonable price.

The other famous drinks produced in Alsace are the white spirits (**alcools blancs**) or **eaux-de-vie**, made from fruits grown in the region. The most famous, **Kirsch**, comes from cherries, but virtually any sort of fruit or nut can be used, including holly berries (**Houx**), William pear (**Poire William**) and pine shoots (**Bourgeon de Sapin**). A wine is first made from the fruit, plus sugar if necessary, and this is distilled to give a clear spirit of 45°–50°. Another spirit, **Marc de Gewürztraminer**, is made in a similar way from the skins and pips remaining after pressing at the beginning of wine making.

Alsace is also famous for its beers, with such brands as **Kronenbourg**, **Mutzig** and **Adelshoffen**, which all provide a good accompaniment to the heavier dishes of Alsace cuisine.

Between 1870 and 1918, when Alsace

was German, her wines were used for blending with light German wines to add fullness, and Alsace wines as such had no market. Between the world wars considerable replanting was undertaken, but the fighting in 1944 destroyed many vineyards, and it was not until after 1945 that Alsace wines as we know them found an outlet.

Partly as a result of the cost involved in replanting with good vines, and partly because so many growers own much less than the 7.5 hectares/ 18½ acres of wine required to make a living from wine making, a good deal of Alsace wine is made by cooperatives. Some of these are excellent, such as Turckheim, Westhalten, Eguisheim (the largest in Alsace) and Kientzheim. There are also many large firms which play the same role as Burgundy's *négociants*, buying in grapes and occasionally young wine from smaller growers to supplement the produce of their own vineyards. Some of the best known, in no particular order, are:

- Hugel
- Trimbach
- Dopff et Irion
- Dopff 'au Moulin'
- Willy Gisselbrecht
- Sick-Dreyer
- Zind-Humbrecht
- J. Becker
- Emile Beyer

However, the fierce independence that is so characteristic of Alsace is well demonstrated by the number of people, often with full-time jobs, who make and sell their own wines at weekends.

Wine making in Alsace is kept as natural as possible, except for the addition of sugar to the grape juice before fermentation to increase the final alcohol level, or chaptalization. The majority of wine makers still use huge old wooden casks and scorn the laboratory technicians so prevalent in Germany. Many do not fine their wines, reckoning that fining strips out the flavour. They go to great lengths to keep the wine away from air contact. Too hot a fermentation can ruin the flavour of a wine, and the more modern cooperatives and big firms have in the main replaced the wooden vats with stainless steel ones, which are easier to clean and to cool down if fermentation temperatures start to rise.

Many of the larger firms have shops in the well-known tourist villages like Riquewihr and Ribeauvillé, where you can buy most of their range of products. Most of the cooperatives also do wine tours for interested groups. But by far the best way to find wines and *eaux-de-vie* to bring home is to visit the *vignerons* in their *caves*, where you can taste and discuss with the maker his thoughts and methods in wine making. Sometimes, if the discussion gets deep, you may be treated to old wines, while the *vigneron* becomes more and more enthusiastic. It is generally unwise to try driving after one of these sessions. Signs to look for are *vente directe* (sales direct to the public), *vente au détail* (retail sales), *dégustation* (wine tasting) and *propre récolte* (own vintage). You may also come across a display of bottles with prices, a useful guide as to whether or not you should venture in.

The *Route du Vin* (Wine Road, see Chapter 6) is well sign-posted and connects all the best villages from the point of view of wine tasting and buying, though some of the prettiest villages are bypassed.

Kientzheim is the headquarters of the Confrérie de Saint-Etienne, Alsace's 'medieval' wine fraternity. Its *chapitres* (chapters) are held in the château, where there is an excellent Wine Museum (see p. 124).

Tourist offices publish route maps for the Wine Road and will provide details of *viticulteurs* offering wine tastings and selling direct to the public. They will also have dates of the many wine fairs and festivals held throughout the summer and autumn (see Practical Information). The biggest wine fair in Alsace is held in Colmar in August, and the fair in Barr on 14 July (Bastille Day) is particularly well known.

Wine cellar visits and tastings are easily arranged in the villages on the Wine Road

4
In and around Strasbourg

Strasbourg, the capital of Alsace, is one of those rare places that has successfully managed to combine all the advantages of a big international city with the charm and the relaxed atmosphere of a small provincial town. As you stroll beside the river near the cathedral or saunter through the old streets lined with crooked half-timbered houses, as you stop for a coffee on a café terrace or a glass of wine in a cosy *winstub*, listening to the locals gossiping about their neighbours, you could easily be in some pleasant provincial backwater. But a few tables away the initiated will spot a Euro-MP. And a short trip along the River Ill in a sightseeing boat will bring you to the briskly modern buildings of the Council of Europe and the European Parliament. The cosy little drapers and haberdashers, the old-fashioned bookshops selling early children's books full of storks and little girls in outsize head-dresses, are flanked by expensive fashion boutiques proffering the latest creations of chic Paris designers. Round the corner from your cosy *winstub*, one of France's top gourmet restaurants attracts bankers and Eurocrats. As well as friendly family-style hotels, the city boasts a Hilton and a Holiday Inn. And on the outskirts are huge breweries and car plants.

One of the reasons behind the city's dual personality is the geographical convenience of the historical centre's being circumscribed by the River Ill. Inside this central area, which contains the major tourist sights, traffic is light – cars are banned from many streets – and you have little impression of being at the heart of a major commercial and financial centre. Virtually everything of interest is in walking distance of the superb cathedral, though those who don't enjoy walking can take a 'mini-train' from beside the cathedral and a boat trip along the Ill.

At the heart of this central area, the superb **Cathedral of Notre-Dame** is like 'a pinky-red angel hovering over the city', in the words of the poet and playwright Paul Claudel. With its single tall spire pointing upwards like an admonishing finger, it dominates the landscape over much of Alsace, the symbol of a proud and independent city praised by Erasmus as possessing 'a monarchy without tyranny, an aristocracy without factions, democracy without turmoil, wealth without luxury and prosperity without arrogance'. One of the finest of the great Gothic cathedrals, it stands on the site of a Roman temple, built on a mound above the marshy land surrounding the camp of Argentoratum, and an early church commissioned by King Clovis of the Franks.

The first version was begun in 1015, but fire destroyed most of this original Romanesque building, and by the time work started on rebuilding it at the end of the twelfth century, the Gothic style had reached Alsace, and stonemasons and master builders who had worked at Chartres were soon bringing their skills to this new project. After their defeat of their prince bishop (see A Little History), the bourgeoisie took charge of the work themselves, calling on the citizens to contribute to the building fund. A contribution of a horse – he apparently had no money to give – came from the man who was appointed in 1284 to mastermind the whole operation, the brilliant Erwin von Steinbach (see box, p. 74). To this medieval genius we owe the magnificent west front, in the purest of Gothic styles. By the time of Erwin's death building had progressed up to the storey bearing the huge rose window. Half a century later his towers had been completed, but a decision was taken to join them together with a structure acting as a belfry. In 1399 Ulrich von Ensingen, the architect of the cathedral of Ulm in Germany, supervised the building of the octagonal base of the spire, which was completed after his death by Johannes Hültz from Cologne – for the next four centuries it was to be the tallest building in Christendom.

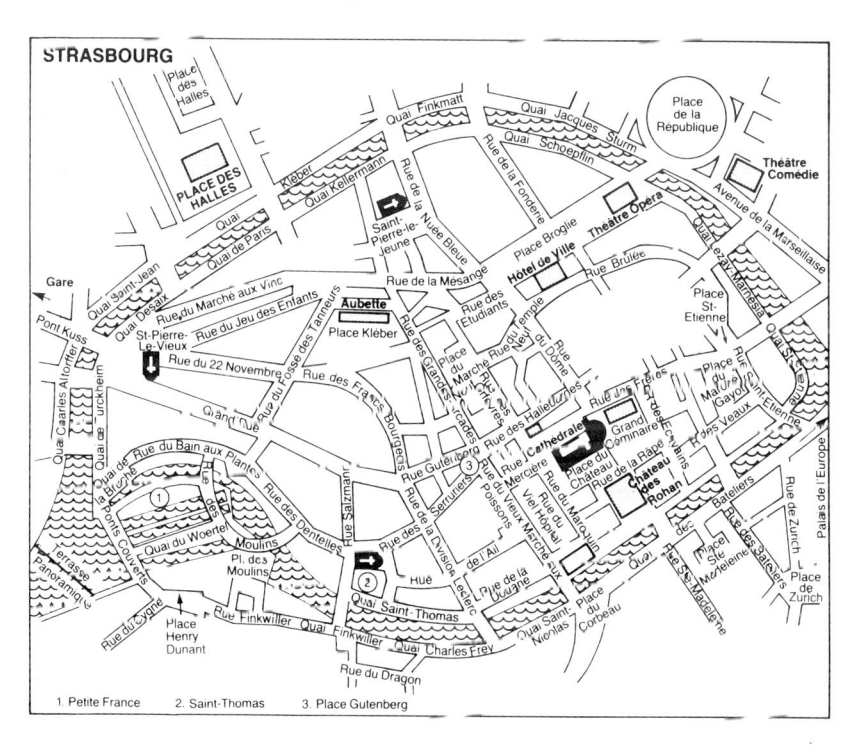

Erwin of Steinbach – the archetypal medieval architect

'Master Erwin', one of the best-known of medieval architects, owes much of his lasting, almost mystical, fame to Goethe, who revered him as the genius who masterminded the building of Strasbourg Cathedral. Goethe's prose poem *On German Architecture* is a panegyric to Erwin, and it is largely thanks to him that enthusiasm for Gothic architecture spread throughout Europe, and that Erwin is often seen as embodying the genius of the Middle Ages. Often compared to Dante, he inspired poets, painters and sculptors, and the legends that grew up round him extended to his whole family.

Particularly popular was his alleged daughter Sabine, who, in the largely mythical accounts of the building of the cathedral, is said to have been responsible for carving the superb sculptures on the Angel Pillar. During the Romantic era she was depicted in many a painting and engraving working on the cathedral, her long hair flowing over her idealized medieval dress. A favourite theme saw her sleepwalking, dizzily high up on scaffolding surrounding the unfinished west front. The whole family gradually came to symbolize the ordinary people who helped to build the medieval cathedrals to the greater glory of God.

Of the real, as opposed to the legendary Erwin, relatively little is known. He may or may not have been known as 'von Steinbach' (there is no contemporary record of the name) and his date of birth is uncertain, though it was probably 1244 or thereabouts. He was certainly working on the cathedral in 1284, and may have started as early as 1277. He is thought to have drawn the original plan of the west front, known as Design B, and now in the Musée de l'Oeuvre Notre-Dame. He was certainly the brilliant moving spirit behind the pure Gothic lines of that glorious façade, and it seems clear that he devoted the rest of his life to supervising the work of the stonemasons and sculptors up to the Apostles' Gallery above the rose window. The third apostle from the left is even believed to be a portrait of him. He may have lived for a while very nearly above the shop, in the house now known as the Maison Kammerzell (p. 78).

But his death on 16 February 1318 meant that his master plan, with its towers and spires, was never completed, even though his son Jean succeeded him as chief architect. Another son, Gerlach or Gerlac, designed the church of Saint-Florent in Niederhaslach and is buried there. But it was Sabine, who may never have existed, who captured the imagination of a later era.

A magnificent rose window surmounts the richly decorated west front of Strasbourg's cathedral, masterminded by Erwin von Steinbach

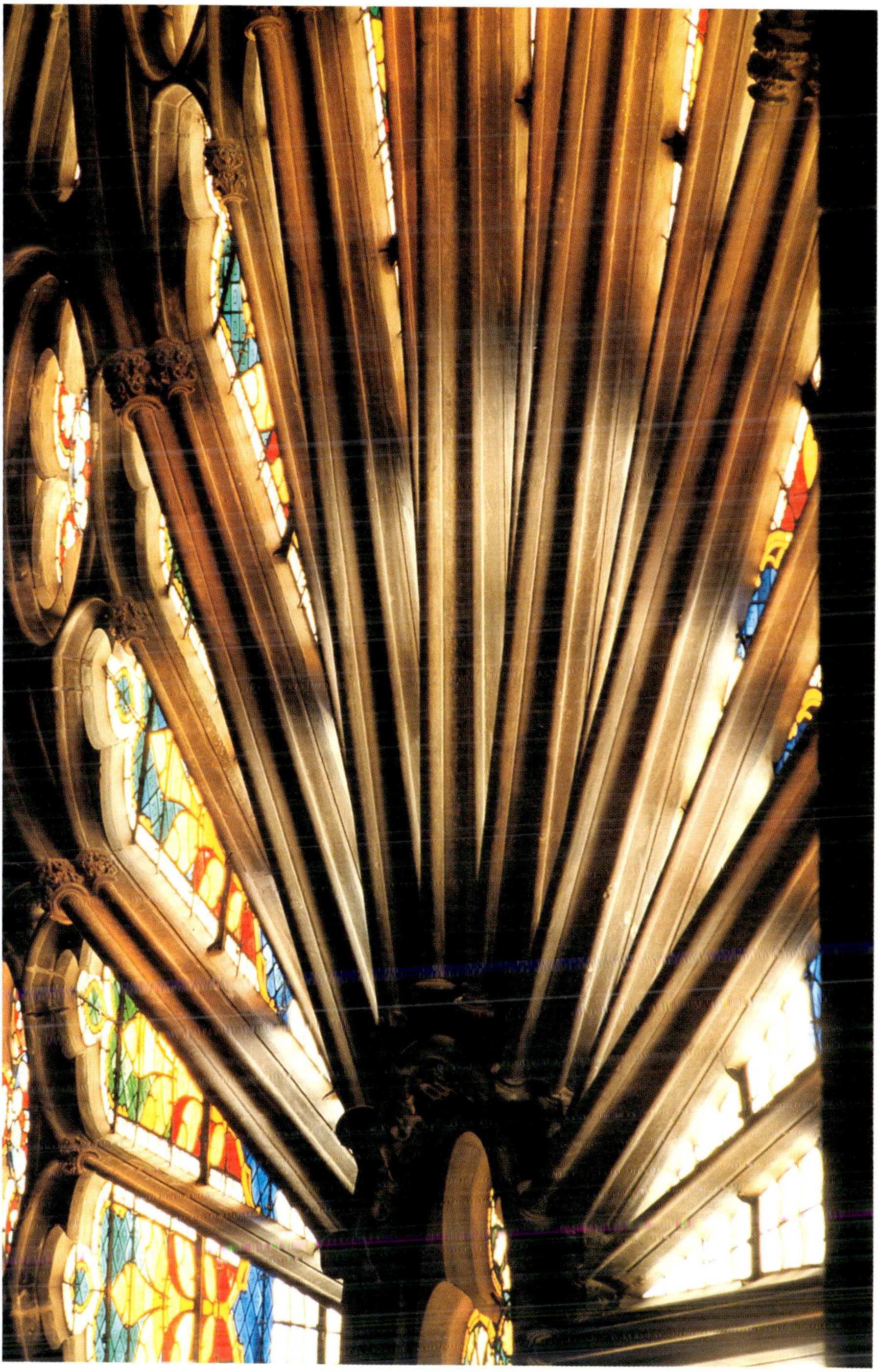

The spire, so much of a symbol of the cathedral now that the oddity of its having no twin seems insignificant, very nearly vanished for ever during the French Revolution: Saint-Just and other revolutionary leaders ordered its destruction, but a local locksmith conceived the brilliant scheme of making a huge Phrygian cap out of metal and covering the spire with it, so that this symbol of Liberty would cause the enemies of the Republic on the other side of the Rhine to quail. His wily suggestion carried the day and the spire was saved. But revolutionary fervour did lead to the destruction of some three hundred statues on the west front. The shellings of 1870 and 1944 caused some damage, but after several restoration programmes, and the replacement of the missing statues, you can once again share the emotion of Goethe, who spoke of the cathedral 'thrusting up a huge wall to Heaven, like the most sublime, wide-spreading Tree of God, proclaiming the glory of the Lord . . . with its thousand branches, millions of twigs and leaves like grains of sands by the sea . . .'

To experience this impression to the full, approach the cathedral from the **rue Mercière**, lined with picturesque houses. The west front looks particularly splendid on summer evenings, when the surging crowds have left the cathedral square and the setting sun picks out every detail of the stonework. The decorative scheme, with a steep gable above the central portal, carved with lion cubs symbolizing the tribes of Israel climbing up to the throne of Solomon, beneath a Virgin and Child supported by twin lions, while God the Father looks down from above, was probably devised by that great scholar and theologian Albertus Magnus, who was in Strasbourg in 1278, two years before his death. Among the rich carving on the three portals, the right-hand figures are particularly striking: the Devil, very much the Seducer with his neatly rolled hair and smirking expression, offers an apple to a clearly captivated Foolish Virgin, who is apparently about to strip for him, blissfully unaware of the slimy toads and snakes crawling up his back beneath his fashionable robe.

The figures on either side of the **South Portal**, too, are memorable. Both the Church Triumphant and the Synagogue, a graceful blindfolded figure, are copies, as the fourteenth-century originals, like much of the cathedral's statuary, has been removed to the **Musée de l'Oeuvre Notre-Dame** to prevent further damage from pollution. A visit to the museum opposite the south side of the cathedral, with its stepped medieval gable and later Renaissance gable, is a must. Feeling rather like a private house, with its many rooms on different levels, it gives you an excellent opportunity to study superb medieval and Renaissance sculpture at close quarters, along with the room where the masons' lodge met, a good stained glass collection and much else besides. On display are some of the original plans for the cathedral.

The South Portal is used for visits to the **Horloge astronomique** (astronomical clock), a mid-nineteenth-century version of the original fourteenth-century clock. The key time to see it in action is 12.30, but you must get there early to be sure of an unimpeded view. The seven different storeys indicate the month and year, the time by the sun, and GMT, while angels turn over hour glasses, a cock crows thrice, and the twelve apostles parade before Christ. Opposite the clock, the **Pilier des Anges** (Angel Pillar, also called the Pillar of the Last Judgement) is a superb piece of Gothic work, its eight slender columns peopled with graceful angels blowing trumpets and the evangelists, carved with great realism. Equally superb is the **Pulpit**, carved by Hans Hammer in 1485 for the famous preacher Geiler von Kayserberg (see box, p. 41). To see this magical transformation of stone into lace to full effect, you must attend a *son-et-lumière* performance (nightly from 1 April to mid-October, in both French and German). Even if you do not speak either language (there is a long-term plan to produce an English version), you will still be impressed by the play of light on the old stones and the sonorous voices of the top actors who take part, with an intelligent musical accompaniment; the booklet giving the French and German texts has a brief summary in English. The fine **organ case**, with its carved and painted organ loft, also looks magnificent as the light plays on it. I have no space to do justice to the cathedral's other riches, which repay a lengthy visit (though the cathedral unfortunately shuts between 11.30 and 12.15). The steep staircase (over three hundred steps) leading up to the platform at the foot of the towers stays open over lunch, and the views are magnificent in fine weather.

Opposite the South Portal is the **Château des Rohan**, an elegant eighteenth-century palace built for Cardinal Armand de Rohan-Soubise, one of several members of his family to be prince-bishop of Strasbourg. Designed by the royal architect Robert de Cotte, it is particularly lovely when seen from the banks of the **River Ill**. You can visit the very grand rooms lived in by the cardinal, all white and gold, and the museums now housed here. The **Musée des Beaux-Arts** (fine arts) has a particularly good collection of Italian paintings and includes Nicolas de Largillière's *La Belle Strasbourgeoise*, an elegant lady with a peculiarly broad-brimmed hat, a small spaniel in her arms and a smile as enigmatic as the Mona Lisa's. The **Musée des Arts décoratifs** (decorative arts) is famous for its collection of faïence and porcelain by the Hannong firm from Strasbourg, and for its clocks. The **Musée archéologique** (archeology) was closed for renovation when this book went to press; check whether it has reopened. Also closed was the **Galerie alsacienne** of work by local artists.

In the same square is another museum, the **Musée d'Art moderne**. Only a small proportion of its many interesting paintings, by Klimt and local painter Hans Arp among many others, can be shown here, but Strasbourg will one day have a brand-new Museum of Contemporary Art, on a site beyond the Petite France district (see below). Also in the square is the **Cabinet des Estampes** (Print Room).

Opposite the west front of the cathedral, the **Pharmacie du Cerf** is said to be the oldest chemist's shop in France: it dates from the thirteenth century. But it is still not as picturesque as the superb Renaissance **Maison Kammerzell** a few steps from the cathedral (see box, p. 78).

The Maison Kammerzell

A few steps away from the cathedral is the mainly Renaissance Maison Kammerzell, known to the Strasbourgeois as simply 'la Kamm'. Now a restaurant with a stylish small hotel attached, it has been superbly restored and offers a glimpse of how the whole cathedral square must once have looked. The original building dates back to at least 1427, when it was owned by a cloth merchant called Hans Jörger. As with all the houses round the cathedral, its ground floor was used as a shop, while the upper floors were stockrooms and living quarters. A goldsmith had his workshop there at one point, and it may have been he, rather than Jörger, who built the sandstone ground floor with its three arched windows protected by wooden shutters, which would once have been lowered on ropes to form a counter for displaying wares. The date 1467 is carved over the narrow Gothic doorway.

Just over a century later, in 1571, Martin Braun, a wealthy cheesemonger, bought the house from another cloth merchant. In 1587 he decided to rebuild the upper storeys and lit the house with no fewer than seventy-five windows, twenty-five to each floor. The rich carved decoration dates from this period. In 1604 one of Braun's daughters married Robert Königmann, who had been brought up in the nearby rue Mercière. He may have had English ancestry, as he was referred to as 'the Englishman'. He introduced the lucrative tobacco crop to Alsace, in a hamlet near Strasbourg still called 'Cour des Anglais'.

The house stayed in the Königmann family down to 1670, then was owned by a series of merchants. At various times the ground floor was a grocer's, a tallow chandler's, a bookshop, even a fashionable shoe shop. In the mid-nineteenth century it was bought by a German grocer, Philipp Franz Kammerzell, whose name has stuck to it. It fortunately escaped damage during the Franco-Prussian War and in 1879 was sold at auction to the Oeuvre Notre-Dame, the medieval foundation whose role is to maintain the fabric of the cathedral. It put up the money to restore it in the 1880s and 1890s, commissioning artists and sculptors to copy early engravings of the Renaissance decorative scheme.

In the early years of this century the ground floor was a *winstub*, whose manager commissioned a local artist, Leo Schnug, to decorate the Gothic vaulting of the ground floor and the walls of the first floor. Using ochre and wine-coloured paint applied directly on to the stonework, he depicted scenes from Sebastian Brant's *Ship of Fools* (p. 81) and figures from classical mythology in medieval dress. His rumbustious paintings can still be seen today. And in the house next door, housing the kitchens, private dining and seminar rooms and the hotel bedrooms, you can admire fragments of fourteenth-century wall paintings, and a fifteenth-century wall safe, complete with elaborate lock mechanism.

The single spire of Strasbourg's Gothic cathedral, visible from all over Alsace, points upwards like an admonishing finger

The Devil, the cathedral and the wind

As you gaze up in awe at the façade of the cathedral, you'll probably find yourself pulling your collar up or wrapping your coat round you – the square is usually windy, even in the height of summer.

Legend has it that when the Devil heard about the splendours of the new cathedral he decided to visit it to see these alleged marvels for himself. So he summoned the wind, and rode on its back to Strasbourg. When he got there and saw with his own eyes how truly beautiful it was, he flew into a rage at the thought that such a superb building should be dedicated not to the powers of darkness but to those of light. He stormed off in a fury, leaving the wind behind. And it still roams there centuries later, waiting like a faithful steed for its passenger to return.

If you walk past the **Portail Saint-Laurent**, the Late Gothic north portal, and take the **rue des Frères**, you come to a quiet area where few tourists venture. It leads to the attractive **place Saint-Etienne**, with several half-timbered houses, past the tiny **place du Marché-Gayot**, surrounded by lively cafés and restaurants.

The **rue des Veaux** and the **rue des Ecrivains** will bring you back to the riverside and, just beyond the Château des Rohan, the **landing stage for sightseeing boats**. From here you can visit the very picturesque **Petite France** district on a mini-cruise that will also enable you to see the **Palais de l'Europe**, housing the **Council of Europe** and the chamber where the **European Parliament** holds its monthly plenary sessions (a new parliament building is planned). Another alternative is to take the **mini-train** to the Petite France from the south side of the cathedral. If you prefer to walk, stop first to enjoy the little network of picturesque streets between here and the cathedral: the **place du Marché-aux-Poissons**, the **place du Marché-aux-Cochons-de-Lait** and the **rue Maroquin**. Then return to the path beside the river and walk past the landing stage and on beneath the bridges. This pleasant riverside walk will enable you to see the **Grande Boucherie**, housing the **Musée historique**, an interesting collection that again was closed for renovation in 1990. Just beyond it, the fourteenth-century **Ancienne Douane** (customs house) stages art exhibitions. The **Pont du Corbeau** holds gruesome memories: here those convicted of killing their children or their parents were put to death by being swung down into the water in iron cages. The **Cour du Corbeau** on the other side of the river is more cheerful: it still looks much as it did when it was a medieval inn surrounding a busy courtyard. The **Musée alsacien** (popular art and customs) is again housed in several attractive buildings. This very interesting museum includes reconstructions of rooms in rural houses and paints a vivid picture of life in Alsace over the centuries, with costumes and painted furniture and a wide range of folk art.

Back on the other side of the river, the **Eglise Saint-Thomas**, where Albert Schweitzer played the organ (see box, p. 144), is dominated by the **tomb of Maréchal de Saxe**, commissioned by a grateful Louis XV from the sculptor Jean-Baptiste Pigalle.

The riverside walk continues to the **lock** in the delightful **Petite France** district, its narrow streets with their picturesque houses crisscrossed by stretches of river. Straight ahead, the **Maison des Tanneurs**, a good restaurant, is a fine example of the dwellings lived in by the tanners who used to hang their hides out to dry on the upper galleries or verandahs. This whole area is crowded with tourists but still charming, and has any number of restaurants and tearooms. The **rue du Bain-aux-Plantes** and the **rue des Moulins** bring you to the **quai du Woertel**. At the far end you reach the **Ponts Couverts**, a misleading name as the bridges are not covered, though they do have three defensive towers. The views are good from here, and still better if you climb up to the **Terrasse panoramique** on top of the **Barrage Vauban**, a defensive dam built in the seventeenth century. The Petite France is spread out before you, its old houses reflected in the still waters, and in the distance, the soaring spire of the cathedral.

Walk back via the **rue des Dentelles**, the **rue de la Monnaie** and the **rue des Serruriers** to the **place Gutenberg**, with its statue of the great man (see box, p. 42) and a fine Renaissance building housing the **chamber of commerce** and the **tourist office**. From here you can explore the old streets leading to the **place Kléber**, all traffic-free (**rues Gutenberg, de la Lanterne, du Vieux-Seigle, du Vieux-Marché-aux-Grains, du Saumon, des Chandelles**). The place Kléber, which contains the tomb of its eponymous general, beneath a monument to him, is Strasbourg's main square, but is otherwise rather dull, though it is due to be spruced up. One side is taken up with **L'Aubette**, a red sandstone neo-classical eighteenth-century building where the local garrison had to report at dawn (*l'aube* in French) for their day's orders. Virtually all the decoration by Hans Arp and his wife Sophie Taeuber-Arp was labelled 'decadent' by the Nazi occupiers and destroyed. But the square does still have its famous **Kohler-Rehm** tearoom. Thousands of drawings by the Alsace

---

The Ship of Fools – a medieval bestseller

Das Narrenschiff, a lively poem satirizing what the author saw as the corrupt nature of men and women, and the ludicrous actions it leads them to commit, was one of the publishing success stories of the Middle Ages. It was written in German by Sebastian Brant, an Alsace lawyer, poet and theologian who was born in Strasbourg in about 1458. A Humanist, he spent much of his career writing and lecturing in Basel, then an important intellectual centre, but returned to Strasbourg in 1499 and died there in 1521.

In 1494 his *Ship of Fools* was published in Basel by Johann Bergmann from Olpe, one of the most important of medieval printer-publishers, who commissioned Albrecht Dürer to produce many of the 116 woodcuts that certainly contributed to the book's popularity. It is divided into short chapters and written in a straightforward, vivid style that is well captured by Dürer's illustrations, each set within a margin of interlaced motifs. The 'fools' of the title, wearing a dunce's cap adorned with long asses' ears and little bells, are caught in all sorts of grotesque or ridiculous postures, like the madman proudly riding a lobster, while a bird swoops down to observe the sight.

The book was a runaway success – so much so that pirated editions were being sold in Nuremberg within a few months of publication. The famous Alsace preacher Geiler of Kaysersberg based some of his fiery sermons on the poem, and it was soon translated into Latin as *Stultifera Navis*. Translations into other languages followed, including English: Alexander Barclay, the Scots poet and monk, published a very free version, *The Shyp of Fools of the Worlde*, in 1509, and another rather more faithful translation by Henry Watson appeared the same year.

cartoonist and satirist Tomi Ungerer (better known in the United States than in his native land) are on temporary display in the **rue de la Haute-Montée**. The early Gothic **Saint-Pierre-le-Jeune**, on the site of Roman catacombs, has a fine rood screen and peaceful cloisters.

The **rue de l'Outre** and the **place du Temple-Neuf**, where the *chocolatier* **Christian** occupies the ground floor of a magnificently painted house, lead to another network of picturesque old streets north of the cathedral, dotted with cosy *winstubs*. To the east, the **place Broglie**, where the Christmas market (see box, p. 85) is held outside the **Hôtel de Ville** (Town Hall), once the residence of the Counts of Hanau-Lichtenberg, also houses the **Banque de France**, the site of the mayor's house in which France's national anthem was first sung (see p. 45). Beyond the **Hôtel du Gouvernement militaire**, the early nineteenth-century **Théâtre municipal**, adorned with Ionic columns, stages mainly opera. Across the canal, the huge **place de la République** is surrounded by buildings dating from the German occupation after the Franco-Prussian War. The imposing **Palais du Rhin**, with its imperial eagles, was briefly the imperial palace. The **Préfecture**, the **Théâtre national de Strasbourg** and the **Bibliothèque nationale** (university library) complete the square.

A bronze statue by David d'Angers in the place Gutenberg commemorates Gutenberg's invention in Strasbourg of movable type

The boats offering mini-cruises on the Ill pass through a lock as they enter the picturesque Petite France district

Beyond here the modern **Synagogue**, beside the leafy **Contades Gardens**, was built as a symbol of peace and reconciliation after the Holocaust. For a real breath of fresh air you must continue to the **Parc de l'Orangerie**, designed by Louis XIV's master gardener André Le Nôtre. Concerts are held in the creamy-white **Pavillon Joséphine**, built for the Empress when she visited the town. Also in the gardens is a reconstructed half-timbered farmhouse, a perfect setting for the excellent **Buerehiesel** restaurant (see Hotels and Restaurants). On the other side of the **avenue de l'Europe** are the curving modern buildings of the **Palais de l'Europe** (see opposite). Inside, the large entrance hall with a curving staircase and fountain is impressive. A bus will bring you back from here to the town centre. And another bus from the centre will take you to the **Port autonome** (commercial harbour), where boat trips are organized. After that, an evening cruise on the Ill, with dinner, would round off some busy sightseeing. Alternatively, you might like to have a drink or dinner in the lively **Krutenau** district, combining it with a walk across the **Pont Sainte-Madeleine** to see the **Château des Rohan** illuminated, and a look in the interesting fashion boutiques in the **rue Sainte-Madeleine**, which again has several restaurants and *winstubs*.

Strasbourg's museums

In most places in France museum opening times are a complex jungle in which the unwary venture at their peril, for they are liable to find themselves locked out just when they thought they had planned everything perfectly. But Strasbourg's museums have sensibly banded together to coordinate their opening hours, which makes it all much easier.

They are open throughout the year 10–12 and 2–6 every day except Tues and some public holidays. In 1990 they decided to offer evening visits once a week at 8.30, lasting about 1½hrs and accompanied by an official guide, with a different evening for each museum. Check if this excellent scheme has been continued.

The **Château des Rohan**, once the palatial residence of the prince-bishops, houses several museums:

- the **Musée archéologique** (archeology), on the lower ground floor, was about to reopen after extensive renovation as this book went to press
- the **Musée des Arts décoratifs** (applied art), in the right wing, is particularly famous for its porcelain collections and its astronomical clocks
- the **Musée des Beaux-Arts** (paintings) on the upper floors has some major canvases by Flemish and Dutch Old Masters as well as a good collection of French, Italian and Spanish paintings and a department of modern French painting, including the work of some local artists
- the **Cabinet des Estampes** (prints and drawings) has over twenty thousand items and also a rich library of art books and journals, including a collection of titles on folk art

The city's other museums are:
- the **Musée alsacien** (popular art and crafts), 23 quai Saint-Nicolas

- the **Musée d'Art moderne** (modern art), 5 pl. du Château; a small collection due to be resited (see below)
- the **Musée historique** (history of Strasbourg), pl. de la Grande-Boucherie, in a Renaissance building; this was shut for renovation in 1990: check locally
- the **Musée de l'Oeuvre Notre-Dame** (medieval and Renaissance art, especially sculpture), 3 pl. du Château
- the **Musée zoologique** (zoology), 29 blvd de la Victoire

A brand-new **Museum of Contemporary Art** is due to open in a modern building near the Barrage Vauban in 1993 or 1994. It will include the city's collection of the work of Hans (or Jean) Arp, the Strasbourg painter and sculptor who was a friend of Kandinsky and exhibited with the Blauer Reiter group, then became a Dadaist and Surrealist.

You can also visit the **Palais de l'Europe**, housing the **Council of Europe** and the **European Parliament**, on weekdays year-round; and when there is no session in progress, you can watch a film with commentary in the nine Common Market languages.

Strasbourg's Christmas Market

Strasbourg's famous Christmas market, the *Christkindelsmärik*, dates back to the Middle Ages, when stalls would be set up round the cathedral for local craftsmen to demonstrate their skills and sell their wares. It would start on or about 6 December, the Feast of St Nicholas, a major saint's day in the Roman Catholic calendar and celebrated particularly by children, as indeed it still is in Alsace. But with the coming of the Reformation St Nicholas was demoted and from 1570 onwards the market was called after the Infant Jesus (*Christkindel* or Christ Child).

The market's reputation spread and it was soon selling products from all over Europe. In the early nineteenth century it moved to the place Kléber and instead of makeshift stalls, the city council decreed uniform wooden huts arranged in neat rows, with counters that could be lowered. The emphasis on Christmas became more marked, with confectionery, toys and decorations given pride of place.

Since 1870 it has been held in the place Broglie, in front of the town hall. It is still a colourful and very popular event, starting early in December and continuing right through to Christmas Eve. Plastic items are inevitably much in evidence these days, but you can still find delightful wooden tree decorations in the shape of traditional biscuits, or angels blowing trumpets or miniature rocking horses. Children love being given a little basket and solemnly filling it with their favourites, each costing only a few centimes or francs. You can choose from a mouthwatering range of edible goodies too, or even buy a Christmas tree from the forests in the Vosges.

Around Strasbourg

Several of the villages and small towns close to Strasbourg make a pleasant excursion from the city – their many restaurants are popular with the Strasbourgeois for Sunday lunch or for supper on summer evenings – or can be visited on the way to a more distant destination.

North of Strasbourg

Peaceful, unexpectedly rural **La Wantzenau** beside the Ill has some delightful houses and several well-known restaurants. But in the early-summer asparagus season they take a back seat while *le tout Strasbourg* heads for **Hoerdt**, a large village with some fine half-timbered buildings that has become famous for the *repas d'asperges* served in its many restaurants (see Chapter 2). The asparagus crop was introduced to Hoerdt in the nineteenth century by its pastor, who had learnt of its ability to flourish on poor sandy soil when he was a missionary in North Africa. Nearby **Weyersheim** has a neo-classical church with a good eighteenth-century organ and brightly coloured houses, some of them picturesquely set beside the Zorn, a tributary of the Ill, which still provides freshwater fish for the restaurants in and around Strasbourg.

Onions are the culinary speciality associated with the little town of **Brumath**, famous for its September Foire aux Oignons (Onion Fair). It was the capital of a Gallic tribe who were briefly masters of much of Alsace, then became a Roman city. Artefacts from both periods, the results of excavations in the sixties, are displayed in a small museum in the cellars of what was, in the eighteenth century, the residence of the powerful Hanau-Lichtenberg family. Their chapel has been converted into the town's Protestant church.

West of Strasbourg

In the western suburbs **Cronenbourg** is the home of the eponymous beer. Just beyond here, starting at **Oberhausbergen**, near the site of the battle in 1262 that enabled the merchants of Strasbourg to expel their prince-bishop, a signposted tourist route, the **Route des Forts**, follows a line of fortifications built by the Germans after the Franco-Prussian War.

You can follow two other tourist routes in this area. The **Route du Tabac** (Tobacco Road) takes you through the region's main tobacco-growing villages, and the **Route du Kochersberg** through the rich agricultural land round the **Kochersberg** itself, a hill just over 300 metres/ 1000 feet high. Tobacco was allegedly introduced into the region by Robert Königmann, one of the seventeenth-century owners of the Maison Kammerzell in Strasbourg (see box, p. 78), but it is only one of the many crops that flourish in the Kochersberg's exceptionally fertile soil. Driving, biking or walking through this peaceful area of lush meadows and golden wheatfields – it is known as 'Alsace's granary' – you will see large, well-kept farms in traditional half-timbered style, usually grouped into prosperous-looking villages. Apart from the odd interesting church, like the Romanesque one in **Willgottheim**, with a Gothic portal, and many wayside crosses, there are no 'sights' to be seen in the Kochersberg, but the villages – **Gougenheim**, **Quatzenheim**, **Wingersheim**, for instance – are full of Alsace charm with their immaculate seventeenth- and eighteenth-century houses, dating from the wholesale rebuilding necessitated by the Thirty Years' War, which devastated the whole area. The **Maison du Kochersberg** in **Truchtersheim** stages temporary exhibitions on the history of this little-known part of Alsace, with special emphasis on traditional rural crafts and architecture. This is also an area of large, comfortable inns, with one of the top restaurants in Alsace, the **Auberge du Kochersberg** in **Landersheim**.

Just south of the Kochersberg lies **Marlenheim**, a large village popular with the people of Strasbourg for its excellent family-run restaurant, **Le Cerf**, and for its *Fête du Mariage de l'Ami Fritz*, a lively celebration on the Feast of the Assumption (15 August). The locals dress up in regional costume and act out, to the strains of folk tunes played by groups of musicians from the neighbouring villages, a famous wedding scene from one of the patriotic novels written in the nineteenth century by a long-lasting double act, 'Erckmann-Chatrian', the joint name used by Emile Erckmann and Alexandre Chatrian, both of them born just outside Alsace. The event takes place to the accompaniment of plentiful quantities of the local wine, a Pinot Noir usually referred to simply as *'rouge de Marlenheim'*, though legend has it that it was a local rosé that saved the village in the Middle Ages, when marauding Swedish troops became so drunk on it that they were deflected from their avowed intention of razing it to the ground.

Marlenheim marks the official starting point of the Wine Road (see Chapter 6) and has a marked 'vine path' (*sentier viticole*) through the sunny vineyards on the **Marlenberg**, a hill just outside the village. The village itself, once the residence of the Merovingian kings, is full of picturesque houses and has a Baroque church with a Romanesque relief over the side door depicting Christ with St Peter and St Paul.

Wangen and **Westhoffen** both have attractive houses and the pretty **Kronthal**, a valley whose quarries provided the pinkish sandstone for Strasbourg Cathedral, brings you to **Wasselonne**, an ancient town on the River Mossig where you can see the tower and fortified gateway of a large medieval château burned down during the seventeenth century. Beyond here the N4 leads on to **Marmoutier** and **Saverne** (see Chapter 5) and the **Mossig Valley** to the pleasant little resort of **Wangenbourg-Engenthal**, perched at about 500 metres/1640 feet, see Chapter 7).

South of Strasbourg

Tobacco, wheatfields and vineyards to the west, cabbages and marshes to the south. In fact the area south of Strasbourg is also on the Tobacco Road, but it is better known as the **'Pays du Chou'** (Cabbage Land), the label given to a signposted itinerary starting and ending in Strasbourg and reaching first the small town of **Illkirch-Graffenstaden**, interesting chiefly because it was here that the Strasbourgeois finally capitulated in 1681 and signed the treaty that annexed the city to France, thirty-three years after the Holy Roman Empire officially handed over Alsace under the Treaty of Westphalia.

Cabbage fields are visible on all sides as you cross the agricultural plain between here and **Obernai** on the Wine Road. The *choucroute* industry accounts for many a livelihood hereabouts and the grateful villagers of **Geispolsheim** duly acknowledge the fact with their annual *Fête de la Choucroute* (Pickled Cabbage Festival). The many half-timbered houses are interesting to social historians because virtually all of them bear carved inscriptions specifying not only their date but their owners' names and trades or professions. In June they act as a backdrop to the village's popular *Fête Dieu* (Corpus Christi) procession. North-east of Geispolsheim and its industrial outskirts is **Entzheim**, the site of Strasbourg's airport, and 4km/2½ miles south-west, **Blaesheim** has more picturesque houses.

South of Illkirch, on the marshy plain between the Rhine and the Ill, **Eschau** is worth visiting for what is left of a convent founded in the seventh century for an enclosed order of nuns whose conduct appears to have been distinctly unholy. You can still see the Early Romanesque church, with later Gothic additions, though much of its sculpture is now on display in the Musée de l'Oeuvre Notre-Dame in Strasbourg. Further south, **Erstein**, set right beside the Ill, has given its name to the **plaine d'Erstein**, the term used for the fertile strip of land running alongside the river that was once again devastated during the Thirty Years' War. The sight of large open sheds with tobacco leaves hanging up to dry will soon convince you that the main crop is tobacco, though watersports of various kinds are increasingly providing an income for the local inhabitants. Just east of Erstein is the **Rhine-Rhône Canal** which, together with draining of the marshy wetlands beside the Rhine, has had a major effect on the ecology of this part of Alsace. But this is still a place for spotting rare species of curlews and other birds, and plants whose survival gladdens the heart of naturalists. To the south, **Osthouse**, once an imperial town, has a Renaissance château complete with moat and medieval towers.

From here the N83 takes you on through the marshy plain to **Sélestat** and the Wine Road (see Chapter 6). Just off the main road, **Ebersmunster** is famous for its cream and pink Baroque church with three unexpected onion domes. It was built by an Austrian architect to replace a very early abbey destroyed in the Thirty Years' War and is beautifully decorated inside with a richly carved and gilded altarpiece, elaborate stucco work and wall paintings – a most unusual sight in Alsace, where Romanesque and Gothic predominate. The church's Silbermann organ is used for Sunday concerts in May.

Key data

Access
Strasbourg is easily accessible from most places in Alsace, by road, rail or regular bus services. The **Compagnie des transports strasbourgeois (CTS)** runs bus services from the city to most of the towns and villages referred to in this chapter: ask for the *'Mon bus bleu'* leaflet at the bus station in the place des Halles, which includes a map showing a dozen different routes, and for individual timetables (or telephone 88 28 20 30). Many of the buses also stop outside the rail station.

Itineraries
The towns and villages north of the city can be visited as days or half-days out or on the way to Haguenau and the Outre-Forêt area. The Kochersberg (reached via the D31 or D41) and Marlenheim and Wasselonne (N4) are conveniently on the way to the Northern Vosges forest or the mountainous area south of Saverne, while the Ried to the south can be combined with an excursion to Sélestat or make a prelude to a Wine Road tour.

STRASBOURG 67000
TO pl. de la Gare (88 32 51 49), 10 pl. Gutenberg (88 32 57 07), Pont de l'Europe (88 61 39 23); address for correspondence: Office du Tourisme de Strasbourg et sa région, Palais des Congrès, av. Schutzenberger
Access Colmar 67km/42 miles, Mulhouse 120km/75 miles, Sélestat 47km/29½ miles; **buses** or **rail** from main centres in Alsace and villages in surrounding area and Northern Vosges
Sights see pp. 84–5

BRUMATH 67170
TO Mairie (88 51 02 04)
Access Strasbourg 18km/11 miles; **rail** from Strasbourg
Sights **Musée archéologique** (local archeology) pl. du Château, open May–Sept only, first two Sun afternoons in month

EBERSMUNSTER 67600 Sélestat
TO Mairie (88 85 71 66)
Access Strasbourg 32km/20 miles, Sélestat 9km/5½ miles
Sights **Eglise abbatiale Saint-Maurice** (Baroque church)

ERSTEIN 67150
TO Mairie (88 98 07 06)
Access Strasbourg 27km/17 miles; **buses** from Strasbourg
Sights **Renaissance château** 4km/2½ miles SE

ESCHAU 67400 Illkirch-Graffenstaden
TO Mairie (88 64 03 76)

Access Strasbourg 12km/7½ miles; **buses** from Strasbourg
Sights Early Romanesque church

GEISPOLSHEIM 67400 Illkirch-Graffenstaden
TO Mairie (88 68 81 88)
Access Strasbourg 12km/7½ miles; **buses** from Strasbourg

MARLENHEIM 67520
TO pl. du Kaufhus (88 87 75 80)
Access Strasbourg 20km/12½ miles; **buses** from Strasbourg
Sights **Eglise Sainte-Richarde** (Baroque church with Romanesque details), **Ancienne Douane** (Customs House)

TRUCHTERSHEIM 67370
Access Strasbourg 16·5km/10½ miles; **buses** from Strasbourg
Sights **Maison du Kochersberg** 4 pl. du Marché, open year-round, Sun afternoons only

WASSELONNE 67310
TO pl. du Général-Leclerc (88 87 17 22 or 88 87 03 28)
Access Strasbourg 25km/15½ miles; **buses** from Strasbourg
Sights **Tour du château** (ruined medieval castle)

The Northern Vosges forests are popular with ramblers and, in the autumn, with gourmets and sportsmen for their fungi and game

5
In and around the Northern Vosges

In the north of Alsace, close to the border with Germany, lie the Vosges du Nord or Northern Vosges, a region of dense forests, romantic ruined castles and outcrops of sandstone fashioned by wind and rain into the curious twisted shapes so aptly known in French as *ruiniformes*. The mountains here are lower than on the western border of Alsace and offer opportunities galore for walks and picnics within reach of even quite small children. And unlike the Wine Road, this part of Alsace is not heavily infested with tourists even in the height of summer. I have seen virtually empty roads in mid-July.

Since 1976 much of the region has been officially designed a 'nature park', the **Parc naturel régional des Vosges du Nord** (see p. 93), whose headquarters are in the castle in **La Petite-Pierre**, a small summer resort that makes a particularly pleasant base for a relaxing holiday. The lack of overt tourism does not mean poor facilities: you will find a fair number of friendly family hotels with comfortable rooms and unpretentious restaurants serving excellent cuisine based on the freshwater fish caught in the mountain streams and meres, on the wild mushrooms and berries picked in the forests, and on the game, both hairy and feathered, that still abound here.

Conservation and an awareness of nature are major concerns in the Northern Vosges, and so is the need to preserve or revive ancient craft skills. You might even like to enrol yourself or your children in one of the many craft classes organized by the nature park authorities during the summer. Riding, angling (for which you will need to buy a temporary permit) and hiking are the main sports activities. A number of farms offer riding lessons and accompanied rides in the forest, as well as modest accommodation and communal meals (see **Practical information**). *Randonnées sans bagages* holidays using the GR 53 hiking trail starting in Wissembourg are a good way of exploring the area without the complications of coping with luggage.

But this is not merely an area for sports and nature enthusiasts. This part of Alsace has many manmade sights as well as natural sites. The border castles are well worth exploring, and the charmingly faded spa of **Niederbronn-les-Bains**, a watering place since Roman times, in a delightful setting on the edge of the forest, and the attractive small town of **Wissembourg** in the north-eastern corner are just two of the places suitable as stopping-off points, days out from Strasbourg, or for a leisurely holiday. Anyone interested in military history will find this a particularly rewarding region to visit. Its strategic site, hemmed in on both north and east by natural frontiers, means that northern Alsace has been fought over for centuries. From **Fleckenstein** and the many other defensive castles perched high up along the northern border to the tragic battlefields of the Franco-Prussian War of 1870-1, like **Geisberg** south of Wissembourg and **Woerth** with its War Museum, and to the Maginot Line fortifications such as **Four à Chaux** near Lembach, this is a major centre of 'military tourism', as it has come to be known.

Then the Northern Vosges boasts several museums specializing in folk art and local customs: the **Maison du Village** in **Offwiller**, the **Musée des Arts et Traditions populaires** in **La Petite-Pierre**, devoted to that seasonal delicacy typical of Alsace, Christmas biscuits, or the **Musée de l'Imagerie peinte et populaire** in **Pfaffenhoffen**. **Niederbronn** has a new archeology museum and in **Obersteinbach** you can visit the **Maison des Châteaux-Forts**, an information centre on the region's castles. On the south-western edge of the region, **Saverne's Château des**

The Parc naturel régional des Vosges du Nord

This well-organized cross between a national park and a nature reserve covers 120,000 hectares/300,000 acres of land stretching up to Alsace's northern border with Germany and includes a small part of Lorraine. It is continued beyond the German border by the Naturpark Pfälzerwald (Palatinate Forest Nature Park).

Its function is to create a greater awareness of nature and the environment by providing information about local flora and fauna, organizing leisure and sporting activities and thus encouraging nature conservation, helping to ensure that local craft skills are passed on to new generations, and running specific conservation projects.

Its headquarters in the castle in La Petite-Pierre, run by helpful staff, stage interesting exhibitions on the park's natural sites and on environmental topics. They are didactic but not preachy and raise interesting questions such as the effect on a region of changes in agricultural methods and of agricultural decline.

The park authorities publish maps of the area, brochures describing suggested walking tours and local museums, and leaflets on the birds and animals, wild flowers and fungi you can find there. Guaranteed to keep nature minded children happy for hours - and teach them some French too. If you can't visit La Petite-Pierre, ask for the main maps and leaflets at tourist offices in the area or write to the *Parc naturel régional des Vosges du Nord*, Maison du Parc, Château, 67290 La Petite-Pierre.

Rohan houses art and local history collections. A quick trip over the border into Lorraine will enable you to visit the **Musée du Sabotier** (Clog Museum) in **Soucht** or the **Maison du Verre et du Cristal** (Glass-making Museum) in **Meisenthal**. **Sarre-Union**, the self-styled capital of 'l'Alsace Bossue', the north-western tip of Alsace jutting out into Lorraine, has a museum focusing on the area's industries and crafts. You might also like to cross the German border to see **Schloss Favorite**, a Baroque château near Rastatt with a famous porcelain collection, or plan a day or weekend in glamorous **Baden-Baden** (see **Days out from Alsace**).

Saverne, a pleasant market town reached from Strasbourg via the Kochersberg (see Chapter 4) or, if you are short of time, by the A4 motorway, makes a good prelude to a visit to the Northern Vosges. With its own forest, the **Forêt de Saverne**, south of the town, its botanical gardens and, a short distance away, the **Col de Saverne**, the mountain pass where Louis XIV was so impressed by the garden-like beauty of Alsace (see Introduction) – it gives you a foretaste of the pleasures to come. This strategic site on the main route through the Vosges to the Rhine was inhabited from an early date and it soon became a major trading post – the modern name is said to be a corruption of Tres Tavernae, meaning 'Three Taverns', where the merchants no doubt conducted their business in convivial surroundings. It played a tragic part in the 'Bumpkins' War' of 1525 (see A Little History), as it was here that nearly twenty thousand of the rebels were slaughtered by the Duke of Lorraine's troops.

Right down to the Revolution the town belonged to the see of Strasbourg, one of whose prince-bishops, the dissolute Cardinal Louis de Rohan, whose involvement in the 'Affair of the Queen's Necklace' discredited Marie-Antoinette and thus helped to bring about the downfall of the *ancien régime*, commissioned Nicolas Salins de Montfort to design a new **Château des Rohan** to replace the earlier residence burnt down in 1757. The result was the austere neo-classical 'Versailles in Alsace' in red sandstone you see today – majestic, impressive, but seeming disproportionately large and palatial in this little town. The palace now houses two museums. One, the **Musée d'Art et d'Histoire**, is a pleasingly eclectic collection of Gothic sculpture, nineteenth-century furniture and decorative art, and eighteenth- and nineteenth-century paintings. The other, the **Musée archéologique**, illustrates the town's Gallo-Roman past.

Saverne has some picturesque old houses, the best known, the seventeenth-century **Maison Katz** in the Grand'Rue, with a two-tier oriel window, now a good restaurant. The lovely Gothic cloisters of the **Eglise des Récollets**, decorated with later wall paintings, are only a short way away. Beside the palace, the **church of Notre Dame**, with a Romanesque porch and belfry, has a finely carved pulpit by Hans Hammer and some good sculpture, including a sixteenth-century marble group of the Virgin Mary and St John weeping over the dead Christ. The town is also famous for its roses: the **Roseraie** (rose garden) boasts a thousand varieties.

Rows of little dormer windows punctuate the crooked roofs of Wissembourg and many other towns and villages in Alsace.

For a good view of the whole town, visit the **Jardin botanique** (botanical gardens, with over two thousand plant species) on the way up to the **Col de Saverne**, and follow the footpath to the **Saut du Prince Charles**, a huge red sandstone rock over which Charles the Bold, Duke of Burgundy, or possibly some other dashing Charles, allegedly made a flying leap on horseback to escape an enemy attacker. Even better views can be had from the ruins of **Haut-Barr Castle**, 5km/3 miles south of Saverne, perched high up on the edge of the **Forêt de Saverne** and often hard to distinguish from the rocky cliff to which it seems to be welded.

If you enjoy clambering about among ruins, two other castles can be reached by footpaths close by – **Géroldseck**, with a tall keep, and **Petit Géroldseck**. A curiosity – the **Tour Chappe** where an eighteenth-century engineer practised an early form of rapid communication by semaphore signalling – is also worth a quick look; a small museum offers some explanatory material. But do allow plenty of time to visit **Marmoutier**, a quiet little town south of Saverne dominated by the monumental deep reddish ochre west front of its Romanesque church, surmounted by octagonal towers and a large square belfry. It was once attached to an abbey church founded as early as the sixth century by a disciple of St Columban, the Irish missionary who brought the Gospel to the Vosges, and is a good example of Alsace's contribution to the Romanesque style. Its sober façade is enlivened by carved beasts and humans, dotted about in shallow niches or perched on the roof – an elongated lion here, crouching ready to spring, a grotesque head there. The nave was rebuilt during the Gothic era and the chancel, Gothic in style, is eighteenth-century, with delightful carvings on the choir stalls.

The large Romanesque church at **Saint-Jean-Saverne**, a village just north of Saverne, has retained its Romanesque interior, with rhythmic foliage decoration on the capitals and surrounding a tympanum depicting the Agnus Dei. It too was originally part of a much larger building, a convent of Benedictine nuns whose tapestries, including a lively *Judgement of Solomon* dating from 1545, were rescued when the convent was pulled down during the Revolution and can now be admired in the church. A pleasant walk brings you up to Alsace's own 'Mont Saint-Michel', with a small white chapel shaded by trees. After enjoying the fine views, you can puzzle over the 'Witches' School', a round depression in the rock where, the locals say, witches used to practise taking off on their broomsticks, and the 'Witches' Hole', the narrow entrance to a cave. The Witches' Sabbath, they say, was held on the **Bastberg**, a hill near **Neuwiller-lès-Saverne**, with another Romanesque church, **Saint-Pierre-et-Saint-Paul**, that survived the destruction of its once magnificent abbey. It has some finely carved capitals and the tomb of St Adelph, to whom the old village's twin-turreted Protestant church is dedicated.

Bouxwiller, at the foot of the Bastberg, looks prosperous, with its well-restored half-timbered houses, some with elaborately carved oriel windows surmounted by a little pointed roof. It was once the seat of the Counts of Hanau-Lichtenberg, whose name is perpetuated in the term often used for this part of Alsace, the **Pays de Hanau**. A fine Renaissance building attached to their former residence now houses both the town hall and a local history museum, the **Musée de Bouxwiller et du Pays de Hanau**, displaying costumes and traditional arts and crafts. More examples of folk art await you at nearby **Pfaffenhoffen**, where the **Musée de l'Imagerie peinte et populaire alsacienne** includes illustrated *Göttelbriefe*, presented to infants at their christening, naïve paintings on glass and cut-out soldiers, their uniforms neatly painted in. Like Bouxwiller, **Ingwiller**, a small industrial town, has an interesting synagogue; topped by a large onion dome, it is slowly being restored, and may house a museum on the region's Jewish community.

Ingwiller is on the edge of the Northern Vosges Nature Park, whose headquarters are in **La Petite-Pierre**, reached by the attractive D56 and D113. Another pretty road, the D919, follows the wooded Moder valley in the nature park to **Wingen-sur-Moder**, the home of the Lalique glassworks. If you are interested in glass, **Meisenthal**, a short drive away in Lorraine, has a **Maison du Verre et du Cristal** in a former glassworks. Its displays include sketches and finished pieces by the brilliant art nouveau artist Emile Gallé, who learnt his craft here. And 4km/2½ miles away at **Saint-Louis-lès-Bitche**, you can visit the fine collections and showroom of the former royal glassworks, dating back to 1767.

A turn off the D919, followed by a short walk, brings you to one of many border castles, medieval **Lichtenberg**, high up on a rocky spur and surrounded by the remains of its fortifications, built in the 1680s to plans by Louis XIV's military engineer Marshal Vauban. A clear leaflet, available from the ticket kiosk, enables you to picture how the whole complex must have looked and it is worth climbing over the ruins to visit the sixteenth-century chapel and the Renaissance water cisterns.

It would be hard to think of a pleasanter place for a peaceful holiday with plenty of outdoor exercise than the little resort of **La Petite-Pierre**. The friendly family hotels strung out along the quiet high street offer lovely views over the surrounding forest, the air is pure, the opportunities for walks and more energetic hikes are legion. Two unusual museums, plus a castle housing the nature park's offices and exhibition rooms, add to its delights.

The original castle dated back to the ninth century and may have been built by one of Charlemagne's sons. But most of the building you see today is either twelfth-century or Renaissance, though it has been altered and restored several times. In the seventeenth century Vauban converted it into a military fortress, and it remained a military establishment right down to 1870. Its most famous inhabitant was Georg-Johannes von Veldenz, Count Palatine of the Rhineland, a sixteenth-century nobleman married to the King of Sweden's daughter Anna, and admired for his European outlook and energetic philanthropy: he helped to establish the region's economic prosperity by granting glassmaking permits to the nearby villages. Known locally as

'Jerry-Hans' (sometimes written 'Jerrihans'), he remains a popular figure and restaurant menus round about may feature *pot-au-feu à l'oie Jerry-Hans*, a fragrant concoction of goose simmered with vegetables, in the same way as their Paris counterparts honour another well-loved character with their *poule au pot Henri IV*.

Tucked in between the eighteenth-century stone houses in the main street of the upper town, the **Chapelle Saint-Louis**, the garrison chapel, has been turned into the **Musée du Sceau alsacien** (Alsace Seal Museum). With its flags and standards hanging from the vaulted roof, its tournament helmets and gentle organ music, it makes an atmospheric setting for a display of seals. By studying the seals, which cover a broader geographical range than the name suggests – Canterbury and the Vatican as well as Alsace and its neighbours – you can trace the history of Europe or explore specific themes, like changing fashions or boat design. This is a good place for learning about landmarks in Alsace's history, like the setting up of the Decapolis (see box, p. 38). A short walk away you can learn more about Alsace and its traditions by visiting the little **Musée des Arts et Traditions populaires** (Museum of Folk Art and Customs), again a misleading name, as this charming museum focuses on a single topic, the love and devotion that goes into the *springerle* and *bredle* (Christmas biscuits) used to decorate the Christmas tree, or sent like Christmas cards to friends and family. You can admire hundreds of biscuit moulds in traditional designs, featuring fish and rabbits, flowers and ears of corn, sailing ships and the swaddled Christ Child, many of them chiefly used for making *spekulazius*, a type of gingerbread with almonds.

The tiny **open-air theatre** beyond the museum is used for performances during the summer season. The **Eglise de l'Assomption**, parts of which date from the early fifteenth century, is a good example of that manifestation of Alsace tolerance, the 'simultaneous church' (see A Little History). The frescoes in the chancel, depicting the evangelists with their emblems and Adam and Eve in the Garden of Eden, date from about 1417, and you can also see the tombstones of Jerry-Hans and his lady.

When you cross the drawbridge into the **castle**, special displays illustrate the impetus he gave to the local economy, present him as a patron of the arts with a fine library, and introduce some of his large-scale projects, which seemed somewhat harebrained at the time, but have been successfully implemented since, like the 'boat lift' at nearby **Arzwiller**. The main exhibition traces the history of the castle and temporary displays treat environmental topics and the survival of ancient farming and craft practices. A small information office supplies maps and leaflets in various languages about the fauna and flora in the nature park, and about cultural and leisure activities. You can climb above the courtyard to the **chemin de ronde** (parapet walk) and gaze over the forest, picking out the rocks whose odd shapes have given rise to graphic nicknames like **'Le Rocher du Corbeau'** (Crow Rock), to which a marked path leads in about 1½ hours. Another path enables you to circle right round the tall ramparts. And you can enjoy many forest walks round here.

In the lower town, you can watch craftsmen at work in the **Cour des Artisans** behind the town hall, and visit displays of their work in the **Maison des Païens**, a small sixteenth-century building looking just like a gingerbread house, in a lovely setting on the site of a Roman watchtower.

A winding forest road brings you to the **Etang d'Imsthal**, 3.5km/2 miles south-east. This peaceful forest pool, surrounded by meadows, is popular with anglers (day permits from the **Auberge d'Imsthal**, see Hotels and Restaurants). Grauſthal, 9km/5½ miles south via D178, D122, is worth visiting for its curious **maisons troglodytiques**, little houses built right into the rock face, some of them lived in as recently as the late fifties, though I find the atmosphere oppressive in this narrow valley at the foot of tall sandstone cliffs. Masonry from the Benedictine monastery founded here in the ninth century and badly damaged during the peasants' revolts of 1525 was used to build the village houses and church.

West of La Petite-Pierre lies the hilly region known as **l'Asace bossue**, forming a 'bump' (*bosse*) jutting out into Lorraine and feeling more like Lorraine than Alsace. Its main town, industrial **Sarre-Union**, was originally two separate towns on either bank of the River Sarre, which were 'united' in the eighteenth century – which explains the odd name. It has some elegant eighteenth-century houses, a splendidly elaborate organ in the Catholic church, and a museum devoted to local crafts and industries, the **Musée régional de l'Alsace bossue**.

*

The small town of **Haguenau**, a convenient centre for visiting the rest of northern Alsace, was a favourite residence of the Hohenstaufen emperor Frederick Barbarossa. Richard the Lionheart was held prisoner in the imperial castle in 1193, after being captured in Austria on his return from an eventful crusade, but his loyal subjects eventually raised the ransom money needed to release him.

In the quite lively traffic-free centre, its streets lined with attractive houses, is the **church of Saint-Georges**. It was originally Romanesque, but rebuilding over a period of three hundred years means that it is now in a mixture of styles, with a Romanesque nave covered by Gothic vaulting. It has two fine fifteenth-century altarpieces, one of the *Last Judgement*, with carving by Veit Wagner, who also carved the pulpit and an extraordinary custodial for the consecrated wafers, soaring upwards in true Flamboyant style. **Saint-Nicolas**, near the **Porte de Wissembourg** on the edge of the historic centre, is Gothic. The elaborate wooden pulpit, organ case and choir stalls were carved for an abbey that was dissolved during the Revolution, and so were the large figures of saints just outside the chancel. The history of Haguenau and its region is illustrated in the **Musée historique** (History Museum), in an amazing Gothick building sprouting towers and turrets. Local art and crafts are the province of the **Musée alsacien**, in the attractive medieval **Chancellerie** (chancellery) on the main square, also housing the tourist office. The museum has a collection of pottery from villages in the **Outre-Forêt**, the area 'beyond the forest'.

One of them, **Betschdorf**, has been well known for its pottery for over two and a half centuries. You will find at least half a dozen workshops still selling the local grey salt-glazed stoneware, hand decorated in distinctive blue patterns: bowls and large plates and dishes, and sets of jugs with miniature goblets for convivial evenings drinking the heady local fruit spirits. The workshops are strung out along the elongated high street, a puzzle until you discover that Betschdorf is made up of what were five separate villages until a couple of decades ago. The **church of Niederbetschdorf** has some lively medieval frescoes depicting the Last Judgement, with angels blowing long trumpets and claw-footed devils hustling the damned into Hell. In the summer you can visit the small **Musée de la Poterie** (Pottery Museum), with examples of work made in the Middle Ages and again when the workshops were able to reopen over half a century after the ravages of the Thirty Years' War forced them to close.

The small industrial town of **Soufflenheim**, on the southern edge of the forest, is also known for its pottery and china. It has been made with the local clay since at least the Middle Ages and similar ware is believed to have been made nearby during the Roman era. You can buy direct from workshops on weekdays, and watch craftsmen and women painting floral motifs on to kitchen and table ware.

A short way from here, peaceful **Sessenheim** was the setting for Goethe's platonic love affair with Friederike Brion just over two centuries ago (see box, p. 101). You can sit beneath the oak tree where the young lovers dawdled in the spring of 1771 and imagine the young poet reading aloud from the recently published German translation of *The Vicar of Wakefield*, in between telling his beloved that she symbolized the charm and beauty of Alsace with her blue eyes and golden hair, dressed in the regional costume of black taffeta apron over a short white skirt and an embroidered white corsage. And as you stroll through the village, picture the scene when the pastor's daughter shyly invited her young man to the local May Festival – an idyllic occasion against a background of general merrymaking that inspired Goethe's lovely lines in *Mailied*: 'Wie herrlich lachtet/mir die Natur!/Wie glänzt die Sonne!/Wie lacht dir Flur!' You can visit the **Goethe Memorial**, a small museum in the former guardhouse, and have lunch or a drink in the cosy **Auberge au Boeuf** (see Hotels and Restaurants), which has its own collection of items connected with Goethe and the Brion family. The tombstones of Friederike's parents can be seen against the wall of the Protestant church, but her own grave is in the village of Rothau, in the Western Vosges, where she moved after their death.

Beyond Betschdorf, tours are organized of the artillery fortifications at **Schoenenbourg**, the biggest link in the Maginot Line to be built in Alsace. They also suffered the heaviest bombardment of any of these sadly inadequate obstacles to a German invasion (see box, p. 49). Over three thousand shells and bombs rained down on them in 1940. During the two-hour visit you glimpse something of the subterranean life led by the six hundred men stationed 30 metres/nearly 100 feet below ground.

Goethe and Alsace

Goethe was sent to Strasbourg by his father, a leading Frankfurt lawyer, to complete his education. After throwing himself over-enthusiastically into student life in Leipzig to forget an unhappy love affair, he had burst a blood vessel and the resulting protracted illness had kept him at home for many months. So his father felt a change of scene was necessary, and the twenty-year-old Goethe arrived in Strasbourg in April 1770.

He took lodgings in the rue du Vieux-Marché-aux-Poissons, in the shadow of the cathedral, and fell under the spell of Gothic architecture. He tells us that he used to climb up to the top of the cathedral, making himself 'dizzy with ecstasy' – some commentators claim that he suffered from vertigo and was determined to cure himself of it. He passionately admired the cathedral's great architect Erwin von Steinbach and later wrote a famous essay, *Von deutscher Baukunst* (*On German Architecture*), singing his praises. This was later incorporated in *Von deutscher Art und Kunst* by the critic and poet Johann Friedrich Herder, whom Goethe met in Strasbourg and who introduced him both to the glories of Gothic art and architecture and to the genius of Shakespeare.

His period in Strasbourg, under the stimulating influence of Herder, had a major impact on the flowering of Goethe's own genius.

No less influential was his love for an Alsace girl, which inspired some of his finest lyric poetry. He fell in love with Friederike Brion, the younger of the two pretty daughters of the pastor of Sessenheim, a village north of Strasbourg, and rode there frequently to visit her. This platonic idyll with a simple country girl (described in detail in his autobiography *Dichtung und Wahrheit*) was one of the happiest times of his life. The *Sesenheimer Lieder* (Songs from Sessenheim) it gave rise to, with their many folksong elements, earned him his early reputation as the first true lyric poet writing in German since the Minnesänger Walther von der Vogelweide.

But the unsophisticated girl who inspired that loveliest of poems *Mailied* and the lyrical lines from *Heidenröslein* – 'Röslein, Röslein, Röslein rot,/Röslein auf der Heiden...' – so familiar from Schubert's *Lied* was too far removed from Goethe's patrician and intellectual background for the relationship to last and he broke it off when he returned to Frankfurt in 1771. The heartbroken Friederike never really recovered – she didn't marry – and Goethe's despair was no less real. It is reflected in the long *Wandrers Sturmlied*, which he wrote when he was back in Frankfurt, in a mood of remorse after receiving a letter from her. The parting is generally believed to have taught him enough of the sorrows of the heart to enable him to write his great *Sturm und Drang* drama *Götz von Berlichingen*, and was perhaps one of the inspirations behind *The Sufferings of Young Werther* and therefore the whole of the Romantic Movement in Europe.

A royal fairytale

Stanislas Leszcynski was born in 1677 in Lemberg (Lwów in Polish) in the Ukraine and elected King of Poland in 1704. But five years later he lost his throne thanks to the machinations of Peter the Great of Russia, who wanted to replace him with Augustus II, the dissolute Elector of Saxony, rumoured to have fathered no fewer than three hundred illegitimate children. Driven out of his kingdom, all his worldly goods confiscated, Stanislas lived in exile in Wissembourg on a pension provided by France.

The old house that was his home can still be seen. It is quite a modest house, but the ex-king lived there with his queen Catherine Opalinska, his elderly mother, Anna Jablonowska, his daughter Marie, and various officials and army officers whose unswerving loyalty had prompted them to share his exile. The only hope for this crowded and impoverished household seemed to be a rich marriage for Marie, who was not a great beauty, but was lively and good-hearted. Stanislas corresponded with a Paris nobleman about a potential match with the Regent of France, the Duc de Bourbon. The duke's wily mistress, the Marquise de Prie, was in favour of the plan, thinking that Marie would be conveniently malleable.

And so poor Marie waited, spending long hours praying in the church of St Peter and St Paul. Then something unexpected happened: a painter turned up from Paris with a commission to paint her portrait. A few weeks later – it was 1725 by then and she was twenty-two – Stanislas burst into her boudoir saying they must both fall to their knees and give thanks to God for his infinite goodness. The Duc d'Antin (the son of Louis XIV's mistress Madame de Montespan) had just arrived from Paris with the incredible news that Marie was to be Queen of France! Madame de Prie had apparently persuaded the Regent – mistresses have long been powerful figures in French history – that the grateful Marie would be as putty in their hands as the wife of the fifteen-year-old Louis XV. The marriage took place by proxy in Strasbourg Cathedral after a period of frenzied preparations: Stanislas had to negotiate a loan from the Governor of Strasbourg to recover the crown jewels, pawned to a moneylender in Frankfurt.

It would probably be untrue to say that Marie lived happily ever after – Louis, whom she bore ten children, grew up to be a thoroughly indolent monarch, heavily under the sway of his mistresses Madame de Pompadour and Madame du Barry. But reigning over the court at Versailles was clearly a greater prize than she can have imagined in her wildest dreams. And the fairytale had the happiest of endings for Stanislas. He briefly regained his throne during the War of the Polish Succession, but eventually renounced it in 1736 and accepted his youthful father-in-law's offer of the dukedoms of Bar and Lorraine, plus a generous financial settlement. Thanks to this, he could indulge his passion for architecture and town planning, and, living a comfortable life in his capital Nancy, he created one of the most beautiful squares in Europe (see Days out from Alsace).

Attractive Wissembourg was the home of the exiled Polish king Stanislas Leszcynski, future father-in-law of Louis XV

Hunspach is one of Alsace's most picturesque villages, full of large black and white half-timbered houses, though not as lively as the Wine Road villages. Some of the older generation still wear traditional regional costume on Sundays. **Wissembourg**, too, is picturesque. Its delightful setting on the River Lauter, very close to the German border, means that it attracts large numbers of tourists, but it is still very pleasant to wander round the old streets, admiring the vast, alarmingly crooked roof of the medieval **Maison du Sel**, used as a salt warehouse, though it was built as a hospital and later became a slaughterhouse. The large Gothic **church of Saint-Pierre-et-Saint-Paul**, built in red sandstone, is oddly dominated by an enormous medieval fresco depicting St Christopher holding the Infant Jesus, uncovered only a few decades ago. But it also has some medieval stained glass and sculpture, including the figure of the Merovingian King Dagobert, a major benefactor of the abbey to which it was once attached. Opposite the church, the Renaissance **Maison des Chevaliers** has a pretty gable, all curlicues, making it look like a stage set. The **Hôpital Stanislas** was the home of the exiled King of Poland, Stanislas Leszcynski (see box). Two sixteenth-century houses in a narrow street, one with an oriel window, house the **Musée Westercamp**, a local history museum that includes a reconstruction of a rural kitchen typical of the Outre-Forêt region and some interesting folk art.

Geisberg, south of the town, was the scene of a particularly ferocious battle during the Franco-Prussian War. It has monuments to the many men who died there on 4 August 1870. But to understand the full horror of those first few days of war in this ever-vulnerable corner of Alsace, you must travel through **Cleebourg**, the centre of northern Alsace's little offshoot of the Wine Road, to **Woerth**. This little town, a prosperous Roman settlement and later the capital of the Hanau bailiwick, earned its place in the history books on 5 and 6 August 1870, when one of the bloodiest battles of that war left over twenty thousand dead. The German Third Army had entered Alsace on 4 August, and at times the French troops were outnumbered four to one. Within a very short time of this heavy defeat, and a doomed cavalry charge at nearby **Moosbronn** (see A Little History), the Germans had taken Strasbourg and conquered the whole of Alsace. The **château des Hanau-Lichtenberg** houses a small museum telling the tragic story of the battle, the **Musée de la Bataille du 6 août 1870**. Children like the models in French and German uniforms.

Nearby, the flower-bedecked village of **Merkwiller-Pechelbronn** was surprisingly a centre of the oil industry until 1970, when drilling had to cease because the oil well ran dry. A small **Musée du Pétrole** (Oil Museum) explains the process used at the refinery and tells the story of Alsace's once-flourishing petroleum business. The local workforce was fortunately able to switch to a new source of wealth: the hot mineral springs, said to be effective in the treatment of arthritis and rheumatism, that were discovered accidentally in 1910 during drilling for oil.

The therapeutic properties of the waters gushing out at **Niederbronn-les-Bains** have been known for much longer. The thermal springs at this sedate little spa were exploited by the Celts and the Romans: those taking the waters today, mainly seeking a cure for rheumatism, gout or obesity, use the **Source celtique** (Celtic Spring) or the **Source romaine** (Roman Spring). In 1989 a new reminder of Alsace's Celtic inheritance came with the launch of a bottled mineral water from Niederbronn, called simply Celtic. If you feel like a flutter, the town has Alsace's only casino, where you can play baccara, black jack, boule or roulette into the early hours. It also has a new archeological museum, called the **Maison d'Archéologie des Vosges du Nord**, displaying artefacts discovered during local excavations, as well as exhibits connected with the iron and steel works run just outside Niederbronn by the De Dietrich family, great local benefactors, who made the town one of France's leading centres of the iron industry in the eighteenth century, until the Revolution caused the temporary collapse of their business.

Heavy damage during the Second World War means that there are few interesting buildings, though there are pleasant walks beside the river and in the well-kept public gardens. But Niederbronn makes an excellent centre for excursions into the forest and to the ruined castles romantically perched along the Franco-German border. To the west are **Wasenbourg** and, just over the departmental boundary in Lorraine, **Falkenstein**, an eerie place said to be haunted. To the north, reached via D53, are **Vieux Windstein, Nouveau Windstein** and **Wineck**, all of which are near two *Grande Randonnée* hiking trails (GR53 and GR531) that pass through this beautiful forested area. The road continues to **Obersteinbach**, where you can find out about the castles in the **Maison des Châteaux-Forts**, a well laid out information centre on the border castles opened in the old presbytery in 1988. Clear displays, labelled in French, English and German, introduce you to their architecture and history, and to the fauna and flora of the Northern Vosges. Charts and relief maps light up at the press of a switch, keeping children happy, and books and maps are on sale. You may find a potter or painter working away in an upstairs gallery, and the tiny Renaissance garden, planted with medicinal herbs, makes a good place to rest before you tackle the stiffish climb up to one of the castles. Nearby are **Petit-Arnsberg, Wasigenstein** and **Lutzelhardt**. Of the other ruins dotted along the border, **Fleckenstein** is the most impressive. Seeming to cling to the sandstone rock, it is a superb eyrie from which to survey the surrounding hills and forests. At nearby **Lembach**, another link in the Maginot Line is open to the public, **Four à Chaux**.

Before you leave the Northern Vosges, try to visit the village of **Offwiller**, only 8.5km/5½ miles from Niederbronn, to see the charming **Maison du Village d'Offwiller**. A village house, run by enthusiastic local people, has been turned into a little museum of folk art and customs, which gives you a good idea of the life led in this peaceful rural area until very recently, and of the traditions that are still maintained.

Key data

Access
Northern Alsace can easily be visited in a series of days out from Strasbourg, from which many places of interest can be reached by train or bus. Haguenau is centrally placed for travel by car or public transport: La Petite-Pierre, Niederbronn and Wissembourg are all attractive places to stay and good walking bases, but are less well served by public transport.

Itineraries
Saverne and Marmoutier can be visited on your way into Alsace from Paris or the Channel ports, or combined with the Kochersberg area. If you decide to visit Baden-Baden in Germany (see Days Out from Alsace), Haguenau, Soufflenheim and Sessenheim can easily be included in your itinerary. Wissembourg, right on the border, is another gateway to Germany. Marked tourist itineraries include the **Route des Châteaux** (Castle Road), the **Route des Vallons et des Thermes** (Vales and Thermal Baths Road) and the **Route des Villages pittoresques** (Picturesque Villages Road).

BETSCHDORF 67660
TO Mairie (88 54 48 00)
Access Strasbourg 45km/28 miles, Haguenau 20km/12½ miles; **buses** from Haguenau
Sights **Musée de la Poterie** (pottery) 4 rue de Kuhlendorf, open May, June, Sept daily except Mon; July and Aug daily

BOUXWILLER 67330
TO Mairie (88 70 70 16)
Access Strasbourg 45km/28 miles, Haguenau 25km/15½ miles, Saverne 20km/12½ miles; **buses** from Haguenau, or **rail** to Obermordern, then 5km/3 miles taxi or walk
Sights **Musée de la Ville de Bouxwiller et du Pays de Hanau** (local history, customs and folk art) pl. du Château, open daily year-round, but afternoons only at weekends

HAGUENAU 67500
TO 1 pl. Joseph-Thierry (88 73 30 41)
Access Strasbourg 30km/19 miles, Wissembourg 32km/20 miles; **buses** from Strasbourg, **rail** from Strasbourg, or Niederbronn, Wissembourg
Sights **Eglise Saint-Georges** rue Saint-Georges; **Eglise Saint-Nicolas** Grand'Rue; **Musée alsacien** (furniture, folk art and customs) 1 pl. Joseph-Thierry, open year-round daily except Tues, afternoons only weekends; **Musée historique** (archeology and local history) 9 rue Maréchal-Foch, open year-round daily except Tues, afternoons only weekends

HUNSPACH   67250 Soultz-sous-Forêts
TO   Mairie (88 80 42 16)
Access   Wissembourg 11km/7 miles; **rail** from Strasbourg

LEMBACH   67510
TO   23 route de Bitche (88 94 43 16)
Access   Strasbourg 50km/31 miles, Haguenau 23km/14 miles, Wissembourg 15km/9 miles; **buses** from Strasbourg
Sights   **Ouvrage du Four à Chaux** (Maginot Line fortifications), open daily mid-Mar–mid-Nov: guided tours only, on the hour every hour from 9 to 11 inclusive and 2 to 5 inclusive Sun and public hols; Mon–Sat, daily at 10 and 3, extra tour at 5 May–Oct, and also at 2 and 4 in July and Aug; **Château de Fleckenstein** open Apr–mid-Nov

LICHTENBERG   67340 Ingwiller
Access   8km/5 miles N of Ingwiller (Saverne 25km/15½ miles, Haguenau 30km/19 miles; **rail** from Strasbourg)
Sights   **Château de Lichtenberg**; open Apr–Nov

MERKWILLER-PECHELBRONN   67250
TO   2 route de Woerth (88 80 77 85)
Access   Strasbourg 48km/30 miles, Haguenau 17km/10½ miles; **rail** from Strasbourg, Haguenau or Wissembourg to Soultz-sous-Forêts (5km/3 miles)
Sights   **Musée du Pétrole** (Oil Museum) 2 rue de l'Ecole; open Apr–Oct, Sun only; at other times by appointment (88 80 77 85)

NIEDERBRONN-LES-BAINS   67110
TO   2 pl. de l'Hôtel-de-Ville (88 09 17 00)
Access   Strasbourg 53km/33 miles, Haguenau 21km/13 miles, Wissembourg 34km/21 miles; **rail** from Strasbourg (sometimes changing in Haguenau)
Sights   **Maison de l'Archéologie des Vosges du Nord** 44 av. Foch; open year-round daily except Tues, afternoons only

OBERSTEINBACH   67510 Lembach
Access   Strasbourg 66km/41 miles, Haguenau 34km/21 miles, Wissembourg 25km/15½ miles; **buses** from Wissembourg
Sights   **Maison des Châteaux-Forts** 42 rue Principale, open afternoons only, daily except Tues, July–Oct; Sun only, Mar and Apr; walks to three ruined castles: **Lutzelhardt**, **Petit-Arnsberg**, **Wasigenstein**, all open year-round

OFFWILLER   67340 Ingwiller
Access   Niederbronn-les-Bains 8·5km/5½ miles
Sights   **La Maison du Village d'Offwiller** (rural arts and crafts) 42 rue de la

108   *Alsace*

Libération; open Sun afternoons July–Oct, at other times by appointment (88 89 30 90 or 88 89 36 56)

LA PETITE-PIERRE   67290
TO   Mairie (88 70 42 30 or 88 70 45 30)
Access   Strasbourg 59km/37 miles, Haguenau 40km/25 miles, Saverne 22km/13½ miles; **buses** from Saverne, **rail** from Strasbourg to Ingwiller, then connecting bus
Sights   **Château** open Easter–mid-Nov: daily except Sat mornings June–Oct; Sat afternoons, Sun and public hols only Easter–June, Oct–mid-Nov; **Musée des Arts et Traditions populaires** (Christmas Biscuits Museum) rue des Remparts, open daily except Mon July–Oct and school holidays; Sun only during term-time Oct–July; **Musée du Sceau alsacien** Chapelle Saint-Louis, rue du Château; same times as previous museum

PFAFFENHOFFEN   67350
TO   Mairie (88 07 70 55)
Access   Strasbourg 36km/22½ miles, Haguenau 14km/9 miles, Saverne 26km/16 miles; **rail** from Strasbourg and Haguenau, or from Strasbourg to Obermodern (4.5km/3 miles), then bus or taxi
Sights   **Musée de l'Imagerie peinte et populaire alsacienne** (Alsace Folk Art Museum) 38 rue du Docteur-Schweitzer; open year-round, Weds, Sat, Sun afternoons only

SARRE-UNION   67260
TO   1 rue des Juifs (88 00 11 30)
Access   Strasbourg 81km/50½ miles, Saverne 37km/23 miles; **rail** from Strasbourg
Sights   **Musée régional de l'Alsace Bossue** (local industries and crafts), open daily except Tues mid-June–mid-Sept, afternoons only

SAVERNE   67700
TO   Château des Rohan (88 91 80 47 or 88 91 18 52)
Access   Strasbourg 39km/24 miles, Haguenau 36km/22½ miles; **rail** from Strasbourg
Sights   **Château des Rohan**, housing **Musées de la Ville de Saverne** (Art and Local History Museum, Archeology Museum), open May–Oct, daily except Tues, afternoons only; **Eglise Notre-Dame**; **Eglise des Récollets**; 5km/3 miles south, **Château du Haut-Barr**, open daily year-round, and **Tour de l'Ancien Télégraphe Chappe** (small museum devoted to visual signalling and its inventor), mid-July–mid-Aug afternoons only, daily except Mon

SESSENHEIM 67770
Access Strasbourg 33km/20½ miles, Haguenau 15km/9 miles; **rail** from Strasbourg
Sights **Mémorial Goethe** (collection connected with Goethe's love affair with Friederike Brion), rue Frédérique-Brion, open daily year-round; **Auberge au Boeuf** (small Goethe museum attached to popular restaurant, see **Hotels and Restaurants**)

SOUFFLENHEIM 67620
TO 20b Grand'Rue (88 86 74 90)
Access Strasbourg 40km/25 miles, Haguenau 15km/9 miles; **buses** from Haguenau, or train from Strasbourg to Roeschwoog (6km/4 miles), then taxi or walk
Sights Local potteries (guided tours sometimes arranged)

WISSEMBOURG 67160
TO pl. de la République (88 94 14 55)
Access Strasbourg 64km/40 miles, Haguenau 32km/20 miles; **rail** from Strasbourg and Haguenau, **buses** from Lauterbourg
Sights **Eglise abbatiale Saint-Pierre et Saint-Paul** (Gothic abbey church); **Musée Westercamp** (local history and archeology, folk art and customs), open daily except Tues, Sun morning and Jan; 3km/2 miles south, **Geisberg battlefield and war memorial**, open daily

WOERTH 67360
TO 2 rue du Moulin (88 09 30 21)
Access Strasbourg 45km/28 miles, Niederbronn-les-Bains 10km/6 miles, Wissembourg 27km/17 miles; **buses** from Strasbourg and Haguenau
Sights **Musée de la Bataille du 6 août 1870** (museum commemorating major battle in Franco-Prussian War) in **Château de Woerth**, open afternoons only, daily Apr–Nov, weekends only Nov, Dec, Feb, Mar (closed Jan)

6
On and around the Wine Road

Alsace's famous Route du Vin or Wine Road starts at **Thann** and meanders gently for about 120km/75 miles through the eastern slopes and foothills of the Vosges to **Marlenheim**, west of Strasbourg. On its way it visits dozens of picturesque villages, many with their medieval or Renaissance houses still happily intact, others, only a short way away, rebuilt after suffering heavy damage during the Second World War. And all along the road you can enjoy views of vine-clad hills, ruined towers and castles perched high up on rocky crags, and in the distance, the celebrated 'blue line of the Vosges' – the rounded outline of Alsace's western mountains, crowned by the blueish-green of its pine forests.

Whether you drive along the signposted route from south to north or vice versa, or decide to concentrate on short stretches of it, or simply to select a few of the most interesting villages (most of them can be easily reached by public transport from Colmar or Strasbourg), you will soon become aware that the Wine Road is very much on the tourist map. Yet in spite of the somewhat self-conscious picturesqueness of the best-known villages, like **Riquewihr** or **Obernai**, it doesn't take long to realize that these are working places. The tourist shops with their kitsch souvenirs, the coy little girls in regional costume waiting to have their photographs taken, the cosy *winstubs* with menus in several languages cannot disguise the fact that the vines are crucial to the local economy, virtually to the exclusion of any other crop. As soon as you wander away from the main streets (most of which seem to be called rue du Général-de-Gaulle) you discover that these are not show villages that come alive only in the tourist season. They are lived in year-round by a hard-working population who are as dependent on the vagaries of the weather as any other farming community, with 'dynasties' who have been tending the same vines for many generations – the Hugels in Riquewihr, the Becker-Beck family in Zellenberg, the Beyers in Eguisheim.

Even Riquewihr, the most tourist-ridden of all the villages, is peaceful on summer evenings, when the coach parties have departed. And on sunny autumn days when the grape harvest is in full swing and you can enjoy a taste of *neia siassa*, the new wine, with a little basket of juicy new walnuts, the roads are as full of tractors pulling trucks piled high with grapes as of luxury coaches. The many festivals held

One of the gaily coloured houses lining Colmar's Quai de la Poissonnerie houses a fishmongering business centuries old

along the Wine Road throughout the year certainly attract tourists from far and wide. But they are essentially popular celebrations, often of very ancient origin, in which the local population joins with gusto, rather than events artificially laid on for the tourist trade.

A number of the villages have interesting churches and chapels as well as their highly photogenic half timbered houses, a few have museums, and at Kintzheim you can visit a monkey reserve and watch demonstrations of birds of prey flying to command. Marked paths called *sentiers vinicoles* meander round the vineyards, while others climb up through the forest to some ruined castle offering spectacular views beyond the plain to the Rhine and the Black Forest. Then there are countless opportunities for wine tastings and for enjoying the local wines as an accompaniment to a meal in a friendly *winstub* or *caveau*, a family hotel or an elegant gourmet restaurant. If you decide to spend a night or two on the Wine Road, the better-known villages have hotels ranging from modest to very comfortable, and it is usually possible to find rooms to let in private houses either right in the villages or on the outskirts among the vines. Self-catering *gîtes* are also available. Another alternative is to base yourself in the very attractive town of **Colmar**, a short drive or bus ride from most of the prettiest villages and full of interest in itself, or in **Sélestat**, with its superb Humanist Libary.

On the whole it is better, especially if you plan to do some serious wine-tasting and buying, not to be too ambitious. Much of the charm of the Wine Road lies in the way it winds sinuously back on itself, slipping off to visit yet another geranium-clad cluster of houses. To see it as an opportunity for ticking off a list of 'sights' is to miss much of this charm – and to restrict your enjoyment of the delicious local wines. It is perfectly possible to taste many of its delights by focusing on a few villages as days out from Strasbourg or Colmar, perhaps combining a wine tasting and lunch in one, followed by a stroll through the vines outside another and a visit to an outlying chapel or ruined castle, with a leisurely glass or two of wine and supper in a third.

While you are visiting Colmar, you might like to leave the Wine Road and head towards the Rhine to visit the little town of **Neuf-Brisach**, fortified by Vauban, and the Maginot Line Museum at **Marckolsheim**.

And if you are planning to taste and buy wine, ask at tourist offices for the annually updated catalogue of vine growers, wine merchants and wine cooperatives, arranged geographically working northwards from Thann, but with alphabetical indexes of firms and places too. It is called *Guide annuaire du vignoble d'Alsace* and has a key in English at the front.

*

The chief glory of the small industrial town of **Thann** is its superb Late Gothic church, the **Collégiale Saint-Thiébaut**, built in local sandstone. Try to see the richly carved west front when the late afternoon sunlight slants on to the three tympanums with their hundreds of biblical scenes. The stonework has recently been cleaned and you can spend many a happy hour 'reading' the sequence of events, like a strip cartoon carved in loving detail. Watch out, for instance, for Adam and Eve digging and spinning, for the waters forming zigzags as God separates them at the Creation, and for the brutish soldiers, their huge feet bare in their sandals, tossing dice for Christ's garments. Just inside the door is a horrifying *Pietà*, with Mary looking not serene and beautiful, but like a haggard old woman whose only child lies dead in her arms.

The church's name commemorates a Bishop of Gubbio in Italy who died in 1160, leaving his ring to a servant. But in his haste to pocket his legacy, the servant clumsily pulled off his dead master's thumb. He hid the precious relic in the knob of his pilgrim's staff and set off for his village in Lorraine. When he reached the spot where the church now stands he lay down to sleep, planting the staff in the ground beside a fir tree, where it promptly took root. As he struggled to pull it out, the lord of Engelbourg Castle rushed up, attracted by three billiant lights shining above the tree. When he heard the story of the episcopal thumb he proclaimed that a miracle had taken place and had a pilgrimage chapel built to mark the spot. The legend is remembered at the end of June when Thann (allegedly a corruption of *Tanne* or *Tannenbaum*, German for fir tree) stages its annual *Crémation des Trois Sapins*, during which three fir trees are blessed, then ceremonially burnt beside the church.

The town suffered heavy damage during both world wars and there is little else of interest to see, except the old cornmarket building, now housing a small local history museum, the **Musée des Amis de Thann**, and a relic of the medieval walls, the **Tour des Sorcières** (Witches' Tower), not to be confused with the **Oeil de a Sorcière** (Witch's Eye), a round section of the lord's ruined castle, which seems to cast a baleful glance over Thann. You can walk up to it in about 20 minutes.

The Gothic church in **Vieux-Thann** has had to be restored many times over the centuries, but still has a medieval *Pietà*. **Cernay**, too, has been ill treated by the many battles fought over this corner of Alsace. It is interesting only as the starting point of the **Route des Crêtes** (Chapter 7) and of the popular steam train that crawls up the **Vallée de la Doller** on summer Sundays (takes just under two hours).

The Wine Road now turns north, soon reaching **Guebwiller**, an industrial town and wine centre on the River Lauch, at the foot of the **Florival**, a valley leading up into the Vosges via **Murbach** (Chapter 7). The valley and its history are the subject of Guebwiller's **Musée du Florival**, in the former **Eglise des Dominicains**, a Gothic church with medieval frescoes often used for concerts. It was built by the monks of Murbach Abbey, who also commissioned the earlier **Saint-Léger**, a Romanesque church in warm pinky-red sandstone with an imposing west front and three large doors. The last of the abbots built the Baroque **Eglise Notre-Dame**, with a famous altarpiece, set in a square adorned with a graceful fountain and surrounded by the abbot's palace and the canons' houses. The Late Gothic **Hôtel de Ville** (town hall) possesses a good example of the oriel windows you often come across in Alsace.

Rouffach, overlooked by the **Château d'Isenbourg**, now a luxury hotel, gives you more opportunities to see oriel windows in the old streets round the church of **Notre-Dame de l'Assomption**, a mixture of Romanesque and Gothic with nineteenth-century additions. The interior is graced with a particularly beautiful Gothic font. Near the church you can admire the former **Hôtel de Ville**, a Renaissance building with twin gables, the slightly earlier **Halle aux Blés** (cornmarket) and another **Tour des Sorcières** (Witches' Tower), this one topped by a stork's nest. In the **rue de la Poterne** is the birthplace of Napoleon's trusty general, Marshal Lefebvre, the son of a local miller.

Beyond **Husseren-les-Châteaux**, the highest point on the Wine Road (beautiful views), lies **Eguisheim**.

As you travel along the Wine Road (or by train between Colmar and Mulhouse) you constantly catch sight of three stern rectangular keeps, known as the **Tours d'Eguisheim** (Eguisheim Towers), perched on a wooded ridge above the vine-clad hills. They are all that is left of a group of three castles built in the eleventh and twelfth centuries as summer residences for the Counts of Eguisheim, the descendants of St Odile (see box, p. 130), and burnt down in the fifteenth century.

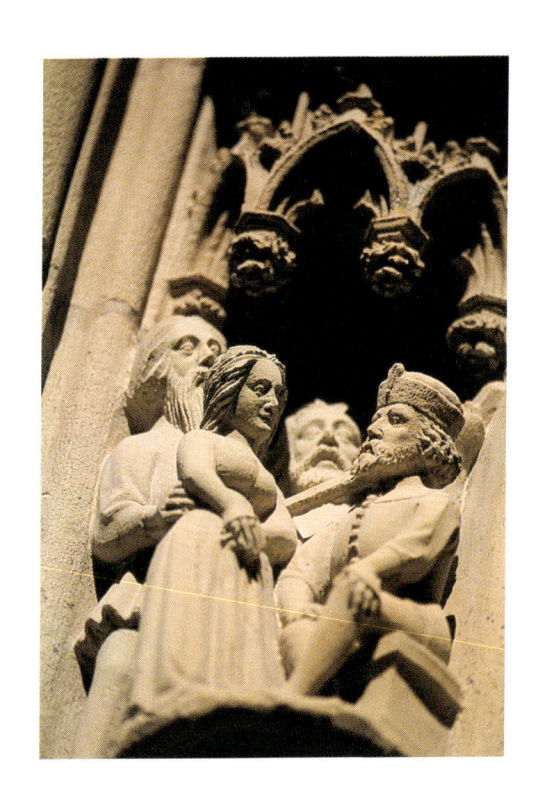

'A strip cartoon carved in loving detail' – hundreds of biblical scenes adorn the west front of Thann's Late Gothic Collégiale Saint-Thiébaut

Eguisheim illustrates the medieval defensive structure of concentric circles of streets surrounded by double ramparts

The Eguisheim family was one of the most powerful in Alsace for centuries and gave the region another saint and its only pope, Leo IX, born Count Bruno of Eguisheim in 1002, and elected to the papal throne in 1048. He was probably born in the family castle, built on the foundations of a stronghold put up by Count Eberhard, the founder of the dynasty and Odile's nephew. Some fragments of the castle can be seen in the walls of the houses in the centre of the village beside the church, whose main doorway bears an inscription to Pope Leo.

Eguisheim escaped war damage and is one of the most attractive of the wine villages, pleasantly peaceful as it has also escaped the over-emphasis on mass-tourism often found elsewhere. It has kept the medieval defensive structure of concentric circles of narrow streets surrounded by ramparts, and as you stroll round the **Rempart du Sud** or the **Rempart du Nord**, following the path trod by the watch, you have a vivid sense of the dangers so often faced by the people of Alsace, huddled inside their walls as the next invader threatened. Many of the houses have inner courtyards. You can inspect one at close quarters if you buy some wine from the Beyer family, whose premises diagonally opposite the church were once the **Hostellerie du Cheval Blanc**, a medieval inn where the valiant Turenne stayed on the eve of the Battle of Turckheim (see p. 122). Most of the present building dates from the sixteenth century but the cellars are twelfth century. The Beyers have been vintners since 1540 and some of the vineyards they own today have been in the family since the Revolution, when they were confiscated from nearby Marbach Abbey as a 'national asset'.

On the other side of the **place du Château**, beyond a **Renaissance fountain** adorned with a statue of Pope Leo, the **parish church** still has its yellowish sandstone belfry in Transitional style, but was rebuilt in the nineteenth century. Its original Romanesque doorway, richly carved and painted, can be seen inside the church. Beneath a Christ in Majesty flanked by St Peter and St Paul is a row of rather elderly-looking Wise and Foolish virgins, and below them, **La Vierge ouvrante**, a rare example of the statues of the Virgin with a hinged panel, like a miniature folding altarpiece, that were proscribed by the Council of Trent.

Eguisheim is a good place for strolling, and you can also climb up to the three towers by following the signposted **Route des Cinq Châteaux** (about a kilometre/just over a half a mile to the ruins). If you are driving you can follow the rest of the Five Castles Road, a circular tour of about 20km/12½ miles, with a marked path leading to the ruins of **Hohlandsbourg**, a Habsburg castle restored by Lazarus von Schwendi, who led the imperial troops against the Turkish armies in Hungary and captured the town of Tokay, from where he allegedly introduced the Tokay vines to Alsace. Another path brings you to the fifth castle, **Pflixbourg**, whose ruins, or so they say, are haunted by a fair princess turned into a dragon by a wicked fairy.

Colmar is sheer delight. Although it is a busy and quite lively town, a major centre of Alsace's wine trade, and has one of France's leading art museums, the network of beautifully preserved medieval streets in the centre has a cosy, villagey feel. Despite an influx of tourists for much of the year, there are plenty of opportunities for peaceful walks beside the River Lauch, which saunters slowly through the town, creating the picturesque district known as **La Petite Venise** (Little Venice). This makes a good starting point for a walk covering Colmar's highlights.

Begin by enjoying the view along the river from the **rue de Turenne**, which has a small **Muséum d'Histoire naturelle** (Natural History Museum). Then walk along the footpath to the **Pont Saint-Pierre** for an even lovelier view that includes much of the Old Town. Turn into the **rue du Manège**, walking past the **Lycée Bartholdi**, on the site of the *Columbarium*, a royal dovecot said to be the origin of the name Colmar. The Colmar-born sculptor Frédéric-Auguste Bartholdi, who carved New York's Statue of Liberty, was also responsible for the **Fontaine Roesselmann**, depicting one of the town's medieval provosts, in the **place des Six Montagnes-Noires**. From here, cross the bridge and turn into the **rue de la Poissonnerie** for a stroll through a picturesque district once peopled by fishermen whose livelihood depended on the fish that swam into the nets they floated in the Lauch. At no. 20 in the **quai de la Poissonnerie** you can even patronize a fishmonger whose family has been in business on the same spot for over four hundred years.

The gaily coloured half-timbered houses make a good backcloth for the busy **food market** held a couple of times a week in and around the

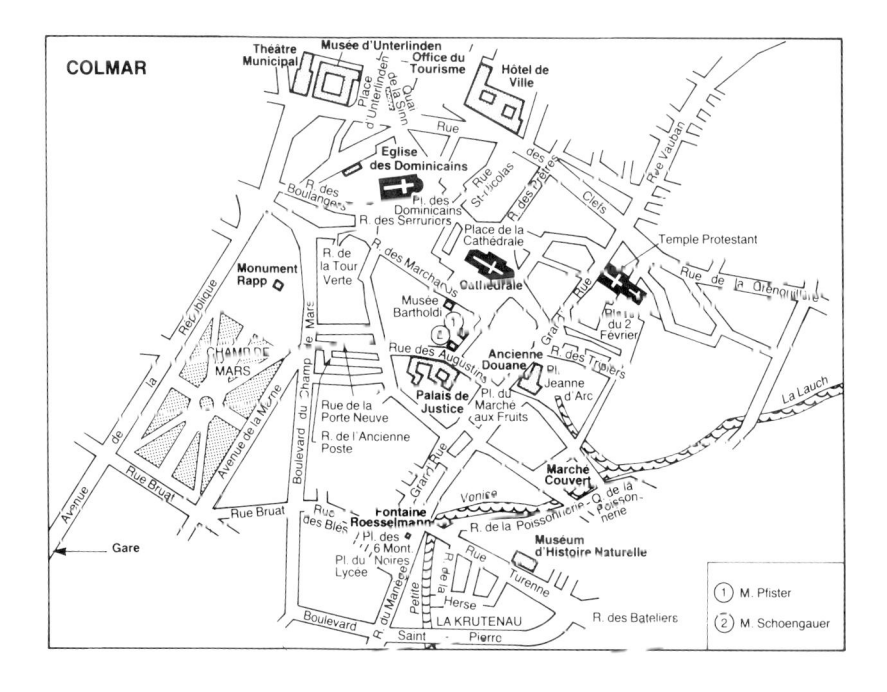

Marché couvert (market building), spilling over into the **rue des Tanneurs**. The houses in this narrow street, the heart of the newly restored **Quartier des Tanneurs**, are painted in paler colours and are taller than in the fishermen's district, with an open verandah on top used for drying hides. The **place de l'Ancienne-Douane** is dominated by the **Ancienne Douane** itself, the Customs or Merchants Hall known locally as the **Koifhus**, a fifteenth-century building with a roof of brightly glazed tiles.

From here **Grand'Rue** leads left to the **place du Marché-aux-Fruits**, with a maze of old streets leading off it. Before exploring them, walk to the right along Grand'Rue, past the early seventeenth-century **Maison des Arcades**, to the **Temple Saint-Matthieu**, a Protestant church, once belonging to the Franciscan order. Built in the late thirteenth and early fourteenth centuries, it is slowly being stripped of its nineteenth-century additions.

Continue to the **place Jeanne-d'Arc**, once a cattle market, then return to the Grand'Rue and walk up the **rue de l'Eglise** to visit the **Collégiale Saint-Martin**, a church always referred to by the local people as 'the cathedral'. Part-Romanesque, part-Gothic, it has some beautiful stained glass and richly carved doorways, and a single tower.

Now spend some time strolling along the **rue Mercière**, the **rue Schongauer**, the **rue des Marchands**, all of them lined with Renaissance houses. Look out specially for the **Maison Pfister** (rue Mercière), dating from 1537 and decorated with painted panels, the **Maison Zum Kragen** (1586, rue des Marchands), with a photogenic carved figure sporting a large collar or ruff (*Kragen* in German), the medieval **Huselin Zum Swan** or Swan House, where Martin Schongauer had his workshop (see box), and the fine oriel window on the corner of the **rue des Augustins** and the **rue Schongauer**. Information on all these houses can be gleaned from the local history rooms in the **Musée Bartholdi** (rue des Marchands), though their contents are due to be moved to the town hall. The museum's main purpose is to display Bartholdi's work in his birthplace, entered via a pretty courtyard.

Just beyond the **place des Ecoles**, at the far end of the rue des Marchands, is the **place des Dominicains**, with the entrance to the thirteenth-century **Eglise des Dominicains**, adorned with beautiful stained glass and now displaying Schongauer's magical *Madonna of the Rose Hedge* (see box). The **rue des Boulangers** brings you to the busy **rue des Têtes** to admire the **Maison des Têtes**, a Renaissance building (now a restaurant) decorated with the elaborately carved heads that give it its name. Take the **rue de l'Eau** to reach the entrance in the **place d'Unterlinden** to Colmar's magnificent museum, the **Musée d'Unterlinden**, housed in a thirteenth-century Dominican convent. The rooms grouped round the cloisters display a wealth of treasures, the best-known the extraordinary altar panels painted by Matthias Grünewald for the hospital run by the Antonine order in Issenheim near Guebwiller. The **Retable d'Issenheim** (Issenheim Altarpiece) is displayed in the convent's chapel, a fine setting for the harrowing *Entombment*, the dead Christ hideously

The River Lauch threads its way through Colmar's picturesque 'Little Venice'

Martin Schongauer

One of the highlights of Alsace for anyone interested in art is the very beautiful *Vierge au Buisson de Roses*, an altarpiece painted in about 1473 by the painter and engraver Martin Schongauer, who was probably born in Colmar, though some authorities claim he was a native of Augsburg and came to the city when very young.

The graceful figure of the Virgin Mary, with her long delicate Gothic fingers and pensive expression, and the Infant Jesus in her arms, wiggling his toes, one hand playing with her long auburn hair, are seen against a gold ground, while in the rose bush trained along a trellis behind them, a host of brightly coloured songbirds trill their paeons of praise for the newborn Saviour. At the top of the altarpiece a pair of blue-robed angels hold aloft a huge jewelled crown. The whole effect is deeply spiritual, yet homely too, with its emphasis on realistic detail, and clearly influenced by Flemish painters like Rogier van der Weyden. Allow plenty of time to enjoy the chaffinch and the robin, the jay and the goldfinch, all singing their hearts out, and the lovingly painted roses and strawberries, peonies and humble meadow grasses.

The altarpiece was stolen during the night of 10/11 January 1972 but miraculously recovered the following year, cut from its frame, in a garden shed near Lyon, just in time for heartfelt celebrations of its quincentenary.

Schongauer was born somewhere between 1430 and 1450. In 1489 he went to live in Breisach, where fragments of his fresco of the Last Judgement in the cathedral have come to light – he died suddenly in 1491 before it was completed. The altarpiece he painted for the Eglise des Dominicains is in the Unterlinden Museum, where it makes an interesting prelude to Grünewald's *Issenheim Altar*.

A number of major museums have paintings attributed to Schongauer, but apart from the two altarpieces in Colmar, the only fully authenticated work by him is a series of over a hundred lovely copperplate engravings on religious themes. One in the Unterlinden Museum is a realistic and very busy scene of a weary Christ bowed down to his knees beneath the weight of the Cross, while soldiers mock, curly-tailed dogs scamper about and a small boy lifts up the skirts of his tunic as he executes a little jig. The engravings were much admired for their technical mastery and must have featured in the pattern books used by painting workshops throughout the German-speaking world, as both paintings and engravings based on his work are very common. They clearly influenced the early style of Albrecht Dürer, whose father is known to have corresponded with Schongauer in the hope of sending the young man to Colmar after he had finished his journeyman's period. But by the time Dürer reached Colmar in 1492 Schongauer had just died, and he was received instead – kindly, we are told – by his brothers Kaspar and Paul, who were both goldsmiths, and Ludwig, also a painter. He noted that he later met a fifth brother, another goldsmith, when he travelled on to Basel.

pockmarked as if by leprosy, and the radiant *Resurrection* – it is hard to believe that this panel, so akin to the work of the Symbolists, was painted as long ago as 1510. Wall charts explain how the various panels folded and at the far end you can see the carved and gilded figures framing the altar, much more medieval in spirit. Don't be so mesmerized by Grünewald's work that you leave too little time for another altarpiece in the chapel, this one painted by Schongauer for the Eglise des Dominicains some forty years earlier and full of life and incident. The rest of the museum's collections are also well worth studying in detail. They include some beautiful Romanesque sculpture and a good range of folk art.

Although this walk will give you a good feel of Colmar, it well repays several days' exploration, and is also a good base for excursions on and around the Wine and Mountain Roads.

Easily visited from Colmar is **Neuf-Brisach**, a little town beside the Rhine, just 5km/3 miles from the German border and a remarkable example of the work of Louis XIV's brilliant military engineer Marshal Vauban. The Peace of Ryswick in 1697 forced Louis to hand over to Austria the fortress of Brisach (now the German town of Breisach-am-Rhein). That left him with an undefended border south of Strasbourg, so he commissioned Vauban to build a new fortified town and offered tax and other incentives to persuade people to move there. The result, completed in 1708, was Vauban's last great work and probably his masterpiece – a perfectly symmetrical octagonal layout, divided into forty-eight squares of equal size and surrounded by a double crown of moats and ramparts. The fortress has never been taken, though it needed extensive restoration after Second World War damage.

Stroll along the chequerboard of streets to the central **place d'Armes**, with a well at each corner and surrounded by attractive houses in classical style. The **church of Saint-Louis** houses a fine eighteenth-century altarpiece and a painted wooden calvary. In the **Pavillon de Belfort**, backing on to the **Porte de Belfort**, one of the two original gates still standing, is the **Musée Vauban**, displaying a model of the town and plans and documents connected with Vauban and his work there. A half hour's walk will take you right round the tall ramparts.

If you are in Alsace on 1 May, you can attend the town's popular *Fête du Muguet* (Lily-of-the-Valley Festival). And at any time of year you may like to cross the border to see frescoes by Martin Schongauer in **Breisach-am-Rhein**'s cathedral (see box, opposite).

A road running beside the **Rhône-Rhine Canal** brings you to **Marckolsheim**, to see fortifications from another era: here Maginot Line casemates (see box, p. 49) have been restored and turned into a small museum and a memorial to those who died on this spot in two world wars.

On summer evenings, and on Christmas and New Year's Eve, crowds of tourists head for **Turckheim**, the next highlight on the Wine Road. They have come to follow the night watchman, dressed in medieval garb, as he does his round of the little town. Clutching lantern and halberd, he strides solemnly beneath three tall fourteenth-century gates, the **Porte de France**, the **Porte de Munster** and the **Porte de Brand**, stopping at intervals to 'cry' the curfew in the local dialect. It makes a pleasant outing, especially if you follow it with a glass of wine in a friendly *caveau*. The town also boasts a memorial to Marshal Turenne, who in January 1675 inflicted a heavy defeat on the imperial troops at the Battle of Turckheim.

A couple of kilometres/just over a mile away is the pretty village of **Niedermorschwihr**, bright with gaily coloured Renaissance vintners' houses and decorative fountains. A road from here leads up to **Les Trois-Epis**, a little health resort frequented for its pure air (it is at 660m/over 2000ft), good walks and lovely views, which doubles as a place of pilgrimage. The 'three ears of corn' that give it its name were allegedly held by the Virgin Mary when she appeared to a local blacksmith in 1491. In her other hand, counterbalancing this harbinger of prosperity, was an icicle, symbolizing the frost that ruins the harvest. Her stern plea for repentance was eventually passed on to the local populace by the frightened blacksmith – though it took another miracle to persuade him to do so – and a pilgrimage chapel was built on the spot where he saw his vision. Les Trois-Epis makes a peaceful base for excursions both along the Wine Road and up into the Mountain Road area.

Pilgrims to **Ammerschwihr** are seeking bodily rather than spiritual sustenance: it lost most of its pretty houses during the fighting at the end of the Second World War, but boasts one of Alsace's finest restaurants, **Aux Armes de France** (see Hotels and Restaurants). **Kaysersberg**, too, has a gourmet restaurant, **Le Chambard**, but its delights do not end there. It is one of the most attractive of the Wine Road villages, its streets lined with Renaissance houses, many of them with elaborately carved and painted façades. It is much visited as the birthplace of Albert Schweitzer (see p. 144). Near the little museum devoted to him is a **fortified bridge**, and further along the high street, the **church of Sainte-Croix**. Its Romanesque doorway is surmounted by a vigorous Coronation of the Virgin, while the interior is thrillingly dominated by a huge wooden medieval calvary, high above the nave, with the crucified Christ flanked by the Virgin Mary and St John. Beyond it, admire the beautiful gilded and painted altarpiece and many other riches, including some fine stained glass. The **local history museum**, reached via a Renaissance courtyard, has an 'opening Virgin' similar to the one in Eguisheim (p. 116). Brooding above the little town is a ruined medieval **castle**, easily reached by a path starting from behind the town hall with its oriel window.

The castle in **Kientzheim** is in the heart of the village. As it was once

Kaysersberg – a ruined castle perched above terraces of vines

The vines penetrate right into the heart of many Wine Road villages, as here in Niedermorschwihr

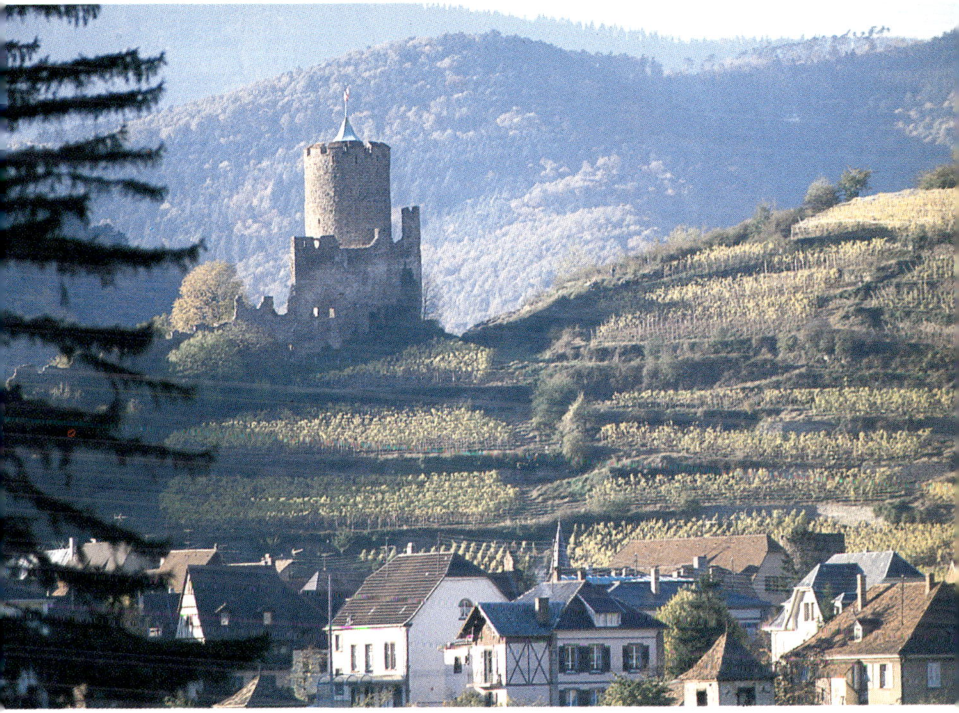

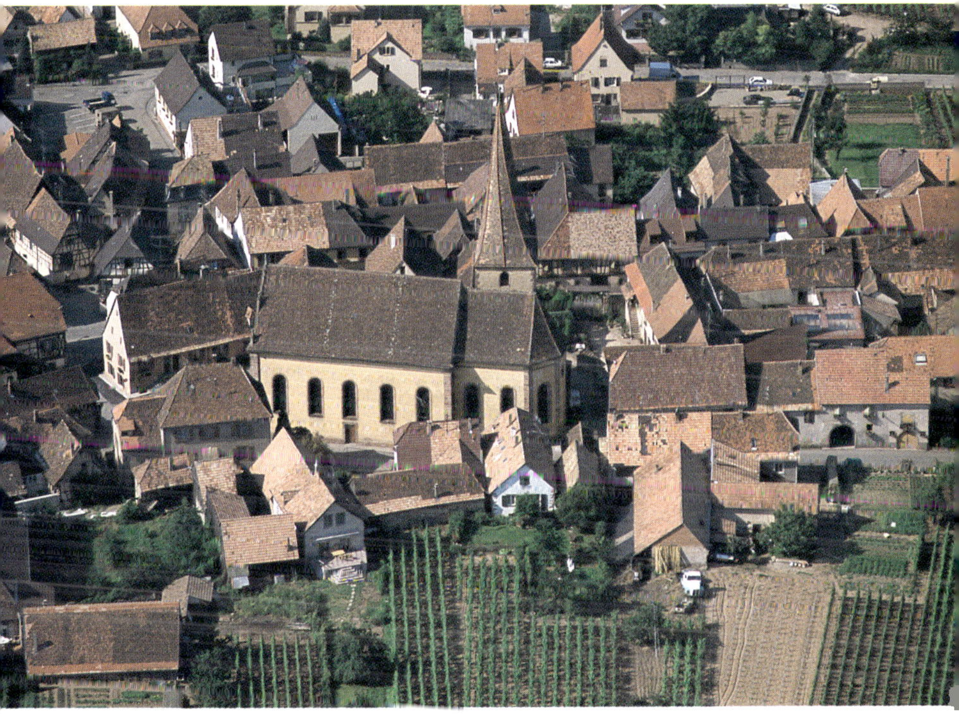

owned by Lazarus von Schwendi, who is said to have introduced one of Alsace's main grape varieties (see p. 116), it is only fitting that it is now the headquarters of the Confrérie Saint-Etienne d'Alsace, an association of wine connoisseurs which holds its regular 'chapters' and 'enthronings' there, and also houses the very interesting and well-displayed **Musée du Vin et du Vignoble** (Wine Museum). Here you will see tools and barrels, corks and glasses – the whole panoply of items connected with the age-old process of wine making.

Sigolsheim, **Bennwihr** and **Mittelwihr** were all virtually wiped out during the fierce fighting that led to the flushing out of the 'Colmar pocket' in 1944–5 (see A Little History). They have been attractively rebuilt in traditional style but cannot compete with **Riquewihr**, the Wine Road's most tourist-frequented village, which miraculously escaped more or less unscathed.

Much of its charm stems from the fact that it still nestles within its medieval walls, lapped by wave upon wave of vines, a little world apart where you can wander at leisure along traffic-free streets (the car parks are outside the walls), admiring picturesque medieval and Renaissance houses before settling down to taste the local wine and enjoy a meal in one of the many restaurants and *winstubs*. The crowds in summer and autumn are not all tourists – Riquewihr is a major centre of the wine trade and boasts one of its best-known dynasties, the Hugel family, who have been making wine from grapes grown in their own vineyards since 1639. Their establishment is one of many immaculate half-timbered buildings in the **rue du Général-de-Gaulle** (also known as **Grand'Rue**), the cobbled high street, with narrow side streets and cul-de-sacs leading off it. As you stroll round (plans available from the tourist office) you will spot oriel windows, carved wooden gables, stone turrets, here a pretty well adorning a courtyard, there a little statue tucked into a niche. Most of the houses are carved with their date, many are painted in bright colours, all are awash with geraniums throughout the summer and autumn. Two of the most attractive face each other as you start to walk up from the **Hôtel-de-Ville** (town hall): the **Maison Liebrich**, with a charming courtyard, dates from 1535, the **Maison Behrel** from a couple of decades earlier.

At the far end of the high street, just before you reach the **Porte supérieure**, a narrow street on the right leads to the **Cour des Juifs**, where you can visit the forbidding **Tour des Voleurs** (Thieves' Tower) to see a medieval torture chamber complete with gruesome instruments. The **Porte du Dolder** has been turned into a small local history and archeology museum. After exploring the village you can find out about the history of Alsace's postal services by visiting the **Musée d'Histoire des PTT en Alsace**, in the Renaissance château of the feudal lords of Riquewihr, near the town hall.

Zellenberg, a sunny village perched on a hill very close to Riquewihr, is the home of another old-established vintners' dynasty – the Beckers have been making wine for even longer than the Hugels, since 1610, and welcome visitors to their wine tastings. The village is peaceful and pretty, and the views over the vines are splendid. It is only 3km/ under 2 miles to the next main stopping point on the Wine Road, **Ribeauvillé**, though you might like to stop off on the way to visit **Hunawihr**'s curious fortified church, surrounded by vines, and its stork-rearing centre, which pioneered the policy of trying to repopulate Alsace with its beloved mascots (see p. 26). True to its nature-conservation image, the village has also created a butterfly centre, where you see hundreds of species living in a lovingly created natural environment within a huge greenhouse.

Ribeauvillé is a small town rather than a village and though it has many attractive houses, the charm of Riquewihr is missing. But the setting is all you could wish for, the long high street offering glimpses high up above the vineyards of the three ruined castles of the powerful counts of Ribeaupierre, who once held sway here. As you walk along the high street, look out for the **Pfifferhüs** (Minstrels' House, see p. 127) and the **Tour des Bouchers** (Butchers' Tower), all that is left of the medieval fortifications. As well as its wines, Ribeauvillé has several other claims to fame. It boasts the spring from which the Carola mineral water is produced – it has been active since 1518 and bottled on a commercial scale since 1888. It also specializes in table linen printed in traditional Paisley patterns, and it claims to be the *Kougelhopf* Capital of the World (see box, p 60).

A pleasant walk of half an hour or so via a marked path starting from near the parish church (you can also reach it from the far end of the high street) brings you up through vines and forest to the castles, **Saint-Ulrich**, **Girsberg** and **Haut-Ribeaupierre**, and the lovely views they command. You may like to continue to the pilgrimage chapel of **Notre-Dame de Dusenbach**, another half-hour's walk.

Yet another castle overlooks the little wine village of **Saint-Hippolyte** with its peaceful old streets. But the huge medieval fortress of **Haut-Koenigsbourg** is definitely not a ruin, and hasn't been since the beginning of the century, when it was reconstructed by an enthusiastic Kaiser Wilhelm in pinkish sandstone. The reconstruction has been severely criticized by art historians and architects, but there is no denying the powerful impression it makes on the lay visitor, with its huge central keep, its twin rows of thick walls, its machicolations and turrets. It certainly says more to children than a romantic ruin, teaching them about life in feudal times, and has become one of Alsace's most popular tourist sights. Inside it is furnished with heavy oak tables, suits of armour, chandeliers made of antlers and hunting trophies, banners and pennants and the like.

Haut-Koenigsbourg can also be reached from **Kintzheim**, whose own castle houses another popular tourist attraction, the **Volerie des Aigles**. Here saucer-eyed children gaze in fascination as carefully trained birds of prey soar into the sky, then swoop down to snatch a chunk of meat from a gloved finger. Nearby are the **Montagne des Singes**, an open-air reserve peopled by several hundred monkeys, and, on the way to Sélestat, the **Parc des Cigognes et Loisirs**, where you can see storks being bred.

Sélestat, one of the ten Decapolis

towns (see A Little History), was the intellectual centre of Alsace in the late fifteenth and early sixteenth centuries, mainly thanks to its famous Latin School and the activities of the Humanists, led by Beatus Rhenanus (see box), whose library you can admire in the **Bibliothèque humaniste**

Beatus Rhenanus and his library

Born plain Bert Bild, the son of a wealthy Sélestat butcher, in August 1485, Beatus Rhenanus is the best-known member of Alsace's important Humanist school. He revealed his great gifts as a scholar when he was still very young, first at Sélestat's famous Latin School and later at the Sorbonne in Paris. He graduated in 1507 and was given a job as editor, proofreader and philologist by Mathias Schurer, a Strasbourg printer who also came from Sélestat. He subsequently moved to Basel, where he worked for the two greatest printers of the age, Amerbach and Froben. In Basel he was in touch with the many leading scholars working there, and became a close friend of Erasmus, whose biography he was to publish. Froben, Erasmus and Rhenanus decided to resuscitate the texts of the Early Fathers, a project which played an important part in spreading the ideals of Humanism throughout Europe.

Thanks to his father's wealth, Beatus Rhenanus was able to start building up a library at an early age. He already owned nearly sixty important volumes by the time he matriculated at the Sorbonne, most of them works of grammar, philology and rhetoric. During his four years in Paris he bought another 188 books, including twenty treatises by Aristotle – you can see them today in Sélestat's Humanist Library, annotated in the margins with his own comments.

By the time he died in Sélestat in July 1547 he had assembled one of the finest libraries of the age. Quite apart from the books he had continued buying throughout his life, it included those he wrote himself, and the many editions of Greek and Roman authors on which he worked. Other titles were gifts from friends and fellow scholars, or had been given in exchange for his own works, which included a much-admired history of Germany and a study of the preacher Geiler of Kaysersberg.

Altogether, his library consisted of over two thousand titles, bound into 670 separate volumes. In his Will he left it to his native town. In 1757 it was added to the library in the archive room at Saint-Georges, which dated back to the Humanist collections left to the town by the church's rector Jean de Westhuss in 1452 – thirty large volumes, each attached to a heavy chain – and added to over the next eighty or so years, when Sélestat was Alsace's leading intellectual centre. In 1840 both collections were moved to the town hall, and half a century later at last found a permanent home in the Halle aux Blés (Cornmarket).

Pfifferdai

Centuries ago the Count of Ribeaupierre (or Rappolsheim) was the official liege lord and protector of the local wandering minstrels, who would gather in Ribeauvillé on 8 September to pay homage to him and to make a pilgrimage to the nearby chapel of Our Lady of Dusenbach. They were gradually joined by other strolling players, acrobats, jugglers and the like, and set up one of the most influential of the region's guilds.

Pfifferdai, the Day of the Fife-Players, is one of the few genuine medieval celebrations to have survived in Alsace. Nowadays it takes place on the first Sunday in September, rather than on the eighth of the month, and is still essentially a popular festival, though it draws crowds of tourists too. A costume parade with floats illustrating scenes from the history of the little town and free wine flowing from the fountain in the main square are just two of the attractions on offer.

In the place de la Sinne a sign on one building tells you that it was once a hostelry where the minstrels held their meetings from 1715 onwards. And in the Grand-Rue you can admire the half-timbered Pfifferhüs, also known as the Maison de l'Ave Maria, because of the carved wooden scene of the Annunciation above its oriel window. Here too the minstrels' guild used to meet, in an atmosphere that was no doubt as lively as you will find today, if you eat in the *winstub* it now plays host to. Among Alsace's star performers who now frequent this popular spot are some of the region's top chefs, drawn by the sturdy regional specialities and joyous ambiance.

Charles-Emile Freppel – bishop, MP and patriot

Born in 1827 in Obernai, Charles-Emile Freppel trained for the priesthood and was in due course appointed Bishop of Angers. He set up a Roman Catholic faculty in Angers and became involved in politics, subsequently being elected a *député* (member of parliament) for the Finistère *département* in Brittany.

Appalled at the projected annexation of Alsace to Germany after the Franco-Prussian War he wrote a famous letter to the Kaiser warning of the consequences. Twenty years later he died, leaving a Will stating: 'I wish my heart to be transported to the parish church of Obernai when Alsace has become French once again.' A statue of him was erected in front of Angers Cathedral, inscribed with these words. At last, in 1918, Alsace regained her freedom, and his heart now rests in a shrine in the church of Saint-Pierre-et-Saint-Paul, much venerated by the local people. A copy of the Angers statue with its inscription stands in the square outside the church.

in the **Halle aux Blés** (Cornmarket). A few minutes' walk away is the **Hôtel de l'Abbaye d'Ebersmunster** in the **Cour des Prélats**, with a creeper-covered turret and a Renaissance doorway. The nightwatchman sets off on his rounds from here on both Friday and weekend evenings. Sélestat has two important churches, the pinkish Romanesque **Sainte-Foy**, with a richly carved porch and an octagonal tower topped by a tall spire, and, very close to it, the reddish Gothic **Saint-Georges**, famous for its beautiful stained glass. You can also see two fortified medieval gates, the **Tour de l'Horloge** (Clock Tower) and the **Tour des Sorcières** (Witches' Tower). As you stroll round the cobbled streets near the churches and peer into the windows of the old-fashioned shops, the hordes of tourists on the Wine Road – and the twentieth century in general – seem far away.

Châtenois, too, has a **Tour des Sorcières**, and there are many interesting old houses both here and in nearby **Scherwiller**, which was virtually burnt to the ground during the Bumpkins' War in 1525 (see A Little History). **Dambach-la-Ville** still has three sturdy medieval gates in its well-preserved ramparts, but once inside the walls, you find surprisingly few tourists admiring its pretty **place du Marché**, its flower-decked fountains and picturesque houses. Do allow enough time to visit the **Chapelle Saint-Sébastien**, just outside the town. Its elaborate Baroque altar in carved wood is a surprise in this humble country chapel, its Romanesque belfry rising out of a sea of vines.

Andlau is a surprise too. From a distance its Romanesque abbey church looks quite plain, but when you get closer you can see that it is adorned with a lively frieze of men and beasts – knights jousting in chainmail, a lion attacking a sheep, a boy riding a dolphin, a donkey with an elephant's howdah on its back, and much more besides. And tucked away at the back is a magnificent Romanesque porch. Notice how the Christ in Majesty on the tympanum seems to have been squashed down to fit into the space, His head hitting the roof. And how the serpent offering Eve the apple is a long, thick creature whose tail touches the ground while its head is up among the apples. The little town is pretty and unspoilt and you can climb up to ruined **Haut-Andlau Castle**.

Barr's pride and joy is its **Musée de la Folie Marco**, a substantial eighteenth-century dwelling with a shady garden that has been converted into a museum furnished in the style of the period. The house has its own vineyard, whose products you can taste in the cellars, together with other local vintages. The old town is picturesque, but much less tourist-frequented than **Obernai**, where Alsace's patron saint Odile was born in about 660 (see box, p. 130). It lies on the River Ehn, a tributary of the Ill, and was once, long ago, when it was the fief of Odile's fearsome father Duke Eticho, called Ehnheim. The ramparts that still surround it make a shady walk on hot summer days, when the narrow streets in the centre, thronged with tourists, can seem unpleasantly airless.

The heart of Obernai is the **place du Marché**, surrounded by half-timbered houses and centring on a modern statue-fountain of St Odile.

On the west side is the mainly Renaissance **Hôtel de Ville** (town hall), with an oriel window and carved stone balcony. Beside it the **Kapellturm** (belfry) was once attached to a medieval chapel: severe in its lower storeys, it breaks out in a froth of lacy carving at the foot of the steeple. On the other side of the square, the Renaissance **Halle aux Blés** (Cornmarket), its steeply pitched roof lit by rows of glassless dormer windows, houses a restaurant and a small **local history museum**. On the way to the **church of Saint-Pierre-et-Saint-Paul**, where a famous Alsace patriot is venerated (see box), stop to admire a decorative Renaissance well with no fewer than six buckets. As well as Monsignor Freppel's heart, the church has an early sixteenth-century altarpiece with a vivid Entombment scene. The horse-minded should now head for Obernai's **Musée du Cheval et de l'Attelage** (Horse and Harness Museum), 4km/ 2½ miles west in the outbuildings of a château set in large grounds.

Nearby **Ottrott**, known for its red wine, is the starting point of an early steam train running back and forth to **Rosheim** on Sundays and public holidays. It is also a good base from which to visit Alsace's most holy spot, the **Mont Sainte-Odile**, high up on a rocky ridge and surrounded by a mysterious wall 12km/7½ miles long, the **Mur des Païens**, probably built by a Celtic tribe in the seventh century BC. The convent crowning the mount dates back to the days of Odile and her father Duke Eticho (see box). It has suffered damage and been rebuilt many times over the years, but is still a major place of pilgrimage, with its own modest hotel. You can visit the **Chapelle Sainte-Odile** to see the saint's tomb and various other chapels beyond the busy courtyard with its well-kept garden (plan available from the reception area). In spite of the crowds, this still feels a very holy place, and the superb views add to the sense of awe.

The pure Romanesque lines of the **church of Saint-Pierre-et-Saint-Paul** in **Rosheim** create a feeling of holiness too. This beautiful church has an octagonal Gothic tower but is best known for its curious Romanesque sculptures dotted about on the roof – a man sitting cross-legged just below the tower, another, with knees drawn up, apparently about to be devoured by a lion but looking stoical, while a third, in the same predicament, is clearly terrified, his hands clenched round his knees, mouth open to scream. Crouching lions and the attributes of the four evangelists also feature in the church's outdoor bestiary, while inside are rows of little human heads, some chubby-cheeked and curly-haired, a few with high cheekbones. Outside the town hall is a Renaissance well, and further along the high street, the twelfth-century **Heidenhüs** is believed to be the earliest surviving house in Alsace.

The region's oldest surviving church is the **Dompeter**, all by itself surrounded by fields at **Avolsheim**, just north of **Molsheim**, whose central square is dominated by the Renaissance **Metzig** (Butchers' Hall), adorned with dragon drainpipes and a graceful clock. The ground floor is now a *winstub*. The square also boasts a Renaissance fountain with a lion bearing the town's coat of arms. A short walk away through pretty side streets is the **Musée Prieuré des**

St Odile

St Odilia or Ottilia, better known by her French name Odile, is the patron saint of Alsace. She was the daughter of a descendant of Duke Eticho, the first ruler of the duchy of Alsace, and was born in Obernai, probably between 660 and 670. Her father, the third duke, is variously referred to as another Duke Eticho, or as Duke Adalric or Duke Atticus. There are several different versions of her legend too: 'The legendary details of [her] story,' remarks *The Penguin Dictionary of Saints* severely, 'put a more than ordinary strain on the reader's credulity.' Perhaps they do, but they have led to her being more venerated in France than almost any other saint.

The Duke's wife, Bereswinde, a sister-in-law of the Merovingian king Childeric II, failed to produce a child for many long years. When the frustrated Duke, desperate for an heir, pleaded with an Irish monk to intercede with God on his behalf, she did eventually become pregnant. But the monk warned him that Bereswinde would give birth to a daughter, who would be a perpetual thorn in his side. When the happy event took place and a daughter was duly born, the Duke, famous throughout the land for his violent temper, flew into a rage. He had discovered that this unwanted daughter was also blind. He ordered one of his henchmen to kill the baby unless she was removed from the dukedom forthwith, never to return. Her mother managed to have her smuggled away by a wet nurse, who took her to her great-aunt, the abbess of a convent near Besançon.

When she was about ten, the Bishop of Regensburg in Bavaria had a dream in which he was commanded by God to travel to the convent to christen a blind girl. He was to give her the name 'Odilia', meaning 'daughter of light'. He set off the next day, and when he anointed her with holy water she miraculously recovered her sight.

Odile's dearest wish now was to return to her family. The Duke would have none of it, and when her brother Hugues plucked up enough courage to bring her home, he was promptly murdered. Eventually the Duke consented to see his daughter, by now a beautiful young woman, and his celebrated temper seems to have cooled off. But it soon burst out again when Odile rejected the fiancé he had chosen for her – a German prince – saying that she could only be a bride of Christ. Furious at the thought of her becoming a nun, he forced her to flee in terror from his castle. The Duke set off in pursuit with a posse of his knights. But when he caught up with her and went to strike her dead a second miracle occurred: a rock split open to let her in, then closed up again to prevent him following her.

The Duke knew when he was beaten. He sent word to Odile that if she came home, he would help her convert his grim fortress into a convent. When the convent was ready she became its first abbess and led a life of holiness and charity, performing countless miracles in curing the blind and the leprous. Since her death in about 720, generations of pilgrims have worshipped at her tomb in the chapel of Sainte-Odile. She was canonized by one of her descendants, Alsace's only pope Leo IX.

Half-timbered houses painted in bright colours, geraniums tumbling from every window – a typical sight on the Wine Road

Chartreux, a local history museum in the prior's house attached to the town's former Carthusian monastery. It includes exhibits connected with the Bugatti factory that used to operate just outside Molsheim; there is also a small museum in the Bugatti premises. On the other side of the square the **rue de l'Eglise** has a pretty house with a Renaissance gable. From here the **rue Notre-Dame** brings you to the large and imposing **Eglise des Jésuites**, its interior blending Gothic and Renaissance. Retrace your steps and you come to the medieval **Tour des Forgerons** (Blacksmiths' Gate), through which you can enjoy a fine view of the Metzig.

Nearby **Mutzig**, famous for its beer, also has a fortified medieval gate, called the **Porte du Bas**, and its château houses a small **firearms museum**. The Wine Road officially ends at **Marlenheim** (see Chapter 4), though it reappears in the north-east corner of the region to take in the **Cleebourg** vineyards near **Wissembourg** (see Chapter 5).

Key data

Access

Most of the villages on the Wine Road are close to one of the major centres, from where adequate bus services operate during the week. Sunday services are rare, and frequency may diminish during the school holidays. The Wine Road itself is well signposted. Roads are generally good, but may be congested with farm machinery and trucks at all times of year, particularly during the grape-picking season, and also with tourist coaches during the summer and autumn. Parking inside the villages is often difficult, sometimes prohibited. It is generally better to leave your car in a car park outside, so that you are free to explore on foot. The narrow roads winding between the vineyards offer few parking opportunities.

As many visitors to the Wine Road sensibly prefer to drink rather than drive, most villages have taxis (ask at tourist offices or hotels and restaurants, or look out for signs in the best-known villages). This can be a convenient way of combining several villages, and an economical one, as they are all close together. Serious gourmets also use taxis to enable them to dine in another village, or to get back after lunch or dinner to Colmar or Strasbourg. Local taxis are also used to pick up visitors from outlying stations such as Ribeauvillé's (4km/2½ miles from the village).

Tourist offices may be able to supply leaflets showing marked paths enabling you to walk from one village to another via the vineyards. Biking is another popular way of getting about on the Wine Road. Inquire at tourist offices about bike-hire arrangements.

Itineraries

The *Route du Vin en Alsace* brochure, showing the Wine Road in detail, is widely available in tourist offices and even tourist shops.

ANDLAU   67140 Barr
TO   Mairie (88 08 22 57 or 88 08 93 01)
Access   Strasbourg 37km/23 miles, Barr 6km/4 miles, Colmar 30km/19 miles, Obernai 12km/7½ miles; **rail** to Barr
Sights   **Abbatiale** (Romanesque abbey church)

BARR   67140
TO   pl. de l'Hôtel-de-Ville (88 08 94 24)
Access   Strasbourg 35km/22 miles, Colmar 42km/26 miles, Sélestat 20km/12½ miles; **rail** from Strasbourg, or Obernai, Sélestat
Sights   **Musée de la Folie Marco** (Renaissance and eighteenth-century furniture) 30 rue Sultzer; open daily except Tues July–Oct, weekends only June and Oct

COLMAR   68000
TO   4 rue des Unterlinden (89 41 02 29)
Access   Strasbourg 71km/44 miles, Mulhouse 42km/26 miles; **buses** from Wine Road villages, Mulhouse; **rail** from Strasbourg, Mulhouse, Sélestat
Sights   **Collégiale Saint-Martin**, pl. de la Cathédrale; **Eglise des Dominicains** (Schongauer's *Madonna of the Rose Hedge*) pl. des Dominicains, open daily mid-Mar–mid-Nov; **Musée Bartholdi** 30 rue des Marchands, open daily April–Nov, weekends only Nov–end-Mar; **Musée d'Unterlinden** 1 rue des Unterlinden, open daily except Tues year-round; **Muséum d'Histoire naturelle** 11 rue Turenne, afternoons only: daily except Mon, Apr–Oct; Weds and weekends only Oct–mid-Dec, Feb, Mar; **Temple Saint-Matthieu** Grand'Rue, open daily except Sun, mid-June–Oct

DAMBACH-LA-VILLE   67650
TO   Mairie (89 92 41 05)
Access   Strasbourg 46km/29 miles, Sélestat 9km/5½ miles; **rail** from Strasbourg, or Obernai and Sélestat
Sights   **Chapelle Saint-Sébastien**

EGUISHEIM   68420 Herrlisheim
TO   22A Grand'Rue (89 23 40 33)
Access   Colmar 6km/4 miles, Mulhouse 39km/24 miles; **buses** from Colmar; **rail** from Strasbourg
Sights   **Parish church**; **Tours d'Eguisheim** (three ruined keeps)

GUEBWILLER   68500
TO   5 pl. Saint-Léger (89 76 10 63)
Access   Colmar 26km/16 miles, Mulhouse 23km/14 miles; **buses** from Colmar and Mulhouse
Sights   **Couvent des Dominicains**, **Eglise Notre-Dame**, **Eglise Saint-Léger**,

all in rue de la République; **Musée du Florival** (local history, ceramics) 1 rue du 4-Février, open weekends year-round; also weekday afternoons (except Tues) April–Nov

HAUT-KOENIGSBOURG see SAINT-HIPPOLYTE

HUNAWIHR 68150 Ribeauvillé
TO Mairie (89 73 60 42)
Access Strasbourg 60km/37½ miles, Colmar 13km/8 miles, Ribeauvillé 6km/4 miles; **buses** to Ribeauvillé from Colmar
Sights **Centre de réintroduction des cigognes** (Stork-rearing Centre) open daily Apr–Nov, afternoon demonstrations; **Serre à papillons** (Butterfly Centre) open daily Apr–mid-Nov

KAYSERSBERG 68240
TO 37 rue du Général-de-Gaulle (89 78 22 78 or 89 47 10 16)
Access Colmar 11km/7 miles; **buses** from Colmar
Sights **Musée de Kaysersberg** (local history) 64 rue du Général-de-Gaulle, open daily Easter, July, Aug; weekends only May, June, Sept, Oct; **Centre Culturel Albert-Schweitzer** 126 rue du Général-de-Gaulle, open daily Easter and May–Nov

KIENTZHEIM 68240 Kaysersberg
Access Colmar 10km/6 miles, Kaysersberg 3·5km/2 miles; **buses** from Colmar, Kaysersberg
Sights **Musée du Vignoble et des Vins d'Alsace** (Wine Museum) in **Château** open daily mid-June–Nov

KINTZHEIM 67600 Sélestat
TO pl. de la Fontaine (88 82 09 90 or 88 82 04 87)
Access Colmar 20km/12½ miles, Sélestat 4km/2½ miles; **buses** from Colmar
Sights **Montagne des Singes** (Monkey Reserve) open daily April–mid-Oct, Weds and weekends only mid-Oct–mid-Nov; **Parc des Cigognes** (Stork-rearing Centre) open daily Apr–Sept; Weds and weekends only Sept–mid-Oct; **Volerie des Aigles** (birds of prey demonstrations) at **Château de Kintzheim** open daily, afternoons only, Apr–mid-Sept; Weds and weekends only Oct–mid-Nov

MARCKOLSHEIM 67390
TO 27 rue du Maréchal-Foch (88 92 56 98 or 88 92 50 01)
Access Strasbourg 50km/31 miles, Colmar 25km/15½ miles, Sélestat 15km/9½ miles; **buses** from Colmar
Sights **Mémorial-Musée de la Ligne Maginot** (Maginot Line Museum) route du Rhin, open daily mid-June–mid-Sept; Sun and public hols only, mid-Mar–mid-June and mid-Sept–Mid-Nov

MOLSHEIM 67120
TO 17 pl. de l'Hôtel-de-Ville (88 38 11 61 or 88 38 52 00)
Access Strasbourg 28km/17½ miles, Obernai 9km/5½ miles; **rail** from Strasbourg
Sights Eglise des Jésuites; Metzig (Renaissance Butchers' Hall), pl. de l'Hôtel-de-Ville; **Musée Prieuré des Chartreux** (local history) cour des Chartreux, daily except Tues, May–Nov; **Musée de la Fondation Bugatti** guided tours usually possible for five people or more (check locally)

MONT SAINTE-ODILE 67530 Ottrott
Access Strasbourg 42km/26 miles, Barr 12km/7½ miles, Obernai 12km/7½ miles; **buses** from Strasbourg; **rail** from Strasbourg to Barr or Obernai
Sights **Convent** open daily mid-Feb–mid Nov and Dec

MUTZIG 67190
Access Strasbourg 28km/17½ miles, Obernai 12km/7½ miles; **rail** from Strasbourg
Sights Musée de Mutzig (Firearms Museum) Closed at time of writing for renovation; check locally

NEUF-BRISACH 68600
TO pl. d'Armes (89 72 56 66)
Access Colmar 16km/10 miles, Mulhouse 35km/22 miles; **buses** from Colmar or Mulhouse
Sights **Musée Vauban** (history of fortifications) 7 porte de Belfort, open daily except Tues, Apr–Nov

OBERNAI 67210
TO Chapelle du Beffroi (88 95 64 13)
Access Strasbourg 25km/15½ miles, Colmar 45km/28 miles, Sélestat 23km/14 miles; **buses** from Strasbourg; **rail** from Strasbourg or Sélestat
Sights Hôtel de Ville (Renaissance town hall), **Kapellturm** (belfry), **Halle aux Blés** (Cornmarket), all in pl. du Marché; **Eglise Saint-Pierre-et-Saint-Paul**, pl. de l'Eglise; **Musée du Cheval et de l'Attelage** (Horse Museum) Domaine de la Léonardsau, open afternoons only, daily except Mon July–Oct

RIBEAUVILLÉ 68150
TO 1 Grand'Rue (89 73 62 22)
Access Strasbourg 60km/37½ miles, Colmar 15km/9½ miles, Riquewihr 5km/3 miles; **buses** from Colmar; **rail** from Strasbourg, Colmar, Mulhouse, then bus (except Sun)
Sights Three **ruined castles** (marked path); **Notre-Dame de Dusenbach** (pilgrimage chapel) (marked path)

RIQUEWIHR 68340
TO 2 rue de la 1ère-Armée (89 47 80 80)
Access Strasbourg 65km/40½ miles, Colmar 13km/8 miles, Ribeauvillé 5km/3 miles; **buses** from Colmar
Sights **Musée d'Histoire des PTT d'Alsace** (history of postal services in Alsace) in **Château**, open daily July and Aug; daily except Tues, Apr–mid-Nov; **Musée du Dolder** (local history) rue du Général-de-Gaulle, open daily July and Aug; Fri and weekends only Easter–July and Sept–mid-Nov; **Tour des Voleurs** rue des Juifs, open daily Easter–mid-Nov

ROSHEIM 67560
TO Mairie (88 50 40 10)
Access Strasbourg 29km/18 miles, Molsheim 6km/4 miles, Obernai 6km/4 miles, Sélestat 29km/18 miles; **rail** from Strasbourg
Sights **Eglise Saint-Pierre-et-Saint-Paul** (Romanesque church), **Heidenhüs** (Romanesque house), both rue du Général-de-Gaulle

ROUFFACH 68250
TO 8 pl. de la République (89 78 53 15)
Access Colmar 15km/9½ miles, Mulhouse 28km/17½ miles; **buses** from Colmar, **rail** from Strasbourg, Colmar or Mulhouse
Sights **Eglise Notre-Dame**; **Chapelle Notre-Dame de Schauenberg** (pilgrimage chapel at Pfaffenheim), open daily May–Nov

SAINT-HIPPOLYTE 68590
TO Mairie (89 73 00 13)
Access Strasbourg 56km/35 miles, Colmar 20km/12½ miles, Sélestat 9km/5½ miles; infrequent **buses** from Colmar and Sélestat, **rail** to Sélestat, then taxi; regular **coach excursions** to Haut-Koenigsbourg Castle
Sights **Château du Haut-Koenigsbourg** (7km/4½ miles W) open daily mid-Feb–early Jan

SÉLESTAT 67600
TO Commanderie Saint-Jean, blvd du Général-Leclerc (88 92 02 66)
Access Strasbourg 47km/29½ miles, Colmar 21km/13 miles; **rail** from Strasbourg, Colmar or Mulhouse
Sights **Bibliothèque humaniste** (Humanist Library) 1 rue de la Bibliothèque, open daily year-round except Sat p.m. and Sun; **Eglise Sainte-Foy** (Romanesque church), **Eglise Saint-Georges** (Gothic church)

THANN 68800
TO 6 pl. Joffre (89 37 96 20)
Access Mulhouse 22km/13½ miles, Colmar 44km/27½ miles; **buses** from Mulhouse, **rail** from Mulhouse
Sights **Collégiale Saint-Thiébaut** (Gothic church) pl. Joffre; **Musée d'Art et d'Histoire locale** (local history) Halle aux Blés, 24 rue Saint-Thiébaut, daily except Mon mornings mid-May–Oct

TURCKHEIM 68230
TO Corps de Garde (89 27 18 08 or 89 27 38 44)
Access Colmar 7km/4½ miles, Munster 12km/7½ miles; **buses** from Colmar
Sights **Porte de Brand**, **Porte de France**, **Porte de Munster**, three medieval gates, through which the night watchman processes from 10 p.m., mid-May–mid-Oct

A detail from the intricate sculpture on the Collégiale Saint-Martin, Colmar's 'cathedral'

7

On and around the Mountain Road

Some of the most beautiful mountain landscapes in France can be enjoyed in the western Vosges, along the border with Lorraine. The rounded peaks, known as *ballons*, though high – the highest, the **Grand Ballon** or **Ballon de Guebwiller** is at 1424m/ 4670ft – are gentle. This is hiking rather than climbing country, with rolling verdant pastures and steely blue-green forests. In the winter the high pastures, the *chaumes* where cattle graze in summer and where you can enjoy a modest meal based on cheese in a *ferme-auberge* or farm-inn (see box, p. 11), become skiing country. The small Vosges ski resorts specialize in cross-country skiing, though downhill skiing is also practised (see Practical Information). Although often sunny, the Vosges are prone to being enveloped in mist at all times of year, so it is always wise to be equipped with warm clothes when you are out walking, even in summer.

In fine weather the views are superb. The finest within easy reach are from the **Route des Crêtes** (literally Ridge Road), a road following the line of the mountain ridge built for strategic purposes during the First World War, now a spectacular tourist route that in winter becomes one long cross-country ski trail. This stretches from **Cernay** northwards to **Sainte-Marie-aux-Mines**, a little textile town that was once at the heart of a silver-mining district, with a southern extension in the shape of the short **Route Joffre** from **Thann** to **Masevaux**, again originally a military road. But further north, the **Val de Villé**, the **Vallée de la Bruche** and **Vallée de la Mossig** are also beautiful, if less spectacular, and this chapter follows the line of the western Vosges up to **Wangenbourg-Engenthal**, a little summer resort popular with the Strasbourgeois and close to Saverne, the gateway to the Northern Vosges, described in Chapter 5.

Apart from a few small specialist museums and churches, some First World War battlefields and the grim remains of the only concentration camp on French soil, **Le Struthof**, this is not an area for sightseeing. But as well as the natural grandeur of the scenery and the many opportunities for walking, skiing and angling in the mountain lakes and streams, it is a good place for getting to know something of the Alsace that lies beyond the picture postcard villages on the Wine Road. The modest little family hotels and the many farm-inns give you a chance to meet local people and to learn of the bitter struggles that

The rounded peaks of the Vosges, popular with hikers in summer, become skiing country in winter

have been fought down the centuries in these beautiful mountains.

The **Route Joffre**, a 15km/9½-mile stretch of beautiful scenery between Thann and Masevaux, was built under the supervision of General Joffre, French commander-in-chief in 1915, who was promoted to the coveted title of Marshal of France a year later. Its purpose was to link the valleys of the **Doller** and the **Thur**. The road follows the south-eastern slopes of the **Rossberg**, whose summit, at 1150m/3770ft, can be reached on foot in a couple of hours from **Masevaux**, a small industrial town on the Doller, allegedly owing its existence to one of St Odile's nephews, called Mason, who built a Benedictine abbey here in the eighth century in memory of his small son. The town is famous for the Passion Play held here annually, in German. The church of Saint-Martin has a fine Silbermann organ (an annual organ festival is staged) and a polychrome medieval *Pietà*.

The area between Masevaux and the **Ballon d'Alsace** (1250m/4100ft), which marks the southernmost tip of the Vosges range, is dotted with mountain lakes, like the **Lac d'Alfeld** and the smaller **Lac de Sewen** in the Doller Valley. The scenery here is Alpine, with superb views in good weather, and there are many marked paths to follow. Close to the **Col du Ballon** is the **Monument aux Démineurs**, commemorating the bravery of those who risk their lives disposing of bombs. A path leads up from the col to the summit, where a statue of the Virgin Mary marks France's western border during the annexation of Alsace to Germany after the Franco-Prussian War. This is farm-inn country, with a host of opportunities for a peaceful night or two or a farm meal.

More farm-inns await you as you embark on the Route des Crêtes proper, starting in **Cernay** (Chapter 6). From the **Col du Silberloch** you can reach **Vieil-Armand**. The French soldiers fighting in the Vosges during the First World War, unable to get

---

The repas marcaire

The farms in the Upper Vosges have had a tradition of serving modest meals since early this century, when hikers would stop off for a wooden tub of milk mixed with *fromage blanc*, each of them drinking from the tub, then handing in on to the next person. After that came cheese and butter made on the farm, and a mound of potatoes in their jackets. Then as transport improved and the Vosges started to attract large numbers of ordinary tourists as well as hikers, the farmers' wives would cook more elaborate meals, based on local recipes.

Nowadays the officially approved *fermes-auberges* (see p. 11) specialize in a filling menu made up of local dishes served with a jug of Alsace wine – excellent value and ideal for keeping you going on a mountain hike, or during a tour of the area by car. There is rarely a choice, so you simply settle down on a wooden bench beside a trestle table and wait to be served the day's specials, perhaps starting with a steaming tureen of soup and continuing through several courses. Some farms in the Munster Valley, which organized its own 'Cheese Road' (*Route du Fromage*) over twenty years ago, serve a special 'Repas Marcaire'. The first course is the local speciality, *Tourte de la Vallée* (see p. 143), with a glass or two of Sylvaner. Then come smoked blade of pork with *roïgabraggeldi*, an unctuous mass of sliced potatoes cooked with finely chopped onions and little chunks of bacon. A generous portion of munster follows, with the traditional bowl of caraway seeds. But make sure you leave enough room for some creamy *fromage blanc*, freshly made on the farm and liberally doused with kirsch, or an open fruit tart, usually made with locally picked *myrtilles*, those tasty dark-blue berries native to mountain regions known in England and Wales as bilberries or whortleberries or whinberries, in Scotland as blaeberries and in the United States as huckleberries.

Ask for the *Route du Fromage* leaflet at tourist offices, or write in advance to the Office du Tourisme-Syndicat d'Initiative Vallée de Munster, pl. de la Salle-des-Fêtes, 68140 Munster.

their tongue round the Alsace name of **Hartmannswillerkopf**, called this rocky spur 'Vieil-Armand' and the name has stuck. Towards the end of the war it was the scene of horrific battles, in which tens of thousands of French and German soldiers were slaughtered by shelling. A sombre monument, its entrance guarded by sword-bearing angels, has been built above a crypt containing the remains of twelve thousand of them. You can visit the small museum and, from a raised platform, pay homage to row upon row of silent crosses. At the far end of the cemetery's central avenue a path leads in about half an hour to the top of the mountain, at an altitude of nearly 1000m/3250ft, crowned by a huge luminous cross marking the spot where the French front ended. If you can wrench your mind away from contemplation of what can only seem senseless carnage, the views are superb from up here.

The road continues towards the **Grand Ballon** (also called the **Ballon de Guebwiller**), the highest peak of the Vosges, which is easily reached by a path from the Mountain Road. Just below the summit is a monument to the 'Blue Devils', light infantrymen who fought here during the First World War. **Le Grand Ballon** is now a small ski resort, and so is **Le Markstein**, with 20km/12½ miles of cross-country ski trails.

From Le Markstein, D430 follows the 'Florival', the poetic name invented for the **Vallée de Guebwiller**, the long valley of the River Lauch, which offers lovely walks in the forest. Another Benedictine abbey was built in **Lautenbach** during the Carolingian era. Its eleventh-century church has survived, though it was partly rebuilt in the fifteenth century. A series of lively carvings, running like an animated cartoon round the Romanesque doorway, depict the story of an adulteress and her punishment (read it from left to right). Inside the church there are more lively carvings on the misericords on the choir stalls, a fine Baroque pulpit, and a painting on panel that may be from the workshop of the Colmar artist Martin Schongauer (see box, p. 120). Further down the valley you can see what may well be the product of Schongauer's workshop in the industrial village of **Buhl**. The nineteenth-century parish church boasts a superb late fifteenth-century altarpiece attributed by some experts to it – it was certainly painted under Schongauer's influence, with its scenes full of movement and action. A light apple green, pinky red and turquoise predominate in these busy scenes, the figures treated with great individuality. In the Adoration of the Magi, the knowing look on the ass's face in the stable is a delight, and so are the curling up, pointed-toe shoes of one of the Three Kings, wearing slinky white tights and a brocaded top elegantly tied with a red bow.

From Buhl, a side road leads to the tiny village of **Murbach**, in a peaceful valley. Its beautiful Romanesque church, of which only the chancel is still standing, was once part of a powerful abbey that came under the personal protection of Charlemagne. The original Benedictine foundation was started by St Pirmin in 727, with substantial financial assistance from Count Eberhard of Eguisheim, whose tomb can still be seen in the church. The first monks are said to have been Scots and Irish hermits who had settled in the area after bringing the Gospel to this remote valley. The abbey was soon rich enough to be able to design new buildings, and Charlemagne, who spent Christmas 775 in Alsace, apparently had a hand in planning and funding the new extension.

By now Murbach's fame was such that it was granted the right to mint its own coinage, and it became a highly aristocratic establishment, its monks all knights and its abbot automatically bearing the title Prince of the Holy Roman Empire. He even had his own army, which was heartily loathed by the local people. But over the centuries the abbey gradually lost its wealth and influence. It was partly destroyed at one stage by the Duke of Weimar's troops, and eventually its last prince-abbot, Casimir of Rathsamhausen, moved in the 1730s to Guebwiller, where he funded the building of the church of Notre-Dame. The monks moved out and the abbey was deconsecrated in 1759. During the Revolution peasants from the valley wreaked their revenge for centuries of domineering rule by tearing everything down but the east end of the church with its transept. It is most beautiful, its pure lines enhanced with some delicate carving inside and out, and doubly so in this quiet wooded valley, conducive to contemplation.

Beyond Le Markstein, the winding D27 runs close to **Schnepfenried**, a small ski resort offering splendid views of **Le Hohneck**. The road continues down the **Vallée de Munster**, famous for its cheese-making (ask at tourist offices for the Route du Fromage or Cheese Road leaflet).

Thousands of soldiers died during the First World War battle at Le Linge in the Vosges

Also well known is the *tourte de la vallée*, a pie or pasty made with pork, onions and eggs, sometimes flavoured with garlic. A forest road from **Sondernach** leads via **Landersen** to **Le Petit Ballon** at 1267m/4155ft. **Metzeral** is a good starting point for walks to the beautiful **Lac de Fischboedle** and beyond it to another lake, the **Lac de Schiessrothried**. In **Muhlbach**, the **Musée de la Schlitte** celebrates the wooden sledges used by woodcutters to transport logs and the various trades connected with timber felling and working.

Munster owes its name to its Benedictine monastery (*munster* in dialect), destroyed during the Revolution. Although not particularly attractive in itself, this little town, whose prosperity once depended on the textile industry, is an excellent centre for excursions in the Vosges valleys, and is also frequented as a spa. To the south, another forest road climbs up to the Petit Ballon, while to the east lies **Gunsbach**, famous as the village where Albert Schweitzer spent his childhood – his father was the local pastor – and where he later built a house of his own. It has been turned into a small museum in his honour (see box, p 144). To the north, a beautiful road via the summer resort of **Hohrodberg** to the **Collet du Linge** brings you to another First World War battlefield, **Le Linge**. Several thousand soldiers lie in the cemetery at the nearby **Col du Wettstein**. Roads from Le Linge continue to **Les Trois Epis** and **Turckheim** (Chapter 6) and via **Pairis** to **Orbey**.

The D417, the main road from Colmar to Gérardmer in Lorraine, winds up from Munster in a series of bends to the **Col de la Schlucht**, the highest pass in the Vosges at 1139m/5736ft, from where a chair lift will take you up to the peak of **Montabey** for panoramic views. A steep road climbs up to **Le Hohneck**, Alsace's second tallest peak (1362m/4467ft), and one of many marked paths will bring you to the lovely **Lac Vert**, its mysterious green waters caused by lichens close to the surface. From this section of the Mountain Road there are fine views of **Gérardmer** and its lakes (see Days Out from Alsace), and from the highest peaks you may be able to see as far as Mont Blanc in clear weather.

Two more lakes are accessible from the road, or by footpath: the sombre **Lac Noir**, with a little restaurant, and the **Lac Blanc** (which looks more black than white in most lights), where a small ski resort is being built. Marked paths link the two lakes and rejoin the Mountain Road. **Le Bonhomme**, too, is a winter and summer resort, with over 50km/30 miles of ski trails, and marked paths to **Le Brézouard** at 1228m/4027ft. From the **Col du Bonhomme** N415 joins the Wine Road at **Kaysersberg** (see Chapter 6). It passes through **Lapoutroie**, the home of a small museum devoted to that typically Alsace product, pure spirits distilled from fruit and berries. Beyond here, **Hachimette** marks the beginning of the 'Pays Welche', where the local dialect is not Alemannic but Romance. In nearby **Fréland** you can visit the interesting **Maison du Pays Welche**, with its own restaurant, to learn about the art and customs of this little enclave of Welche- (i.e. French-) speaking villages, including **Orbey**, a good centre for excursions into the beautiful **Vallée de la Weiss** and the

Schweitzer and Alsace

The great doctor, theologian, musician, philosopher and philanthropist Albert Schweitzer was born in Kaysersberg in January 1875. When he was only a few years old his family moved to Gunsbach in the Munster Valley, where his father became the local pastor. He studied the organ locally and later in Paris, and read theology and philosophy at the University of Strasbourg, later acquiring further degrees in Paris and Berlin.

At twenty-one he made his celebrated decision to devote himself to science, art and music until he was thirty, then give the rest of his life to his fellow men and women. Three years later he was awarded a doctorate for his work on Kant's religious philosophy, and was soon appointed curate at the church of Saint-Nicolas in Strasbourg. By 1903 he was principal of the city's theological college. But he kept up his interest in music, too, publishing a study of Bach in French in 1905 and an essay on organ design the following year.

By this time he had earned an international reputation both as musician and musicologist and as a theologian: his *Geschichte der Leben-Jesu Forschung*, written in German and published in English in 1910 as *The Quest of the Historical Jesus*, had a far-reaching impact on New Testament studies. But he had not forgotten his vow and in 1905 started to study medicine. By 1913, his medical degree behind him, he was ready to set off with his new wife for French Equatorial Africa, where he founded the famous leprosy hospital at Lambaréné that will always be associated with him.

By one of those administrative absurdities that bedevilled the lives of those born in Alsace, he was arrested by the French at the beginning of the First World War, and interned as an enemy alien. But otherwise he spent most of the rest of his life in Africa, except for his regular visits to Europe and North America to give the organ recitals that helped to fund his work in Africa. During these tours he would slip away to Alsace for a period of rest and contemplation in the house he built in Gunsbach with the money he was awarded with the Nobel Peace Prize in 1952.

He died in 1965 at the age of ninety, a revered figure throughout the world. His house in Gunsbach has been turned into a memorial to him, reverently kept as it was when he lived there. There are some faded photographs of Lambaréné too, similar to those you can see in the little museum and study centre in his birthplace in Kaysersberg. It is curiously moving to see that tall figure, upright to the end, with his nurses and patients, and to watch the thousands of visitors who still come to pay homage to Alsace's 'white witch doctor'.

Buying local produce

The markets in Strasbourg and Colmar are a good source of locally grown fruit and vegetables, pine-flavoured and other sorts of honey, local cheeses and *charcuterie*, especially pâtés and tasty sausages. But you should also try buying direct from farms.

Charcuterie, smoked trout, goat's cheese, honey, apple juice, blackcurrants, raspberries and apples, garlic, pigeons and *foie gras* are just some of the local produce sold on farms all over Alsace. The *Société pour la Promotion des Produits du Terroir* (Maison de l'Agriculture, 103 route de Hausbergen, 67300 Schiltigheim) publishes a leaflet called *Savourez la Montagne!* listing such places with their various specialities. Ask for it at local tourist offices or write in advance to the association.

In many farm-inns you can buy cheese made on the premises, and sometimes *charcuterie* and slices or tart made with wild bilberries – excellent ingredients for a picnic.

Val d'Orbey. The Weiss Valley villages are well organized, publishing a newsletter full of practical advice about events in and around the area, and about local craftsmen and women willing to let you watch them at work and to sell their pottery or wrought-iron pieces, their wooden clogs or fragrant honey (ask for it at tourist offices or hotels). There are also possibilities for *randonnées sans bagages* holidays, where you can hike from one peaceful inn to another while your luggage is transported for you. **Pairis**, a small village 4km/2½ miles south of Orbey, was the site until the Revolution of an abbey dating back to the twelfth century; its stone gateway has survived.

The Mountain Road continues from Le Bonhomme along the pastoral valley of the Lièpvrette to the little industrial town of **Sainte-Marie-aux-Mines**. Sainte-Marie was once at the heart of a silver-mining district – hence the name – and in high summer you can visit the sixteenth-century **Saint-Barthélémy Mine** and a small museum devoted to mineralogy and mining. During the first weekend in July, anyone interested in minerals, fossils and precious stones should make sure to attend Sainte-Marie's annual Mineral Fair. And 4km/2½ miles south, the hamlet of **Saint-Pierre-sur-l'Hâte** has a 'Miners' Church', built in the fifteenth and sixteenth centuries.

The ruins of medieval **Frankenbourg Castle**, visible from the N59 beyond industrial **Lièpvre**, can be reached by a footpath. The views from the round keep are superb. On the other side of the road, reconstructed **Haut-Koenigsbourg Castle** (see Chapter 6) makes a dramatic sight, and once you reach D424, two more ruined castles, **Ramstein** and **Ortenbourg**, appear. Paths from little **Huhnelmuhl** lead to both of them. The **'Val de Villé'**, with its eight side valleys, is proud of its individuality – its rural architecture and traditions are jealously preserved (and displayed in the **Maison du Val de Villé** in **Albé**). It is also known as the 'Pays de kirsch', Kirsch Country, as the villagers specialize in distilling fruit spirits from wild cherries and other fruit and berries. **Villé** itself makes a good centre for walks.

From **Villé**, D425 crosses the **Col du Kreuzweg** to **Le Hohwald**, a sunny winter and summer resort, its flower-filled meadows surrounded by pine forests. Nearby **Champ du Feu**, at 1000m/3280ft, is a popular ski resort in the beautiful upper reaches of the **Vallée de la Bruche**. **Waldersbach** honours the memory of the eighteenth-century Alsace pastor and philanthropist Jean-Frédéric Oberlin, an energetic educationalist, who devoted many years of his life to helping to improve the lot of the peasants in this remote spot: the **Oberlin Museum** is in the presbytery he built there. A bleaker memorial, reached from **Rothau**, where Goethe's once-beloved Friederike Brion died, is the Nazi concentration camp set up during the Second World War at **Le Struthof**, where over ten thousand men and women died. One of the huts inside the chilling barbed wire enclosure houses a **Deportation Museum**.

Schirmeck, an otherwise uninteresting industrial town, is a base for excursions into the **Donon** mountain range on the border with Lorraine. **Niederhaslach**'s Gothic church, with its richly carved west front and unexpectedly tall tower, was built by Gerlach von Steinbach, the son of 'Master Erwin', the genius behind Strasbourg Cathedral (see box, p. 74). His tomb is inside the church, which has some fine medieval stained glass. The little pilgrimage **Chapelle Saint-Florent** just outside **Oberhaslach** is allegedly the site of a hermitage built in the seventh century by the saint, who later became Bishop of Strasbourg. There are several ruined castles to be visited here, and at **Nideck**, both the romantic ruins of two castles and a famous waterfall, plunging down a high porphyry cliff.

This forested area, referred to as 'la Petite Suisse d'Alsace', 'Alsace's mini-Switzerland', is popular with the Strasbourgeois for Sunday outings, and the resort of **Wangenbourg-Engenthal**, in a forest clearing, is much frequented when the summer heat becomes trying on the plain. Just outside, at **Obersteigen**, a medieval priory has been converted into a **Medieval Art Centre**. A short walk brings you to the ruins of **Wangenbourg Castle** and there are many pleasant excursions to be enjoyed in the **Forêt de Saverne**.

Lichens close to the surface create the mysterious green waters of the pine-fringed Lac Vert

Key data

Access
The western Vosges are best visited by car or on walking tours, though the Munster and Orbey Valleys are accessible by ordinary bus services from Colmar and the ski resorts can generally also be reached by bus. 'Hiking without luggage' holidays are organized from several centres. Many of the roads are impassable during winter snows.

Itineraries
The main itinerary is the **Route des Crêtes** (Mountain Road), which is continued by the **Route Joffre** to the south. But the Mountain Road can be approached from the plain or the Wine Road via one of the long Vosges valleys. The northern sector, sometimes referred to as the **Vosges moyennes** or Middle Vosges, can easily be combined with a visit to the Northern Vosges, or visited as days out from Strasbourg.

LE BONHOMME 68650 Lapoutroie
Access Colmar 31km/19 miles, Orbey 18km/11 miles; **buses** from Colmar, Kaysersberg, Lapoutroie

FRÉLAND 68240 Kaysersberg
TO Mairie (89 47 57 13)
Access Colmar 18km/11 miles, Kaysersberg 7km/4½ miles; **buses** from Colmar, Kaysersberg
Sights Maison du Pays Welche (popular art and customs), open daily year-round, with restaurant

LAPOUTROIE 68650
TO Mairie (89 47 50 10)
Access Colmar 20km/12½ miles; **buses** from Colmar, Kaysersberg
Sights Musée des Eaux-de-Vie (Fruit Spirits Museum) 85 rue du Général-Dufieux; open daily year-round

LE MARKSTEIN 68610 Lautenbach
TO Mairie (89 82 60 53)
Access Guebwiller 23km/14 miles

MASEVAUX 68920
TO 36 fossé des Flagellants (89 82 41 99)
Access Mulhouse 30km/18½ miles, Thann 18km/11 miles
Sights For information on Passion Play (in German) 4 pl. Clémenceau (89 82 42 66)

MUNSTER 68140
TO pl. de la Salle-des-Fêtes (89 77 31 80)
Access Colmar 19km/12 miles; **buses** from Colmar
Sights At **Gunsbach: Maison Albert Schweitzer** (small museum in Schweitzer's home), open daily except Mon year-round; at **Muhlbach: Musée de la Schlitte et des Métiers du Bois** (Sledge and Timber Trades Museum) 56 rue Principale, open daily July to mid-Sept

MURBACH 68530 Buhl
Access Colmar 28km/17½ miles, Guebwiller 5km/3 miles
Sights Eglise abbatiale (Romanesque abbey church), open daily year-round

NIEDERHASLACH 67190 Mutzig
TO Mairie (88 50 90 29)
Access Strasbourg 39km/24 miles, Saverne 32km/20 miles, Molsheim 15km/9½ miles; **rail** to Urmatt (3km/2 miles)
Sights Collégiale Saint-Jean (Gothic church), open daily year-round

ORBEY 68370
TO Mairie (89 71 30 11)
Access Colmar 20km/12½ miles, Kaysersberg 10km/6 miles; **buses** from Colmar, Kaysersberg
Sights **Musée du Val d'Orbey** (popular art and customs) 97 rue Charles-de-Gaulle, open daily year-round; **Mémorial du Linge** (First World War battlefield memorial), open mid-Apr to Nov

SAINTE-MARIE-AUX-MINES 68160
TO pl. Prensureux (89 58 80 50)
Access Colmar 34km/21 miles, Ribeauvillé 19km/12 miles, Sélestat 22km/13½ miles
Sights **Musée minéralogique et minier** (Mineralogy and Mining Museum) 70 rue Wilson, open July and Aug; **Mine d'Argent Saint-Barthélémy** (sixteenth-century silver mine) chemin de la Sermonette, rue Saint-Louis, open Whitsun, July and Aug

LE STRUTHOF 67130 Schirmeck
Access Rothau 8km/5 miles, Champ du Feu 13km/8 miles
Sights **Concentration Camp Memorial** Natzwiller-Struthof, open Mar to Christmas

VILLÉ 67220
TO Mairie (88 57 11 69 or 88 57 11 57)
Access Strasbourg 54km/34 miles, Sélestat 18km/11 miles; **buses** from Sélestat

WALDERSBACH 67130 Schirmeck
Access Schirmeck 10.5km/6½ miles
Sights **Musée Oberlin** 58 rue Principale, afternoons only, open daily except Tues in July and Aug; Mon, Weds and weekends Mar–July, Sept, Oct

WANGENBOURG-ENGENTHAL 67710
TO Mairie (88 87 32 41 or 88 87 31 46)
Access Strasbourg 41km/25½ miles, Saverne 20km/12½ miles; **buses** from Strasbourg
Sights **Centre régional d'art médiéval** (medieval art centre in thirteenth-century priory) Obersteigen; check with TO for opening times

8
In and around Mulhouse and the Sundgau

Sundgau, the old name for the South County created under Charlemagne, is still used for the rural southern tip of Alsace stretching from the busy industrial city of Mulhouse down to the Swiss border. A land of meres and orchards, of small but prosperous farms and rolling hills, it feels different from the rest of the region. Its peaceful villages are made up of large half-timbered houses, their framework often intricately carved, their coloured walls painted with religious motifs or signs of the Zodiac or curious symbols, some of them of superstitious significance – sorcery is still said to be rife in parts of the Sundgau. Their roofs often dip almost to the ground, for protection against the hard winters often experienced in this extension of the Swiss Jura range of mountains. Some houses have long verandahs or galleries, modelled on those of the Grisons canton of Switzerland, where meat used to be air-cured, though nowadays you are more likely to see them festooned with strings of corn on the cob.

You will soon become aware of the use of different coloured paints, used to denote the religion of the inhabitants: red, pink and a pinkish beige for the Catholics (originally a mixture of lime and ox blood), various shades of green for the Protestants (dyed with plants) and mauve and purple tones (clay mixed with ox blood) for the old-established Jewish community. You can see typical examples of the different styles of rural architecture in the Sundgau in the reconstructed 'village' forming the Eco-Museum near Mulhouse (see box, p. 158).

The people seem different too. Even though many of them travel into Switzerland every weekday to earn their living, they still live in close-knit communities and seem more reserved, less outgoing than the jovial villagers you come across in the *winstubs* on the Wine Road or in the Northern Vosges. Some villages do not even have an inn or small café-restaurant. But the Sundgauviens are helpful to strangers and very willing to tell you about local customs once you have broken the ice. Also different from the rest of the region is the cuisine, with an emphasis on fish from the local meres, especially the carp that has given its name to the Sundgau's main signposted tourist route (see box, opposite).

This is good walking country, with many marked footpaths. Or you may feel like meandering from village to village by horse-drawn caravan (see Key Data). **Ferrette**, a quiet little town makes a good base for walks in what is known as the **Jura alsacien**. From here you can also visit the lovely Romanesque church of **Feldbach**, the Musée paysan in **Oltingue**, and the castle of **Landskron** right on the Swiss border. Sleepy **Altkirch**, with its own museum of local history and folk art, is another convenient base, particularly if you are using public transport – most of the buses serving the Sundgau's villages pass through it or radiate out from it.

Mulhouse, too, is a good jumping-off point for the Sundgau. And although it is not an attractive town in itself – it has long been an industrial centre and was badly damaged during the Second World War – it has excellent museums, open commendably long hours and ranging from one of the world's leading displays of vintage cars to wallpaper and printed fabric collections. While you are visiting the Sundgau, a quick hop over the Swiss border by train or car will bring you to **Basel**, a lively town with much to see (see Days out from Alsace).

Mulhouse has always been proud of its own 'difference'. A free imperial town from the fourteenth century, it became a member of the Decapolis (see A Little History) but later broke away and joined the Swiss federation, so was not handed over to France along with the rest of Alsace after the Thirty Years' War. The city's central square today, the **place de la Réunion**, commemorates the day in 1798, exactly a century and a half after the Treaty of Westphalia, when the Mulhousiens voted to be reunited with their compatriots by becoming part of France. Mulhouse was an early convert to Protestantism – it embraced the Reformation as early as 1532. The Protestant work ethic no

---

The Fried Carp Roads

The pools and meres of the Sundgau have been used for centuries for breeding carp, and in 1975 the local tourist authorities decided to launch **Les Routes de la Carpe frite** (the Fried Carp Roads) to promote a favourite local dish. Thirty odd restaurants in the region joined forces to start up a 'Fried Carp Association', all of them serving the delicacy either every day or on certain fixed days of the week (advance orders are sometimes necessary). Look out for the large blue and white signs depicting a surprised-looking carp about to be speared by a trident, both outside the member restaurants and as signposts beside the Fried Carp Roads. Leaflets listing the restaurants, with notes of their fried carp days and details of their other specialities, are available from tourist offices. Or you can write in advance to **L'Association Le Sundgau, Routes de la Carpe frite**, Chambre de Commerce et d'Industrie de Mulhouse, 8 rue du 17-novembre, 68051 Mulhouse Cedex. The association also publishes leaflets giving the addresses of hotels in the area and telling you where you can buy a fishing permit if you feel like catching your own supper.

---

doubt accounts, at least in part, for its equally early conversion to the industrial era. It became a major textile-manufacturing centre in the mid-eighteenth century, scoring great successes in export markets, and was soon specializing in printed fabrics. By the nineteenth century it had become known as 'France's Manchester' and it expanded rapidly into a large industrial city, presided over by manufacturing dynasties known for their enlightened philanthropy: they built 'La Cité', a model housing estate allowing textile workers to own their houses, dotted with little gardens, that can still be seen today, set up a zoo for their family outings, and provided them with a welfare and social benefits system that was way ahead of its time.

Mulhouse still has a serious, hardworking feel about it. Its solid buildings, many of them rebuilt after heavy war damage, are very different from the pretty village houses or the elaborately decorated houses in the centres of Colmar or Strasbourg. Yet right in the heart of this industrial city, in the **place de la Réunion**, which fortunately survived wartime bombing, is one of Alsace's most fanciful buildings – the Renaissance **Hôtel de Ville** (town hall), painted and gilded all over with allegorical scenes and motifs and statues in *trompe-l'oeil* niches. Hanging on the right-hand wall, overlooking the picturesque **rue Guillaume-Tell**, is a copy of the celebrated *Klapperstein*, a solid stone head with popping eyes and grimacing mouth suspended from a chain. This very heavy object used to be hung round the necks of men and women found guilty of slander, who were then paraded round the streets sitting back to front on an ass. The original can be seen in the **Musée historique** (Local History and Archeology Museum) now housed in this splendid building, which looks distinctly like a stage set. Visiting the museum's collections, which include Stone Age and Bronze Age artefacts discovered during local excavations, toys, furniture and Sundgau folk art, also gives you a chance to see the **Salle de Conseil** (Council Chamber) and other state rooms, all with their original painted beams and ceilings.

A few paces away on one side of the same square, the **Temple Saint-Etienne**, a neo-Gothic Protestant church, is famous for its beautiful medieval stained glass, carefully inserted into the new church when its predecessor was demolished in the mid-nineteenth century. The Renaissance **Maison Mieg** and the seventeenth-century **Pharmacie Au Lys** (chemist's) are just two of the picturesque houses round the square and in the **rue Guillaume-Tell**. Nearby in the **place Guillaume-Tell**, an eighteenth-century building is now the home of the **Musée des Beaux-Arts** (Fine Arts Museum). This newly organized collection offers an opportunity to study the work of Jean-Jacques Henner, Alsace's best-known nineteenth-century painter, born in Bernwiller in the Sundgau, along with that of other local artists and a somewhat mixed bag of Old Masters (including a winter scene by Jan Breughel) and French painters.

Within easy walking distance of the place de la Réunion, but open only during the summer months, is the **Chapelle Saint-Jean**, originally attached to the commandery of the Knights Hospitallers of St John of Jerusalem. Its sixteenth-century wall paintings are allegedly the work of

The Dreyfus Affair

Alfred Dreyfus, the army officer whose trial for espionage divided French society from top to bottom, was born in Mulhouse in 1859, the son of a wealthy Jewish textile manufacturer. He joined the army as an artillery officer and was on the General Staff in September 1894 when a French secret agent fished a memo out of a wastepaper basket in the German Embassy. This listed military documents allegedly handed over to the Germans.

The top ranks of the army were solidly conservative at this time, their members virtually all staunch Catholics. Most of them shared the anti-Semitism then rife in France, mainly because of hostility to recent Jewish immigrants from Eastern Europe. The Dreyfus family, like many of their fellow industrialists in Mulhouse, had opted to retain their French nationality when Alsace was annexed after the Franco-Prussian War. But this did not stand in the way of the army's counter-espionage department, determined to pin the blame on a 'foreign' scapegoat. Captain Dreyfus, one of only a handful of Jewish officers, seemed the obvious choice. There was no evidence whatsoever: the handwriting on the memo bore no real resemblance to Dreyfus's. He was nevertheless identified as the spy.

With the popular press baying for blood, and eager to run a story about a Jewish traitor trying to use his wealth to buy himself out of trouble, the War Office realized that a guilty verdict was essential. So the unfortunate Dreyfus was court-martialled. A crude forgery by Major Henry, a leading light of the counter-espionage department, provided the necessary 'evidence'. Dreyfus was duly found guilty and sentenced to deportation. Refusing to do the decent thing and commit suicide, he spent the next four years enduring the harsh regime of Devil's Island off French Guiana.

Still no motive had been found for his alleged treachery. And his removal had not put a stop to the leaking of military secrets. Eventually new evidence pointed to another officer, Major Esterhazy. But he was rapidly acquitted, and then dragged into the intrigue designed to ensure that Dreyfus's innocence was never revealed. As the Dreyfus family slowly gained support for their campaign to have him rehabilitated, the Dreyfus Affair became the subject of passionate public debate between *dreyfusards* and *anti-dreyfusards*, heightened by publication of the novelist Emile Zola's famous *J'accuse*.

After a series of resignations and Colonel Henry's suicide, followed by Esterhazy's flight to England, the appeal court insisted on a new court-martial in 1899. A prematurely aged Dreyfus was again found guilty, by a majority verdict. But this time 'extenuating circumstances' were referred to, and the sentence was reduced to ten years' detention. A presidential pardon followed and the guilty verdict was quashed in 1906. Amazingly, Dreyfus returned to the army. Although he was fifty-six by the time the First World War broke out, he fought bravely and was awarded the coveted *Légion d'honneur* in 1919.

Hans Holbein the Younger, but were left unfinished because Mulhouse's eager embrace of the Reformation put a stop to elaborate decoration. Also in the chapel is a small museum of medieval sculpture and tombstones.

Near here you can see two more monuments to the city's medieval past, the much-restored **Tour du Diable** and **Tour Nessel**, a pair of towers that once formed part of a fortified residence for the Bishops of Strasbourg. On the other side of the place de la Réunion, in the **rue de Metz**, beyond the **rue du Sauvage**, a busy shopping street (don't miss at no. 3 Mulhouse's famous charcuterie, CCA, a family business dating back to 1886, now with branches in Paris), the **Tour du Bollwerk** is another medieval survivor, a reminder of the fortifications that once ringed the city. But Mulhouse is better known for its modern tower, complete with revolving restaurant, in the nearby **place de l'Europe**, a large pedestrian square whose marble paving reproduces the coats of arms of forty-odd major European cities. The view from the top of the **Tour de l'Europe** takes in both the city and the surrounding countryside. Or you can head for the fancifully named **Jardin suspendu** (hanging garden) for an overview of this piece of sixties town planning by local architect François Spoerry, well known for his admired pastiche of a Mediterranean fishing village, Port Grimaud in the south of France.

Still in walking distance of the place de la Réunion, near the station and the **city tourist office** in the arcaded **avenue du Maréchal-Foch**, the **Musée de l'Impression sur étoffe** (Fabric Printing Museum) is full of interest. Part industrial and social history, part applied art, it enables you to study the development of Mulhouse's pre-eminence in fabrics printed with Paisley patterns, known in French as *indiennes*. Demonstrations of early weaving and printing techniques are staged, and after seeing the superb fabrics on display – the handkerchief collection is popular too – you may well be tempted to buy a scarf or tie from the museum's boutique. The museum is based on a pattern archive started in the 1830s and visitors are occasionally allowed a glimpse of the main reference library with its huge pattern books. Textile designers come from far and wide to study and copy (for a fee) the earliest designs, many of them looking surprisingly modern.

The archives of a private firm also form the basis of the **Musée du Papier peint** (Wallpaper Museum) at Rixheim on the outskirts of Mulhouse. Etablissements Zuber started producing wallpaper at the end of the eighteenth century in the former commandery of the Teutonic Order of Knights. It now makes a fine setting for a museum devoted to a product that has long been a French speciality, with some good examples of the 'panoramic' landscape designs for which Zuber was famous, and exhibits connected with the technology involved.

Even if you aren't normally interested in cars you are liable to be dazzled by the sheer beauty of the vintage models superbly displayed in a vast hangar, adorned with hundreds of twirling art nouveau lamps, that houses the **Musée national de l'Automobile** (National Motor Museum), again on the outskirts, in the **avenue de Colmar**. At first, as you step inside, it all seems to be done with mirrors, but then you realize that the huge space is filled with row upon row of sleek, svelte thirties Bugattis, majestic 12-cylinder Hispano Suizas, sky-blue Mercedes, haughty Rolls-Royce Silver Ghosts. The jaunty early models in canary yellow, emerald green, bright orange and brilliant blue make our modern motorcars seem like poor relations, and I defy anyone not to feel an urge to clamber into the slim white Peugeot 161 two-seater with its red seats arranged in tandem one behind the other and its gleaming brass lamps. This model museum, with its own bar, cafeteria and brasserie, spotless lavatories and good museum shop, was initially the private collection of a pair of apparently model Alsace industrialists, the Schlumpf brothers, who finished up on trial for embezzlement after their business had collapsed and some of the angry workforce had broken into their secret domain and discovered, to their astonishment, what their bosses had been spending the company's funds on.

There is no such extraordinary story behind the **Musée français du Chemin-de-fer** (French Rail Museum), but it too is an enthralling homage to a bygone age of transport. Built just like a real-life station with six tracks, it is peopled with tall steam engines that suddenly clank into noisy life, without actually moving. Once again, even if you didn't think you were a train enthusiast, the romance of the Age of Steam will grab you by the throat as you clamber in and out of a Golden Arrow carriage or climb up on to an overhead viewing platform to admire luxury private trains and the last-ever steam model used in France.

Train spotters, young and old, are often fire engine-mad too, so it was a sensible decision to site the **Musée des Sapeurs-pompiers** (Fire Fighting Museum) next to the Rail Museum.

Row upon row of sleek models, lit by twirling art nouveau lamps, are displayed in Mulhouse's dazzling National Motor Museum

Essentially a collection lovingly built up by a retired fireman, it traces the history of fire engines and fire fighting from the *ancien régime* onwards, with helmets and hoses and other paraphernalia to delight anyone who has ever dreamt the classic small boy's dream of joining the Fire Brigade. Close by, one more museum awaits the technically minded: **Electropolis**, an Electricity Museum with a difference, due to reopen after drastic reorganization in 1992. The idea sprang from a gift to Mulhouse from one of its biggest industrial firms of a turn-of-the-century alternating-current generator. And if a surfeit of museum visiting has now set in, yet another gift to the city from enlightened industrialists should cure the condition: a visit to the **Parc zoologique et botanique**, a 'green' zoo, set in an attractive park on the south-eastern outskirts.

North of Mulhouse, the **Ecomusée de Haute-Alsace** (see box, p. 158) makes an interesting prelude to a tour of the villages of the Sundgau. And a drive or bus ride to the east of the city through the game-filled **Forêt de la Harth**, stretching between the A5 motorway and the Rhine, will bring you to **Ottmarsheim**, a little town with an important hydro-electric power station on the **Grand Canal d'Alsace**, and one of Alsace's oldest and most unusual churches, consecrated by the local pope Leo IX in 1049. It is built on an octagonal plan, with a dome, on the model of Charlemagne's Chapel Palatine at Aachen, inspired by S. Vitale in Ravenna. This sober building, beautiful in the purity of its lines despite Gothic additions, was originally attached to a Benedictine monastery that was pulled down during the French Revolution.

South of Mulhouse lies the **Sundgau**, and the countryside becomes pretty as soon as you leave the city. Much of the farming here is still practised on traditional lines, and the modern policy of digging up hedges to form huge fields happily seems to have bypassed this peaceful area, with its neat chequerboard pattern of fields interspersed with woods and copses and orchards, brilliant with blossom in spring, often gently misty.

This is not an area for intensive sightseeing, but for driving, biking, walking or taking local buses along pretty roads such as the D21 via **Steinbrunn-le-Bas**, which has one of Alsace's top restaurants converted from a sixteenth-century mill, or the D432 southwards from **Altkirch** to **Ferrette**. But there are a few sights to be seen. The quiet market town of **Altkirch**, its old centre huddled on a hill overlooking the River Ill, has a small **Musée sundgauvien** (Sundgau Museum), in the former bailli's residence, an attractive Renaissance building next to the eighteenth-century **Hotel de Ville** (town hall). The Sundgau painter Jean-Jacques Henner is again well represented here, along with other local artists, local history and archeology collections and folk art and customs. The neo-Romanesque church has a painting depicting the Count of Ferrette, a member of a powerful family whose sway extended over much of southern Alsace in the Middle Ages and whose castle was once on this spot, receiving St Morand. The saint's tomb is just outside Altkirch in the **Chapelle**

Saint-Morand, much visited as a pilgrimage centre.

West of the town, the pretty village of **Ballersdorf** has some old houses typical of Sundgau architecture, and there are more of the same, well restored, in **Gommersdorf**, an elongated village just south of the little town of **Dannemarie**. From here the attractive D7bis road passes through a series of peaceful villages to **Mooslargue**, well known for its golf course, and on to the source of the Ill at **Winkel**. Just beyond here, in tiny **Lucelle**, overlooking a lake right on the Swiss border, you can still see a doorway and various other fragments of the important Cistercian abbey that was dismantled during the Revolution and sold off in bits. Its porch ended up fronting the church in **Raedersdorf**, topped by a stork's nest and a few minutes' walk from the village's small stork-breeding centre.

Close to here, **Lutter** has a carefully restored tithe house and a reconstructed half-timbered Sundgau house turned into a charming hotel by the owners of the friendly Auberge paysanne (see box, p. 158). Rural crafts and traditions are the subject of the little **Musée paysan** in the nearby village of **Oltingue**. Housed in another good example of traditional regional architecture, with a long verandah running along one side, it owes its existence to the enthusiasm of the village priest, a passionate collector of the sort of everyday objects that had been used for centuries in rural districts but were gradually disappearing.

Tools and kitchen utensils, marriage garlands and ceremonial head dresses, biscuit moulds and candlesticks, painted wooden furniture and examples of humble folk art create a vivid feeling of life in this remote corner of rural Europe as you wander through the small rooms and the reconstructed smithy next door, the blacksmith's tools all set out and the floor made in traditional style with miniature tree trunks laid side by side. A modest restaurant-tearoom serves light meals and you can visit the church to see one of Alsace's finest organs. The same dynamic priest has encouraged the organization of 'heritage concerts' using this newly restored organ, now officially classified as a historic monument. Just outside the village, on the way to the **Chapelle Saint-Martin**, are the mysterious **Glockenlöcher** or 'bell holes'. Here, so legend has it, the chapel's bells were hidden during the Thirty Years' War to prevent them getting into the hands of the marauding Swedish army. A more poetic version of the story has the bells burying themselves there to escape the requisitions carried out during the Revolution. The **Chapelle Saint-Brice**, built by monks from Murbach Abbey, has an interesting polychrome altarpiece.

South of **Leymen** on the Swiss border, there are fine views to be had from the ruins of **Landskron Castle**, a medieval fortress refortified by Marshal Vauban, now surprisingly inhabited by a colony of monkeys, a popular tourist attraction. On the other side of the border, **Mariastein** has a famous pilgrimage chapel. The attractive D12B from Leymen leads to **Huningue** (which likes to boast of being a 'three-border town' and was again fortified by Vauban), skirting round the Swiss city of Basel.

From here the D473 returns to the 'Alsace Jura' and the little town of

The open-air Eco-Museum

In 1972 a group of students in Mulhouse formed an association called **Maisons paysannes d'Alsace** (Rural Houses in Alsace) and started restoring uninhabited timber-frame houses in the south of the region. Devoting most of their spare time to the project, they worked on twenty-five buildings over the next eight years, either restoring them *in situ*, or, if this proved impractical, carefully numbering each component of the framework and dismantling it, ready to be reconstructed elsewhere.

The dismantling was not quite as daunting as it sounds, because in the old days peasants could be forced at any moment, at the whim of their feudal lord, to move off his domain. So they sensibly made sure that they could take their home with them, building it of interlocking timbers with an infill of mud or clay, or of pebbles from the river bed bonded with clay. Then if and when the order came to move on, the infill was knocked out and the frame taken apart and subsequently rebuilt.

In 1980 the *commune* of Ungersheim near Mulhouse offered the association 10 hectares/25 acres of disused industrial land. Over the next four years nineteen of the timber frames lovingly stored in garages and outhouses were rebuilt on the site and on 1 June 1984 Alsace had a brand-new open-air museum, which quickly caught the public's imagination and proved a huge success. By 1990 fifty-five houses rescued from all over Alsace formed a 'village' where visitors can study different types of rural architecture and building techniques, and watch traditional crafts being practised. During the weekend from about Easter to the end of September, you can see people baking bread, using an oil crusher, making clogs or ropes, even doing the laundry by the old, backbreaking methods. You can chat with the blacksmith or the wheelwright and go for a ride in a cart pulled by a pair of yoked oxen, admire a herd of little black pigs and visit stork-rearing pens, sample regional fare in a reconstructed inn or eat local cheeses and *charcuterie* on wooden boards, handed out by serving wenches in traditional costume. It may sound kitsch, but it's all great fun and highly instructive too – and it would be hard to think of a more imaginative way of making use of a stretch of post-industrial wasteland.

The earliest house, a fortified dwelling from Mulhouse, dates back to the twelfth century, and the Eco-Museum includes examples of buildings right down to the nineteenth century. In some cases the infill is left incomplete, so that the different building methods and materials can be easily understood even by small children. Plans and leaflets are available from the main entrance.

If you decide to stay at the friendly Auberge Paysanne at Lutter, near Ferrette (see Hotels and Restaurants), you can admire the superb 'hostelry' reconstructed by the Litzler family with advice from the Eco-Museum staff and ask to see photographs of the numbered pieces of timber carefully laid out in the carpenter's yard, like a gigantic jigsaw.

A stork, Alsace's mascot, obligingly perching on the roof of one of the reconstructed houses in the Eco-Museum

Ferrette, the seat of the Counts of Ferrette, a title still held by the Grimaldi, the princely ruling family of Monaco. Perched high up on a hill at the centre of a network of footpaths marked by the Club vosgien, it is peaceful and charming with its narrow street climbing up from the central square to the ruins of its two castles. Before you start the climb, notice the early nineteenth-century house on one side of the square, carved by the original owner, a local lawyer, with a little boy reading a book and a winged angel holding a snake coiled round the *oeil de boeuf*. The **rue du Château** passes a pretty garden adorned with a curious Virgin and Child with three arms, the Renaissance town hall (housing the tourist office) and another curiosity: a little house that was once the workshop of an ironmonger and is proudly decorated with three-dimensional models of iron stoves and stove pipes. A steep path then takes you up from the villagey **place des Comtes** to the two **ruined castles**, one medieval, the other sixteenth-century, both offering lovely views over wooded hills into Switzerland and beyond the Rhine to the Black Forest.

North of Ferrette, **Feldbach**, nestling in a peaceful valley, has a beautiful little Romanesque church, founded by one of the Counts of Ferrette, along with a convent of enclosed Benedictine nuns. Recent restoration has stripped it of later additions and decoration, and it can now be seen in all its original purity, with its half-domed apse and Corinthian capitals. The convent was damaged many times over the centuries, by wars, peasants' revolts, even an earthquake, and eventually dismantled during the Revolution, but you can still see the Gothic **Maison du Prieuré**.

The area between Ferrette and Altkirch is studded with pretty villages, some of them, like **Grentzingen**, beside the Ill. And most of them have cosy inns where you can taste one of the local carp dishes or spend a peaceful night or two.

Key data

Access
The main places of interest in the Sundgau can easily be reached by car from Mulhouse or Altkirch, both of which have adequate regular bus services to many of the villages. The area can also be combined with a visit to Basel (see Days out from Alsace), or visited on the way into Alsace from Switzerland. Mulhouse itself is on Alsace's fast main rail line linking Strasbourg and Colmar with Basel. Roads are generally good.

Itineraries
D432 from Mulhouse to Ferrette via Altkirch takes in many of the prettiest villages. D7bis from Dannemarie to Mooslargue is another attractive road enabling you to enjoy the scenery of the 'Alsace Jura'; it can be combined with D10bis to Pfetterhouse, and with D463 to Feldbach. The tourist office in Ferrette publishes a booklet listing walks in the area. These basic routes are all covered by bus services, though they make detours to surrounding villages.

A popular way of visiting the villages near the Swiss border is to travel by horse-drawn caravan, stopping off for meals in the local inns. Inquire at tourist offices about itineraries.

ALTKIRCH 68130
TO Tour Bloch, pl. X-Jourdain (89 40 02 90)
Access Mulhouse 18km/11 miles; buses, rail from Mulhouse
Sights **Musée sundgauvien** (local history, popular art, archeology) open afternoons only: daily except Mon in July and Aug; Sun only rest of year; **Chapelle de la Litten** (pilgrimage chapel) at Aspach

FELDBACH 68640 Waldighoffen
TO Mairie (89 25 80 55)
Access Mulhouse 38km/23½ miles, Altkirch 17km/10½ miles; buses from Mulhouse or Altkirch
Sights **Eglise de Feldbach** (Romanesque church)

FERRETTE 68480
TO 38 rue de Château (89 40 40 01)
Access Mulhouse 27km/17 miles, Altkirch 20km/12½ miles; buses from Mulhouse or Altkirch
Sights **Châteaux de Ferrette** (ruined castles) accessible year-round

HUNINGUE 68330
TO 4-6 rue des Boulangers (89 67 36 74)
Access Mulhouse 32km/20 miles
Sights **Musée de Huningue** (local history) rue des Boulangers, open afternoons only, first and third Sun in month (except Aug)

LANDSKRON
Access Saint-Blaise 11km/7 miles, then 15-20 mins walk; buses from Mulhouse, Altkirch, Ferrette to Oltingue (12km/7½ miles)
Sights **Château de Landskron** (ruined castle) accessible year-round

MULHOUSE 68100
TO 9 av. Foch (89 45 68 31)
Access Strasbourg 114km/71 miles, Colmar 42km/26 miles, Basel 35km/22 miles; buses from Colmar, Altkirch and many villages in Sundgau; rail from Strasbourg, Colmar, Sélestat, Thann, Altkirch
Sights **Electropolis** (history of electricity) 55 rue du Pâturage, open afternoons only, daily except Mon; **Musée national de l'Automobile** (vintage cars) 192 av. de Colmar, open daily June–Oct; daily except Tues rest of year; **Musée des Beaux-Arts** (painting and sculpture) 4 pl. Guillaume-Tell, open daily except Tues (late opening Thur); **Musée français du Chemin-de-Fer** (railway history) 2 rue Alfred-de-Glehn, open daily year-round; **Musée historique** (local history and

archeology, toys, Sundgau folk art) 4 rue des Archives, open daily except Tues (late opening Thur); **Musée de l'Impression sur étoffes** (fabric printing) 3 rue des Bonnes-Gens, open daily June–Sept; daily except Tues rest of year; demonstrations at 3 p.m. in three summer months; **Musée lapidaire Saint-Jean** (Renaissance sculpture and frescoes in former chapel) Grand'Rue, open May–Oct only, daily except Tues; **Musée du Sapeur-Pompier** (history of fire-fighting) 2 rue Alfred-de-Glehn, open daily year-round; **Temple Saint-Etienne** (medieval stained glass) pl. de la Réunion, open May–Oct, daily except Tues

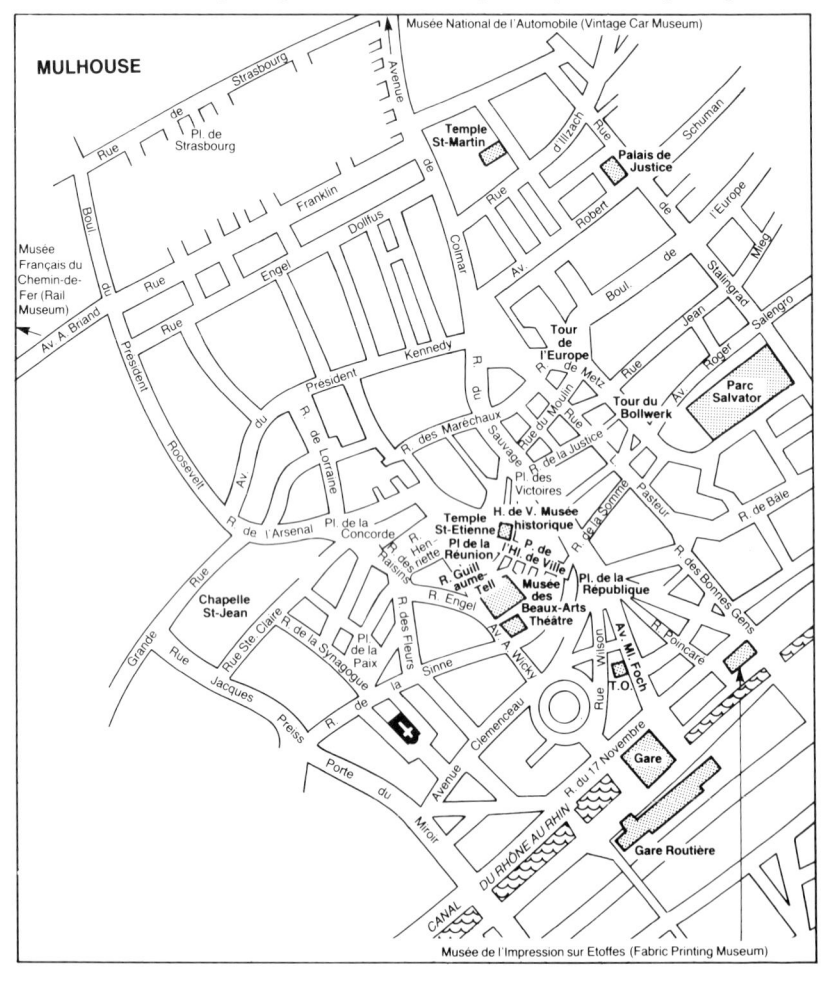

OLTINGUE 68480 Ferrette
TO Mairie (89 40 70 11)
Access Mulhouse 45km/28 miles, Altkirch 20km/12½ miles, Ferrette 8km/5 miles; **buses** from Mulhouse, and Altkirch, Ferrette

Sights   **Chapelle Saint-Martin** (Romanesque chapel); **Eglise d'Oltingue** (parish church with famous organ); **Musée paysan** (rural life, popular art and crafts) 150 rue Principale, open Tues, Thur and Sat afternoons and Sun all day, mid-June–Oct; Sun afternoons only Oct–mid-Dec and Mar–mid-June

OTTMARSHEIM 68490
TO   Mairie (89 26 06 42)
Access Mulhouse 15km/9½ miles, Colmar 45km/28 miles; **buses** from Mulhouse
Sights **Eglise d'Ottmarsheim** (Early Romanesque abbey church)

RIXHEIM 68170
Access Mulhouse 6km/4 miles; **buses** from Mulhouse
Sights **Musée du Papier peint** (Wallpaper Museum) 28 rue Zuber, open daily except Tues year-round

UNGERSHEIM 68190
Access 15km/9½ miles from Mulhouse (turn off D430 between Pulversheim and Bollwiller); **buses** from Mulhouse
Sights **Ecomusée de Haute-Alsace** (see box). Open daily year-round

Morimont close to the Swiss border, many times ruined and restored

9
Days out from Alsace

The previous chapters will, I hope, have made it clear that Alsace offers a wealth of delights both to those seeking short breaks and to those embarking on a more leisurely holiday. But it can also act as a springboard for brief trips across the border into Switzerland – Basel, with its riverside cafés and many museums, is only a short distance from Mulhouse and the Sundgau – and Germany, where you can easily visit the fashionable spa of Baden-Baden and also Freiburg-im-Breisgau, an attractive university town, and perhaps explore the Black Forest surrounding them and test your palate by comparing the wines made in the villages in the Rebland with those you have been enjoying in Alsace. Then you can cross over the western Vosges to spend a day in the lakeside resort of Gérardmer in Lorraine, or visit Lorraine's two main cities, Metz and Nancy. Or you might like to visit one of them on your way to or from Alsace.

All these places can be reached by public transport from at least one of the three main towns in Alsace. For drivers and bikers there are many roads linking Alsace to Switzerland and Germany. In the restaurant suggestions in this chapter, places where it is advisable to book in advance are given with the full telephone number for anyone dialling from Alsace (including the international and regional code where relevant).

Baden-Baden

A short train ride from Strasbourg or an easy drive or bike ride from northern Alsace brings you to Baden-Baden in Germany, once *the* watering-place for the crowned heads of Europe and still fashionable, with chic boutiques and jewellers, luxury hotels and a splendidly elaborate casino. It makes a pleasant day trip in itself, or can be combined with the Black Forest and the nearby wine villages. Or you might feel like a night out in the casino: even if you aren't a gambler, the grand rooms are full of interest, aesthetic and historical, and it's fun to watch what's going on at the tables.

The town's fame as a spa dates back to the Romans, who first discovered the therapeutic properties of the local hot springs and built thermal baths in about AD 80. The remains of the marble imperial baths (**Kaiserbad**) have survived beneath the **Stiftskirche**, but aren't open to the public because the springs are still gushing out water so hot (68°C or over 154°F) that you would need protective clothing. But you can visit the **Römerbad** in the Römerplatz, apparently built for the ablutions of the Roman legions. What is left of these baths is beneath the superb **Friedrichsbad**, built between 1869 and 1877 in palatial Renaissance style. By then Baden-Baden had been a mecca for Europe's royalty for a good eighty years and the baths still seem fit for a royal palace with their brightly coloured cupola, their slender pillars, arches, elaborate tiled walls and frescoes. The décor was restored and the baths equipped with the latest in modern technology in the eighties. You might like to try the popular *Römisch-Irische Bad* (Roman-Irish baths), open to 10 p.m. most evenings and specializing in two-hour sessions starting with a shower and continuing through warm- and hot-air (68°C) rooms, massage, steam bath, thermal jet spray and a brief plunge into an ice-cold bath. Equally relaxing and invigorating is the 'thermal landscape' in the less glamorous (and less expensive) **Caracalla-Therme**, the latest incarnation of the old Augustinabad.

Even if you don't fancy indulging in the pampering atmosphere of the baths, you can taste the waters at the **Trinkhalle** (pump room), its terracotta-coloured façade adorned with a row of Corinthian capitals. It was built in the 1830s and 1840s and decorated with large frescoes illustrating local legends and heroes by the Romantic painter Jakob Götzenberger. If you time your visit for spring or autumn you can pep up your system with a 'grape juice cure'.

After such hedonistic pleasures, you may decide that a serious attempt at money-making is in order. The **Kurhaus** (**casino**) is a short walk away through the well-kept gardens, or you can approach it via a leafy arcade of luxury shops – any pounds you may have shed at the baths are likely to go straight back on again if you are tempted by the window displays at **Rumpelmayer's**, the famous confectioner's that, originally in Dresden, had a fashionable tearoom in Paris.

The 'Conversation House', as it was originally called, was built in the 1820s, but it owed its true fame to a Frenchman, Jacques Bénazet, the son of a humble farrier in the Pyrenees, whose career and livelihood were threatened by Louis Philippe's decision in 1838 to close down the gaming rooms round the Palais Royal in Paris, for many of which Bénazet had the concession. He promptly moved to Baden-Baden and set about turning the town into Europe's premier spa. His son inherited the concession and commissioned the palatial décor that you can still enjoy in all its splendour. Guided tours (mornings only) take you through the **Winter Garden**, partly modelled on the Grand Trianon at Versailles, adorned with marble and gold leaf, the **Florentinersaal**, once a ballroom, the **Fürstenzimmer**, with paintings of the Margraves of Baden, the pretty **Salon Rouge** with an elegant painted ceiling, and the little **Salon Pompadour**, very French with its gilt and mirrors. All these grand rooms, full of paintings and Meissen vases, look their best under the light of the chandeliers, so do try to come back in the evening: a day ticket costs only a few marks and there is nothing to stop you looking rather than gambling. As you watch the cosmopolitan crowd grouped tensely round the blackjack, baccara, poker and roulette tables, imagine the haunted figure of Dostoevsky, an obsessive gambler, constantly having to borrow to be able to keep playing. Among those who baled him out was Turgenev, whose beloved Pauline Viardot had a house and music school in a nearby valley.

Baden-Baden also has a pretty **theatre**, opened in style with the first performance of Berlioz's *Béatrice et Bénédict*, and a famous **racecourse**. Perched above the Kaiserbad is the **Neues Schloss** (New Castle), originally a Renaissance palace built for the Margraves of Baden, later a ducal summer residence. It has a small museum and it is worth climbing up to the terrace for its lovely views over the gardens on the **Florentinerberg**, full of tropical plants watered by the hot springs, and on to the Black Forest. On the way down you can visit the **Stiftskirche**, a Gothic church badly damaged by fire at the end of the seventeenth century and partly rebuilt, with a huge sandstone Late Gothic *Crucifixion* by Nikolaus Gerhaert of Leyden. It also houses the tomb of some of the local margraves, including 'Türkenlouis', Markgraf Ludwig Wilhelm, who led his armies to victory over the Turks.

Not far from Baden-Baden on the way to Rastatt you can visit the lovely Baroque **Schloss Favorite**, built as a summer residence for Türkenlouis's widow Markgräfin Augusta Sybilla in the early eighteenth century. The elaborate rooms, adorned with marble and marquetry and mother-of-pearl inlays, are on a pleasingly small scale and the guided tour enables you to see the **Spiegelkabinett**, lined with hundreds of mirrors.

The **Lichtentaler Allee**, once one of the most fashionable promenades and carriage drives in Europe, is lined with azaleas and rhododendrons and many rare trees and plants. It leads to the **Kloster Lichtental**, a convent of Cistercian nuns dating back to the Middle Ages. In the Gothic **Fürstenkapelle** is the tomb of the margravine who founded the convent, carved by an artist from Strasbourg.

Excursions into the Black Forest are run by the tourist office from April to November and there are regular bus services to the spick-and-span wine villages along the **Badische Weinstrasse** (Baden Wine Road). In **Neuweier**, a village-cum-suburb only 5km/3 miles from the town centre, you can buy local wine in flat circular bottles, or in curious *Affenflaschen* adorned with hand-gilded monkeys carved in relief.

Nearby **Steinbach** was allegedly the birthplace of 'Master Erwin', the medieval architect of Strasbourg Cathedral (see box, p. 74). You can drive along the **Schwarzwaldhochstrasse** (Black Forest Mountain Road), which climbs up to 1000 metres/3250 feet, or go for a hike in the **Merkur** with its many marked paths (reached by a funicular).

The casino has a full-scale restaurant, the **Boulevard-Terrassen**, as well as **Mirabell** for snacks and light suppers, or the traditional German coffee-and-cakes in the afternoon. Also good for light lunches and cakes is **Café Confiserie Heinz König** (12 Lichtentalerstrasse), a tearoom furnished with antiques. **Badener Weinkeller** (2 Maria-Viktoria-Strasse), open evenings only, offers local dishes in a lively cellar restaurant. **Le Bistro**, in Sofienstrasse close to the casino, is a cheerful copy of a Paris bistro.

The villages in the vine-growing area are full of attractive inns. In **Neuweier**: **Der Altenberg** (6 Schartenbergstrasse, tel 07223-57236) and **Gasthaus zum Lamm** (34 Maubergstrasse, tel 07223-57212). **Merkurius** in **Varnhalt** (2 Klosterbergstrasse, tel 07223-5474) is a well-known restaurant; **Gasthaus zum Adler** (tel 07223-57241) has a cosy *Winzerstube* (the Rebland equivalent of an Alsace *winstub*). In **Umweg** there is **Der Bocksbeutel** (103 Umwegstrasse, tel 07223-58031).

TO Haus des Kurgastes, Augustaplatz 8

Basel

Basel or Basle (Bâle in French) shares an airport with Mulhouse and is also easily reached by train from there and from Colmar and Strasbourg, as it is on the main line linking Alsace's three main towns. Although it is Switzerland's second city and a busy commercial and banking centre, it has a pleasantly relaxed feel, largely because of its setting on the Rhine and the many riverside café-restaurants where you can enjoy a coffee or a meal before setting off to explore the old streets round the cathedral or visiting the city's museums. The centre is easily visited on foot, and you might like to plan a trip down the Rhine on a riverboat too.

The Roman legions had an important garrison here and Basel became a major intellectual centre during the Reformation, having joined the Swiss federation in 1501. Many of Europe's best-known early printers set up shop here, including Johann Bergmann, who published Sebastian Brant's *Ship of Fools* (see p. 81), Johann Amerbach and Nikolaus Kessler, whose edition of St Jerome's letters was again illustrated by Albrecht Dürer during his period in Basel in 1492–3. These highly educated printer-publishers helped to spread the ideas and ideals of Humanism, and Erasmus lived in the city for many years, studying and teaching at the university. He died there in 1536 – you can admire his tomb in the cathedral. Among many other scholars who made Basel their home was one of Alsace's finest intellects, Beatus Rhenanus from Sélestat (see p. 126).

It is now a prosperous city, its wealth based on industry as well as banking. But although your main impression is of a comfortable, bourgeois society as you stroll about, it rather surprisingly has a reputation for wild merrymaking. In January winter is driven out of the Klein-Basel district during a frenzied ceremony presided over by three revellers dressed as mythological creatures: *Vogel Gryff* (Griffon, complete with scaly wings), *Wilde Mann* (a Wild Man of the Woods, bedecked with holly and fir branches) and *Leu* (Lion). And for three days from the early hours of the Monday following Ash Wednesday, the city stages its famous Carnival.

A short walk from the main station (**Bahnhof SBB**, where the tourist office will give you a map) brings you via the **Elisabethenstrasse** to the **Klosterberg**, a lively old street with busy cafés, art galleries and antique and craft shops. From here the Theaterstrasse leads to the large modern **Theatre**, the square in front of it enlivened by the **Tinguely Fountain**, a square pool full of animated fountain-sculptures by the Swiss sculptor Jean Tinguely. Wrought-iron contraptions, looking like the brainchildren of some mad inventor, spray water through hoses or scoop it up by the panful and sieve it through giant colanders. Behind the fountain is the **Kunsthalle** (Steinberg 7, open late Wed), a cross between an art gallery, a museum and an arts centre.

St Alban-Graben, beyond the **Freie Strasse**, a busy pedestrian shopping street, has two museums. The **Antikenmuseum** (no. 5) has a large collection of Greek and Roman antiquities. On the other side of the road, fronted by an imposing arcade with carved capitals, is one of Europe's major art museums, the **Basler Kunstmuseum** (no. 16). Beyond the courtyard, adorned with Rodin's *Burghers of Calais* and work by Hans Arp (who died in Basel in 1966) and other sculptors, the main entrance hall (modest snackbar with a few tables outside) leads to several floors of paintings, including an important collection of Old Masters, and a representative selection of nineteenth- and twentieth-century artists (some fine Monet *Waterlilies*, Léger, Picasso and many others). The paintings are displayed in a series of small, cosy rooms that are rarely crowded. I particularly like a little Breughel of a wooded river valley, with a ghostly landscape in the distance, and an *Ascension* by Altdorfer, the risen Christ appearing in a halo of light at the top, against a dripping forest landscape, while the dazzled soldiers gradually wake up below.

This is also a good place for reminding yourself about major Swiss artists like the medieval Konrad Witz or Henry Fuseli (originally Füssli), both of whom are well represented, and enjoying the largest gathering of canvases by Hans Holbein outside the Queen's Collection in Britain.

Just beyond the museum, **St Alban-Vorstadt** has a number of attractive houses, some with oriel windows elaborately carved, and several antique shops. Turn left into the leafy **Mühlenberg** for a pleasant walk downhill past creeper-covered houses to **St Alban-Tal**, still seeming like a peaceful village beside the Rhine.

Here you can admire the heavily rebuilt **St Alban-Stift**, originally an eleventh-century monastery, beside **St Alban-Kirche**, the monastery church. Walk past the church and you come to a pretty square, then a series of quiet streets of sixteenth-century houses threaded through with the rushing waters of a mill-stream. For you soon come to an old water mill, its huge wheel still intact, recently converted into the **Basler Papier-Mühle** (**Paper and Printing Museum**, closed Mon). In this welcoming little museum, covering what were once two flour mills, you can still see the mill machinery in action and visit rooms devoted to papermaking.

A short walk away is the **Museum für Gegenwartskunst** (**Contemporary Art Museum**, St Alban-Rheinweg 58, closed Tues), where spacious modern exhibition areas house good temporary shows as well as the permanent collection.

A few coins to the ferryman and you are ensconced in a tiny flat-bottomed boat being drawn across the Rhine on an overhead wire cable. The **St Alban-Fähre** (St Alban's Ferry) is just one of four ferries in the centre of Basel – a curious anomaly in this busy modern city. A walk beside the river or along the **Oberrheinweg**, lined with comfortable houses, brings you to a row of café-restaurants with terraces overlooking the river and fine views of the cathedral high up on the opposite bank. Cross back over from this district (known as **Klein-Basel** or Little Basel) by the **Mittlere Brücke** (Central Bridge), then climb up the **Rheinsprung**. Beyond the elaborate façade of the eighteenth-century **Weisses Haus**, turn right into the **Martingasse** to see a brightly painted fountain and the **St Martinskirche** (Church of St Martin). Retrace your steps and turn right to follow the **Augustinergasse** past the **Naturhistorisches Museum** (Natural History Museum, no. 2) and the **Museum für Völkerkunde** (Ethnology Museum, same address) and the **Schweizerisches Museum für Volkskunde** (Swiss Folklore Museum, Münsterplatz 20).

The **Münsterplatz**, with picturesque half-timbered houses, is dominated by the red sandstone **Münster** (Cathedral), its west front adorned with large groups of sculptures, many of them reminiscent of the work on the cathedrals in Strasbourg and Freiburg-im-Breisgau. The original early Romanesque building, dating from the tenth and eleventh centuries, later modified in Transitional style, was badly damaged by fire and then virtually destroyed in an earthquake in 1356. The rebuilt Gothic building suffered during the Reformation, when it was demoted to a parish church. The cathedral houses **Erasmus's tomb** and has a wealth of Romanesque and Gothic sculpture, as well as early tombstones in the crypt.

The winding **Münsterberg**, with chic fashion boutiques and art galleries, leads down to the busy **Freie Strasse**. A short walk away is the **Barfüsserplatz**, whose church has been turned into a museum of local history. Or walk along the Freie Strasse to the **Marktplatz**, the traffic-free market square, overshadowed by the dark red Renaissance **Rathaus** (**Town Hall**). Beyond here lies the **Fischmarkt** (**Fish Market**), famous for its Gothic fountain. The **Spalenberg** and **Spalenvorstadt**, with attractive old houses, brings you to the **Spalentor**, one of the medieval city gates.

Elsbethenstübli (Elisabethenstrasse 34), offering a range of inexpensive set lunches, makes a cosy stop for a quick meal between the station and the town centre. The busy restaurant in the **Kunsthalle** building (Steinenberg 7, tel (19-41-61) 23 42 33) is divided into three: a cheerful *Stube* or tavern, its traditional décor enlivened by frescoes featuring naked ladies; and two more elegant dining rooms with modern paintings. The **Basler Kunstmuseum** has a tiny snackbar and the **Café Papiermühle** in the Paper and Printing Museum is a good place for a light meal. The historic **Gasthof Zum Goldnen Sternen** (St Alban-Rheinweg 70, tel (19-41-61) 23 16 66) is only a few paces from the ferry. On the other side, the posh **Hotel Merian am Rhein** (Rheingasse 2, tel (19-41-61) 681-0000) has a well-known fish restaurant, **Café Spitz**, and the less expensive **Rhyterrasse** overlooking the river. The **Hotel Krafft am Rhein** (Rheingasse 12, tel

(19-41-61) 691-8877) again has a terrace beside the river for light meals and a restaurant, **Le Petit Bâle**. Also in this row of riverside terraces, **Da Pippo** (Rheingasse 8, tel (19-41-61) 691-2220), a vegetarian restaurant-cum-tearoom.

About 10km/6 miles south of the city in the Rebberg at **Aesch** is the well-known and mostly expensive **Nussbaumer** (tel (19-41-61) 78-16-85, closed Mon and Tues).

TO Blumenrain 2; at main station

Freiburg-im-Breisgau

The lively university town of Freiburg-im-Breisgau in Germany, popular as a centre for excursions into the Black Forest, suffered badly during the Second World War but still has many medieval buildings, and its beautiful cathedral fortunately escaped damage. It now shares Basel and Mulhouse's rechristened 'Euro-Airport', with a direct bus link. It is only 52km/32½ miles from Colmar, from where a bus service connects with trains from Breisach-am-Rhein, worth visiting for Martin Schongauer's fresco of the Last Judgement (see box, p. 120). If you decide to combine a visit with Baden-Baden, the two are about an hour apart by car or train.

Freiburg was founded in the early twelfth century by one of the local counts, but came under Habsburg rule in 1368. Its university dates from a century later. It was there that, in 1507, the cartographer and cosmographer Martin Waldseemüller, working with Matthias Ringman, a Humanist from Alsace, produced a map for the Emperor Maximilian on which the term 'America' was first used. A couple of decades later Freiburg provided a refuge for Erasmus and other scholars driven out of Basel by the Reformation. The city was taken by Swedish troops during the Thirty Years War, then became French in 1677 when it was captured by Louis XIV's armies. Vauban drastically rebuilt it as a fortress town, but by 1698 it was back in Austrian hands. Its frontier position meant further damage during the Franco-Prussian War and again during the First World War. In 1918 it became part of the new republic of Baden. Bombing in 1940 was followed four years later by a devastating air raid in which three thousand people died and the Old Town was virtually wiped out.

The best way to visit Freiburg is on foot, though do keep an eye open for the **Bächle**, the miniature canals or drainage channels running through the old streets in the centre. They date back to the Middle Ages and were designed to ward off the danger of fire, as well as acting as drinking troughs for horses and other animals.

A few minutes' walk from the station (**Hauptbahnhof**) along the **Eisenbahnstrasse** is the **Colombipark**, reached by a vine-shaded path. Here you can visit the **Museum für Ur- und Frühgeschichte** (Prehistory and Early History Museum, open daily) in the **Colombischlössle**, a large mansion built in the local equivalent of Victorian Gothick, and learn about the history of the whole of the Rhine region and its peoples, including Alsace and the Alemanni.

On the far side of the public gardens, **Rathausgasse** has some good shops. It leads to the **Rathausplatz**, blessed with two town halls. The sixteenth-century **Altes Rathaus** (Old Town Hall), with a painted façade, was converted from several earlier buildings. The mainly Renaissance **Neues Rathaus** (New Town Hall) boasts a fine oriel window below which is a stone carving of what appears to be a mermaid with twin tails, plus a scene depicting a lady with a unicorn. On the other side of the square, the **Martinskirche** was once attached to a Franciscan monastery. Behind the church, the terracotta Late Gothic **Haus zum Walfisch** was the home of Erasmus for two years from 1529.

Beyond the busy **Kaiser-Joseph-Strasse**, **Münsterstrasse** leads to the cathedral square, the **Münsterplatz**, surrounded by cafés and wine bars. A colourful open-air food market is held here (mornings only). The dark red sandstone **Münster** (cathedral) is one of the loveliest in Germany. The transepts are Late Romanesque, while the nave, designed by one of the master builders who worked on the cathedral in Strasbourg, is firmly Gothic, supported by flying buttresses and adorned with sculpture and gargoyles, and the chancel Late Gothic.

The richly carved west porch (unexpectedly fenced off, but you can reach it from inside the cathedral) is reminiscent of Strasbourg with its busy tympanum, its Wise and Foolish Virgins, its Virgin and Child over the portal, and, beside the square, a smirking Satan and Sensuality, with serpents and other creatures crawling up her legs and back. The porch is topped by a single tower with an openwork spire. In fine weather it is worth climbing up the tower (usually closed Mon) for the views over the town and the Black Forest.

The interior is richly decorated too, with a moving fourteenth-century **Holy Sepulchre** and a wooden **Adoration of the Magi** at the entrance to the chancel, whose chief glory is a **triptych** by Hans Baldung Grien. But to see this and other important works of art you have to take one of the compulsory guided tours.

Although the square lost most of its buildings during the Second World War bombing, you can still see the bright red **Kaufhaus** (Merchants' Hall) dating from 1520 and enlivened with huge statues of Habsburg grandees above the gallery. Beside it is a Baroque palace, now the archbishop's residence. The **Kornhaus** (Cornmarket, also used as a *Metzig* or Butchers' Guild), the **Alte Hauptwache** (Old Guardhouse), and the house designed for himself by the eighteenth-century painter and architect J.-C. Wentzinger, which will one day open as a local history museum, can all be admired round the square.

Kaufhausgasse and **Augustinergasse** lead to the **Augustinermuseum** (Augustinerplatz, closed Mon, late opening Wed), housed in a former monastery. The lofty, bare rooms make an impressive setting for works of art like the early fifteenth-century **Staufen Altarpiece**, with its plump-faced Virgin, the **Passion Altarpiece** painted half a century later by the 'Master of the Housebook', and an oddly modern-looking **Virgin and Child** by Hans Baldung Grien, dating from about 1520.

Beyond a little bridge by an old oil mill, the **Museum für Neue Kunst** (Museum of Modern Art, Marienstrasse 10a, closed Mon) includes some good examples of German Expressionism and *Neue Sachlichkeit*

('New Objectivity'), the movement reacting against it. Just beyond here, the **Adelhauser Neukloster** (Dominican Convent), with a Baroque church, now houses the **Museum für Völkerkunde** (Ethnology Museum, Gerberau 32, closed Mon).

Fischerau, where the local fishermen's community once lived, brings you to the **Martinstor**, one of the medieval city gates, astride the main shopping street. On the far side, the **Bertoldsbrunnen**, a modern fountain replacing one destroyed in 1944, marks the beginning of the **Bertoldstrasse**, leading to the Baroque **Alte Universität** (Old University) and the university church, once a Jesuit college.

For local cuisine, **Kleiner Meyerhof** (Rathausgasse 27, closed Sun). In the cathedral square, **Oberkirch's Weinstuben** (no. 22, tel (19-49-761) 31011, closed Sun). A few steps away, **Weinstube Zur Traube** (Schusterstrasse 17, tel (19-49-761) 32190, closed Sun and for lunch on Mon), with a fixed-price 'regional menu'. At nos 18–20 in the cathedral square, **Bier und Speck**, for a glass of beer and an inexpensive local dish, and **Ratskeller** (no. 11, tel (19-49-761) 37530, closed Sun for dinner, Mon). The fairly expensive **Zum Roten Bären** (Oberlinden 12, tel (19-49-761) 36913) claims to be the oldest inn in Germany. For vegetarians, **Tessiner Stuben** (Bertoldstrasse 17, closed Sun), and **Hotel Victoria** (Eisenbahnstrasse 54).

TO Rotteckring 14

Gérardmer

The summer and winter resort of Gérardmer, famous for its three beautiful mountain lakes in a magnificent setting in the Vosges just over the border from Alsace in Lorraine, is equidistant from Strasbourg and Basel – about an hour's drive through the mountains in each case. It is only 52km/32½ miles from Colmar, with which there are frequent bus links (via Munster and the Col de la Schlucht). It suffered appallingly during the German retreat in 1944 and therefore has none of the grand turn-of-the-century or the Edwardian-style buildings you would expect from a place that boasts of having France's oldest tourist office (opened in 1875).

But with its comfortable modern hotels, its many restaurants, its sports opportunities and beautiful surroundings it makes a pleasant day or weekend excursion, perhaps combined with a drive along the Route des Crêtes (see Chapter 7). In the spring, the meadows and hillsides are magically carpeted with daffodils (annual Daffodil Festival in April).

A small museum is devoted to the Vosges forests, the **Musée de la Forêt** (6 rue du 152e RI) and the **Maison du Commerce et de l'Artisanat vosgien** (pl. de l'Eglise), a craft centre, displays the table linen for which Gérardmer is well known.

The three lakes – **Lac de Gérardmer**, **Lac de Longmer** and the smaller **Lac de Retournemer** – were carved out by the melting glaciers of the Ice Age, which also created the **Saut des Cuves** waterfall, cascading down through granite rocks, leaping from the 'basins' or 'vats' (*cuves* in French) hollowed out by their headlong flight (3km/2 miles east). Near here is the **Pierre de Charlemagne**, a large rock on which a weary Charlemagne allegedly took a breather when out hunting in the forests that then covered the whole region. You can buy walking maps and hire bikes at the tourist office; one-day angling permits are sold in various shops in the town and at some of the campsites; and there are boats and water bicycles for hire on the two larger lakes.

Au Grand Cerf, in **Grand Hôtel Bragard** (pl. du Tilleul, tel 29 63 06 31) offers good (mostly fish) cuisine in a spacious hotel dining room, with tables outside in fine weather, and good-value *menus* **La Réserve**, overlooking the lake, again with tables outside, is more expensive (tel 29 63 21 60). Just over 3.5km/2 miles south, **La Belle Marée** at **Les Bas-Rupts** (144 route de La Bresse, tel 29 63 06 38, closed Mon) also specializes in fish, at reasonable prices.

TO At the station

Metz

Metz is a surprise. The first time I went there I expected to find a rather dull town, mindful of its centuries-old role as a commercial centre and its position at the heart of a region dependent on heavy industry, now very much in decline. But it turned out to be a pleasant place adorned with gardens and riverside walks. The historic centre round **Saint-Etienne cathedral** is both small and reasonably traffic free, largely thanks to the ring roads encircling it, built at the turn of the century by the Germans, on the site of the old ramparts. The period of German occupation also gave the city its **Ville allemande**, the area round the station built as a *Neustadt* (New Town) in an odd mixture of neo-Romanesque, neo-Gothic and neo-Renaissance styles – worth a look as a curiosity.

Metz – pronounced Mess – boasts of three thousand years of continuous history. Its site at the point where the Moselle and Seille rivers meet was inhabited in the late Bronze Age and by the Roman era it had become a major centre. It went on to be the capital of the Merovingian kingdom of Austrasia, an important intellectual centre during the Carolingian era and a free imperial city in the Middle Ages. Its frontier position has given it a 'garrison town' role for centuries and it is still a major military headquarters. But don't think that that makes it seem forbidding. The narrow streets in the centre with their odd-sounding names – En Chaplerue, En Fournirue, En Nexirue – are full of chic boutiques and it is fun strolling round this pedestrianized, essentially medieval area, its main streets the **rue des Clercs** and the **rue Serpenoise**.

At one end of the network of old streets is **Saint-Etienne**, a Gothic cathedral based on two Romanesque churches, which were rebuilt in the thirteenth century and joined together to make a single mighty cathedral, famous for the height of its nave and its lovely stained glass, some of it superb examples of medieval craftsmanship, some designed by contemporary artists, including Chagall and Jacques Villon.

Opposite the south façade in the eighteenth-century **place d'Armes** is the classical **town hall**, and beyond it the **Musée d'Art et d'Histoire**, conceived on the time-machine principle. The city's architectural, art and history collections have been combined to form a 'total museum', complemented by military and natural history museums. It is all very stylish and unstuffy, with constant emphasis on the details of everyday life from the Gallo-Roman period onwards.

A short walk from the cathedral past the large market buildings brings you to the river. The **Pont des Roches** leads to the **Ile de la Comédie**, where graceful eighteenth-century buildings surround the **place de la Comédie**. Beyond the **Pont Moyen** various paths and steps lead up to the **Esplanade**, a leafy promenade offering lovely views over the countryside. On one side is the eighteenth-century **Palais de Justice** (law courts), built as a residence for the governor of the 'Three Bishoprics' (Metz, Toul and Verdun). Between here and the neo-Gothic **Palais du Gouverneur**, another legacy of the German era, Metz has recently acquired an **arts complex** designed by the Spanish architect Ricardo Bofill.

This part of the town also has two important religious buildings. **Saint-Pierre-des-Nonnains**, believed to be France's oldest church, was built on the foundations of a Roman basilica. The **Chapelle des Templiers**, an octagonal oratory once part of the commandery built for the Knights Templars at the beginning of the thirteenth century, has been incorporated into the new arts centre.

Beside the River Seille you can admire the **Porte des Allemands**, a good example of medieval military architecture. And as you stroll round the old streets in the centre you will come across a number of tall medieval houses, round the arcaded **place Saint-Louis**, for instance.

A few paces away from the cathedral, **La Gargouille** (29 pl. de Chambre, tel 87 36 65 77), a cheerful bistrot with turn-of-the-century décor. **Maire** (1 rue du Pont-des-Morts, tel 87 32 43 12), rather elegant, with a terrace overhanging the river, part of it glassed in, and, on the other bank, **Les Roches** (27/29 rue des Roches, tel 87 74 06 51), specializing in fish. For a gastronomic experience, cross three bridges from the centre to eat at **La Dinanderie** (2 rue de Paris, tel 87 30 14 40); the *menus* are good value. For a glimpse of the Messins, **A la Ville de Lyon** (7 rue des Piques, tel 87 36 07 71), between the east end of the cathedral and the river: listed décor, mainly imaginative cuisine and plenty of atmosphere.

TO Pl. d'Armes

Nancy

Nancy, the capital of the Lorraine region, has what is often said to be the most beautiful town centre in France and several interesting museums. It is roughly equidistant from Strasbourg and Colmar (148km/92½ miles and 140km/87½ miles) and is on the main line from Paris to Strasbourg: trains take about 1¼ hrs between the two towns, or just over 2 hrs from Colmar with a change in Strasbourg. Nancy and Metz are only 56km/35 miles apart (about 40 mins by train).

Nancy's history is closely linked to that of the Dukes of Lorraine, whose stronghold and later capital it was for centuries. They built the medieval **Ville Vieille** (Old Town), centring on their palace and surrounded by mighty fortifications, and warded off an attempt to seize the duchy by Charles the Bold, Duke of Burgundy, who was killed fighting at the gates of the town in 1477. The end of the sixteenth century saw expansion with the building of the **Ville Neuve** (New Town) beyond the original bastion, designed on a regular grid pattern and surrounded by its own wall. The Thirty Years' War brought great devastation, followed by rebuilding. The town acquired some fine seventeenth-century mansions at this time. But in the 1730s Duke François III was persuaded by Louis XV to give up Lorraine in return for the sunnier duchy of Tuscany. It is to his successor that Nancy owes the lovely **place Stanislas**, laid out by Stanislas Leszczynski, the exiled King of Poland, who was granted the dukedoms of Bar and Lorraine when his daughter Marie unexpectedly married the young French king (see box, p. 102).

A short walk from the station towards the centre takes you through a busy shopping area (look out for confectioners selling the local specialities – *bergamotes de Nancy* or *craquelins* or *macarons des religieuses*). Then suddenly you find yourself in an airy square adorned with graceful *hôtels*, magnificent gilded wrought-iron gates, railings and balconies, and frothy Rococo fountains. Starting in 1752, Stanislas worked with his architect Emmanual Héré and his ironsmith Jean Lamour, both of them local men, to build this perfect square. One side is taken up with the vast **Hôtel de Ville** (town hall), whose staircase has a wrought-iron balustrade by Lamour. On the other sides are matching buildings, in one of which Marie Antoinette stayed on her way to Paris in May 1770 to marry the Dauphin, later Louis XVI. It now houses the luxury **Grand Hôtel de la Reine**. Another is the city's **theatre** and yet another the **Musée des Beaux-Arts** (Fine Arts Museum, no. 3, closed Tues), with good painting collections, including Delacroix's *Death of Charles the Bold*, and glass by the local firm of Daum, which has a shop a few minutes' walk away in the rue Héré.

In the centre of the square is a **statue of Stanislas**, replacing his patron and son-in-law Louis XV, to whom he also dedicated the small **Porte Royale** at the end of the rue Héré, a triumphal arch leading to the **place de la Carrière**, with long avenues of plane trees, built in the sixteenth century as a jousting ground but redesigned by Héré and surrounded by eighteenth-century houses. A stroll through this peaceful square brings you to the **Palais du Gouvernement**, once the residence of the dukes. To your right a gateway leads into the **Parc de la Pépinière**, with a statue by Rodin of the landscape painter Claude Lorrain, who was born near Nancy.

Turn left out of the square to visit the **Ville Vieille**, with sixteenth- and seventeenth-century mansions in the **Grand-Rue**. At no. 64, the mainly Gothic **Palais Ducal** (Ducal Palace), its doorway resplendent with the equestrian figure of one of the dukes, houses the **Musée historique lorrain** (Museum of Lorraine History, closed Tues). This has rich local history collections, rooms devoted to Stanislas's town-planning schemes and an almost complete set of etchings by Jacques Callot, who was born in Nancy in 1592.

Most of the dukes are buried in the **Eglise des Cordeliers**, beyond the palace. (Stanislas tactfully chose to be buried in the church of **Notre-Dame-du-Bon-Secours** in the avenue de Strasbourg – here you can also see the monument surrounding the heart of his beloved daughter Marie, who outlived him by only two years.) At the far end of the Grand-Rue, the mighty **Porte de la Craffe**, one of the city's medieval gates, has a collection of gruesome instruments of torture and medieval sculpture (closed Tues).

A ten-minute walk to a residential district the other side of the railway line brings you to the **Musée de l'Ecole de Nancy** (38 rue du Sergent-Blandan, closed Tues). A comfortable house, built at the turn of the century for one of the patrons of the art nouveau 'School of Nancy', has been turned into a showcase for their work, with Gallé glass, Majorelle furniture and lamps, jewelry and fabrics. The tourist office publishes a leaflet pinpointing the most important houses of the period, including one built for Louis Majorelle.

On your way to or from the place Stanislas: **L'Excelsior** (50 rue Henri-Poincaré), a lively brasserie near the station with genuine art nouveau décor. The **rue des Maréchaux** near the place Stanislas (known locally as *'rue goumande'*) has restaurants to suit all pockets, the best of them **La Gentilhommière** (no. 29, tel 83 32 26 44, closed weekends), in the house where Victor Hugo's father was born. **Le Comptoir du Petit Gastolâtre** (1 pl. Vaudémont, tel 83 35 51 94, closed Sun and Mon), a chic bistrot near the place Stanislas, and, in the square itself, **Le Foy** (no. 1, tel 83 32 21 44, closed Wed). **Mirabelle** (24 rue Héré, closed Mon) has an inexpensive *menu*. For a drink and a sandwich or salad, the strategic café tables round the place Stanislas.

TO 14 pl. Stanislas

Hotels and restaurants

For general advice on staying and eating in Alsace, see Practical Information and Alsace Cuisine. I have no space to provide comprehensive lists of hotels, and especially of restaurants, with which Alsace is so well endowed. Instead I have aimed to suggest a range of pleasant restaurants, the majority medium-priced, but with some more expensive places (especially in pricey Strasbourg) for a special meal, and, whenever possible, some inexpensive restaurants, tearooms and *winstubs* too. In selecting hotels, I have concentrated on traditional, family-run hotels with a friendly local ambiance. Those who prefer chain hotels will find them in the main towns, but although staff are generally friendlier than in such places elsewhere, they give you little feeling of being in a region with a strong personality, and as such seem to me less appropriate for readers of this book.

A rough price guide is indicated by the symbols F, FF, FFF and, for restaurants, FFFF. These corresponded in 1990 to the following range:
hotels: (for a double room without breakfast) F = 75–150 francs per head; FF = 175–300 francs per head; FFF = over 300 francs per head
restaurants: (for a two- or three-course meal without wine) F = 100 francs or below on average; FF = 100–150 francs; FFF = 150–250 francs; FFFF = over 250 francs

As always in France, prices may vary considerably within one establishment. Even very expensive restaurants often have a good-value *menu* (fixed-price menu with limited choice) that enables you to sample the artistry of their chefs, yet pay as little as half the price of three or four courses selected from the *carte*. And a modest restaurant may offer an expensive *menu gastronomique* (perhaps available only on Sundays and public holidays). Similarly, hotels may have a few small and modest rooms alongside spacious and much more expensive ones – part of the charm of Alsace's traditional hotels is their lack of uniformity. As prices may change without warning, always check locally, or ask for confirmation when making a hotel booking.

When writing direct to a hotel or restaurant, use the postcode given in the top right-hand corner of each entry. A code by itself means that you simply put this before the place name (e.g. 67000 Strasbourg or 68340 Riquewihr). A code plus another name means that you must put the place name first, followed on the next line by the postcode and the second place name (e.g. Lutter, then 68480 Ferrette). If you are telephoning from elsewhere in France, dial 16 and wait for a second tone before dialling the telephone number given in brackets. Restaurants without a telephone number are places to drop in to for a meal: they are not suitable for booking in advance or planning a trip round. Fax numbers, if any, are included after the telephone number.

ALTKIRCH 68130
Terrasse (F) 44–6 rue du 3e-Zouaves (89 40 98 02). Small and modest, with restaurant.
Restaurants
Auberge sundgovienne (F–FFF) 3km/2 miles W, route de Belfort, **Carspach** (89 40 97 18), cl. Mon, for lunch Tues, Christmas. Regional cuisine in dining room of modern hotel.
La Couronne (F–FF) 9 rue de Steinsoultz, again at **Carspach** (89 40 93 09) cl. Tues for dinner, Wed, part of July, part of Aug. Friendly inn, popular for fried carp.

AMMERSCHWIHR 68770
A L'Arbre vert (F–FFF) 7 rue des Cigognes (89 47 12 23), cl. mid-Feb to mid-Mar. If you can't get a table at the famous *Armes de France*, you'll still enjoy a good meal of traditional dishes here; a few rooms.
Aux Armes de France (FFF–FFFF) 1 Grand-Rue (89 47 10 12), cl. Wed, Thur for lunch, Jan. One of Alsace's top restaurants, in a village that was virtually flattened by bombing in 1944, now rebuilt in traditional style; mostly excellent *nouvelle* variants on regional recipes, friendly atmosphere, plus a few comfortable rooms (FF).

ANDLAU 67140 Barr
Au Canon (F) 2 rue des Remparts (88 08 95 08). Modest, in 18thC building; most rooms overlook garden; pleasant, unpretentious restaurant (FF–FFF, cl. Wed).
Kastelberg (F) 2 rue du Général-Koenig (88 08 97 83). Modern building on outskirts furnished in traditional style; quiet rooms with balconies overlooking vineyards; adequate *winstub* and restaurant.
Restaurant
Au Boeuf rouge (F–FFF) 6 rue du Dr-Stoltz (88 08 96 26), cl. Wed for dinner, Thur, second half June. Friendly family-run restaurant in 16thC coaching inn; *winstub* (F) upstairs.

BALDENHEIM 67600
La Couronne (FF–FFFF) 45 rue de Sélestat (88 85 32 22, fax 88 85 36 27), cl. Sun for dinner, Mon, second half July. Family-run village inn in Ried near Sélestat; good modern cuisine based on regional dishes.

BARR 67140
Du Manoir (F–FF) 11 rue Saint-Marc (88 08 03 40). Comfortable rooms in traditional hotel with attractive garden; no restaurant.

Restaurants
A la Couronne (FF–FFF) 4 rue des Boulangers (88 08 25 83), cl. second half Jan. Good range of *menus*, all including modern versions of regional dishes.
Winstub Gilg (FF–FFF) 2km/1 mile away at **Mittelbergheim** (88 08 91 37), cl. Tues for dinner, Wed, Jan, first half July. Usually reliable, rather rich classical cuisine, plus local specialities.

BEBLENHEIM 68980
La Basse Cour (FF), 10 rue Jean-Macé (89 47 91 49), cl. Mon, Tues, Wed. Lively inn near Riquewihr, open till early hours and serving straightforward meals with local wines.

BERGHEIM 68750
Wistub du sommelier (FF–FFF) 51 Grand-Rue (89 73 69 99), cl. Sun, Feb. Half-timbered 18thC building housing one of Alsace's best-known *wistubs* (the southern version of a *winstub*), run by prize-winning wine waiter; regional cuisine and the finest local wines served by the glass in friendly panelled dining room.

BETTENDORF 68560 Hirsingue
Au Cheval blanc (F–FF) 4 rue de Hirsingue (89 40 50 58), cl. Wed for dinner, Thur, second half Feb, second half July. Typical Sundgau inn offering fried carp, trout stuffed with *choucroute* and other local dishes; a few modest rooms (F).

BOUXWILLER 67330
Heintz (F) 84 Grand-Rue (88 70 72 57), cl. most of Jan, second half June. Small hotel with pool, garden and terrace for outdoor meals; adequate cuisine (F, cl. Sun for dinner, Mon).

BRUMATH 67170
L'Ecrevisse (FF–FFFF) 4 av. de Strasbourg (88 51 11 08), cl. Mon for dinner, Tues, mid July to mid-Aug. Old-established family-run restaurant, rightly popular for inventive variants on regional dishes; also a few attractive rooms (F).

CLIMBACH 67510 Lembach
Au Cheval blanc (F–FF) 2 rue de Bitche (88 94 41 95), cl. Tues for dinner, Wed, first half July. Half-timbered inn near Wissembourg, with friendly service and hunting décor – this area on the edge of the forest is popular in the shooting season.

COLMAR 68000
Amiral (FF) 11a blvd du Champ-de-Mars (89 23 26 25). Once a malthouse, now a comfortable hotel with courtyard terrace, conveniently opposite Colmar's main carpark on edge of Old Town, but with quiet rooms set back from road; some charming attic rooms on two floors.
Maréchal (FF–FFF) 4–6 pl. des Six-Montagnes-Noires (89 41 60 32, fax 89 24 59 40). Delightful rooms, furnished with antiques, in half-timbered 16thC building in picturesque Petite Venise district; some overlook river, and so does cosy dining room, with terrace for summer meals.
Park (F) 52 av. de la République (89 41 34 80). Nondescript modern building but opposite leafy park midway between station and Old Town; comfortable modern rooms (those on main road are noisy), restaurant.

Rapp'hôtel (F) 1-5 rue Weinemer (89 41 62 10). Amusing façade painted in sherbert colours; small and plain, but well-planned modern rooms; spacious, quite elegant dining room with Napoleonic battle scene mural (F–FF, cl. Wed).
Saint-Martin (F–FF) 38 Grand-Rue (89 24 11 51), cl. Jan and part of Feb. Ideally situated in heart of Old Town opposite Koifhus; usually pleasant service; mainly small but well-furnished rooms, some overlooking peaceful courtyard, with bird's-eye views of old roofs.
Terminus-Bristol (FF) 7 pl. de la Gare (89 23 59 59, fax 89 23 92 26). Very comfortable traditional hotel opposite station, with well-known restaurant and less expensive 'inn' (see Restaurants).
Turenne (F-FF) 10 route de Bâle (89 41 12 26), cl. Christmas and New Year period. Friendly small hotel close to Petite Venise; small but well-planned rooms, cosy *winstub*-type breakfast room.
5km/3 miles SE at **Wettolsheim**:
Auberge du Père Floranc (F–FF) 9 rue Herzog (89 80 79 14, fax 89 79 77 00), cl. first half July, mid-Nov to mid-Dec. Friendly family-run inn, with large and popular restaurant (F–FFF, cl. Mon, and Sun for dinner in winter); some rooms in main building, others in spacious annexe beyond pretty garden.

Restaurants
It is wise to book at all of these:
Au Chaudron (F–FF) 5 pl. du Marché-aux-Fruits (89 24 56 18), evenings only, cl. Sun, mid-July to mid-Aug. Restful little place a few paces from Koifhus, mainly light cuisine and smiling service.
Boulevard 15 (F–FF) 15bis blvd du Champ-de-Mars (89 24 24 44), cl. Sun. Stylish bistrot under same management as Hôtel Amiral (see Hotels).
Au Fer rouge (FF–FFF) 52 Grand-Rue (89 41 37 24), cl. most of Jan. One of most attractive of Colmar's many attractive buildings, right by Koifhus, houses one of Alsace's finest restaurants, offering delectably light cuisine, not exorbitantly priced if you stick to *menus*, plus unstuffy service.
Chez Hansi (F–FF) 23 rue des Marchands (89 41 37 84), cl. Wed for dinner, Thur, mid-Jan to mid-Feb. Again in heart of Old Town, and very typical of Alsace with its cosy ambiance, waitresses in local costume and good choice of regional dishes; a few sought-after tables outside.
Les Maison des Têtes (FF) 19 rue des Têtes (89 24 43 43), cl. Sun for dinner, Mon, mid-Jan to mid-Feb. Amazing Gothic/Renaissance building, covered with carved heads that give it its name, is the setting for a quite elegant restaurant offering both regional specialities and *nouvelle* recipes; shady little courtyard for your apéritif.
Le Rendez-vous de chasse (FF–FFF) In Terminus-Bristol hotel (see Hotels) (89 41 10 10). Very grand and very well run, with often inventive cuisine (affordable if you don't stray from *menus*).
Schillinger (FFF–FFFF) 16 rue Stanislas (89 41 43 17), cl. Sun for dinner, Mon, most of July. Colmar's top restaurant, elegant and very professional, serves classical cuisine with many light touches.
Aux Trois Poissons (F–FFF) 150 quai de la Poissonnerie (89 41 25 21), cl. Tues for dinner, Wed, late June, first half July. Right by river and few doors away from fishmonger's that dates back to Middle Ages, so wonderfully fresh fish is special-

ity of this friendly and unpretentious restaurant in picturesque street.
Other restaurants
Bartholdi (F–FF) 2 rue des Boulangers, cl. mid-Nov to mid-Dec. Conveniently close to Eglise des Dominicains in network of pedestrian streets; popular with locals for mainly Alsace dishes.
L'Auberge (FF) Terminus-Bristol's second restaurant specializes in straightforward *winstub* dishes.
Chez Hansala (F) 38bis rue des Marchands. Tearoom annexe of *Chez Hansi*, useful for light lunch.
La Petit Gourmand (F–FF) 9 quai de la Poissonnerie. Tiny restaurant-cum-tearoom in purple half-timbered house, with tables on little terrace beside river.
Winstubs
Au Koifhus (F–FF) pl. de l'Ancienne-Douane, cl. Mon, Feb, first half Mar. Relaxed atmosphere, convenient situation by Koifhus.
La Krutenau (F–FF) 1 rue de la Poissonnerie, cl. Thur, Feb. Small and friendly, with terrace over river for hot summer evenings.
S'Parisser Stewwele (F–FF) 4 pl. Jeanne d'Arc, cl. Tues, mid-Feb to mid-Mar. Lively and popular with local clientele, near Temple Saint-Matthieu.
Unterlinden (F–FF) 2 rue Unterlinden, cl. Sun for dinner, also Tues in winter, part of Jan. Tourist-frequented (opposite superb museum of same name) but not tourist trap: carefully cooked regional repertoire, cosy ambiance, range of *menus*.

DAMBACH-LA-VILLE 67650
Au Raisin d'or (F) 28 rue Clemenceau (88 92 40 08), cl. Jan. Small family-run hotel in heart of pretty village; restaurant (F–FF, cl. Wed for dinner, Thur) serves regional cuisine.
Restaurants
Caveau Nartz (F–FF) 12 pl du Marché (88 92 41 11), weekends only except July and Aug, cl. Jan–Apr. Delightful crooked old house, straightforward regional dishes at low prices, wine by the glass.
A la Vignette (F–FF) 8 pl. du Marché, cl. mid-Jan to mid-Feb, Mon for dinner, Tues. Modest restaurant-cum-*winstub*.

DIEFMATTEN 68780 Sentheim
Au Cheval blanc (F–FFF) 17 rue de Hecken (89 26 91 08), cl. Mon, Tues for dinner, second half July. Good family-run restaurant in converted Sundgau farm.

EGUISHEIM 68420 Herrlisheim-près-Colmar
Auberge alsacienne (F) 12 Grand-Rue (89 41 50 20), cl. Dec–Mar. Half-timbered building in heart of village; rooms furnished in traditional style; regional cuisine in restaurant (FF–FFF, cl. Tues).
Restaurants
Auberge du Rempart (F–FF) 3 rue du Rempart-Sud (89 41 16 87), cl. Mon, Jan. Cheerful *winstub* ambiance and décor; tables outside beside fountain in summer.
Caveau d'Eguisheim (FF–FFFF) 3 pl. du Château (89 41 08 89), cl. Tues for dinner, Wed, mid-Jan to Mar. Owned by association promoting excellent local wines, with regional cuisine to match.
Au Dagsbourg (F–FF) 41 rue du Rempart-Nord (89 41 51 90), cl. mid-June to mid-July; also four modest rooms (F).

ENSISHEIM 68190
La Couronne (FF–FFFF) 47 rue de la 1ère-Armée-française (89 81 03 72), cl. Sun for dinner, Mon, second half July. Renaissance building, mostly *nouvelle cuisine*; convenient for Eco-Museum; a few comfortable rooms (F).

FEGERSHEIM 67640
La Table gourmande (FF–FFFF) 43 route de Lyon (88 68 53 54), cl. Sun for dinner, Mon. Excellent fish cuisine in attractive old inn in village south of Strasbourg; good value.

FELDBACH 68640 Waldighoffen
Au Cheval blanc (F–FFF) 1 rue de Bisel (89 25 81 86), cl. Tues for dinner, Wed, first half July. Convenient stopping-off place for meal when visiting the Sundgau's loveliest church.

FERRETTE 68480
Cheval blanc (F) 3 rue Léon-Lehmann. Modest restaurant with tiny garden, useful for quick meal.
Le Felseneck (F–FF) 42 rue du Château, cl. Mon, Feb. Pleasant terrace shaded by lime trees at foot of path leading up to châteaux; friendly service, adequate cuisine, with some carp dishes; a few rooms (F).
8km/5 miles E at **Lutter**:
Auberge paysanne (F–FF) 24 rue de Wolschwiller (89 40 71 67), cl. second half Feb. Friendly inn with modest rooms and good restaurant (F–FFF, cl. Mon) has opened charming 'hostelry' in reconstructed half-timbered Sundgau dwelling; pretty rooms with old beams, sunny garden.

LE GRAND BALLON 68760 Willer-sur-Thur
Goldenmatt (FF) (89 82 32 86), cl. mid-Nov to Easter. Family hotel with restaurant close to Alsace's highest mountain.
Le Grand Ballon (F) (89 76 83 35), cl. mid-Nov to mid-Dec. Modest rooms frequented by hikers and skiers in chalet-style hotel with popular restaurant (F–FFF).

GRAUFTHAL 67320 Drulingen
Au Vieux Moulin (F) (88 70 17 28), cl. Jan, first half Feb. Modest family hotel peacefully set beside lake in valley near La Petite-Pierre; restaurant (cl. Mon for dinner, Tues).

GUEBWILLER 68500
Taverne du Vigneron (F–FF) pl. Saint-Léger, cl. Mon for lunch, Jan. Busy wine tavern close to Saint-Léger church.
6km/4 miles W at **Jungholtz**:
Auberge de Thierenbach (FF) (89 76 93 01), cl. Jan. Peaceful inn with restaurant (FF–FFF).
Les Violettes (F–FFF) (89 76 91 19), cl. most of Jan. Very comfortable rooms with forest views, good regional cuisine (FF–FFFF, cl. Mon for dinner, Tues).

HAGUENAU 67500
Europe (F–FF) 15 av. du Président-Leriche (88 93 58 11, fax 88 93 21 33). Modern and comfortable, close to Forêt de Haguenau, with pool and restaurant.
6km/4 miles S at **Marienthal**:

Relais Princesse Marie Leczinska (FF–FFF) 1 rue Rothbach (88 93 70 39), cl. Sun for dinner, Mon, most of Feb, first half Sept. Marienthal has been a place of pilgrimage since the Middle Ages, and hungry pilgrims should book a table at this delightful inn specializing in game; pool.
4km/2½ miles W at **Schweighouse-sur-Moder**:
Auberge du Cheval blanc (F–FFF) 46 rue du Général-de-Gaulle (88 72 76 96), cl. Sat, for dinner Sun, most of Aug. Typical Alsace inn with painted ceiling, friendly atmosphere, classical cuisine plus regional dishes.

HARTMANNSWILLER   68500 Guebwiller
L'Amphitryon (F–FFFF) 49 route de Cernay (89 76 71 83), cl. Fri, for lunch Sat, second half Jan, first half June. Popular restaurant in **Meyer** hotel (F).

HÉSINGUE   68220 Hégenheim
Au Boeuf noir (FF–FFFF) 2 rue de Folgensbourg (89 69 76 40), cl. Sat for lunch, Sun for dinner, Mon, most of Aug. Good restaurant in village near Basel, on edge of Sundgau.

HIRTZBACH   68118
Ottie Baur (F–FFF) 9 rue De Lattre (89 40 93 22), cl. Mon for dinner, Tues, first half July, first half Jan. Mixture of classical and regional cuisine in Sundgau.

LE HOHWALD   67140 Barr
Grand Hôtel (F–FF) rue Principale (88 08 31 03, fax 88 08 33 15), cl. mid-Nov to mid-Dec. Traditional hotel in peaceful mountain setting, with garden, tennis court and miniature golfcourse; restaurant (FF–FFF).
Marchal (F) 12 rue Wittertalhof (88 08 31 04), cl. Nov, first half Dec. Popular with families skiing or walking in Vosges; restaurant (F–FF, cl. Tues for lunch).
5km/3 miles away at **Col du Kreuzweg**:
Zundelkopf (F) (88 08 30 41). Modest family hotel restaurant at 750m/2,500ft.

HUSSEREN-LES-CHÂTEAUX   68420 Herrlisheim-près-Colmar
Husseren-les-Châteaux (FF–FFFF) rue du Schlossberg (89 49 22 93, fax 89 49 24 84). New hotel with rooms on two floors, each with private balcony, built in series of terraces overlooking vines; pool, sauna, restaurant (FF–FFF).

ILLHAEUSERN   68150 Ribeauvillé
Auberge de l'Ill (FFFF) (89 71 83 23), cl. Mon for dinner (also Mon lunch in winter), Tues, Feb. One of France's top restaurants, in idyllic setting beside Ill, beneath weeping willows. Superlative cuisine, at not unreasonable prices, and smiling, unstuffy atmosphere; advance booking essential.
3km/2 miles W at **Guémar**:
La Clairière (FF–FFF) 46 route d'Illhaeusern (89 71 80 80), cl. Jan, Feb. Delightful little hotel designed by former head waiter at 'Auberge' to put up his ex-bosses' diners (no restaurant); tennis court.

ITTERSWILLER   67140 Barr
Arnold (FF) 98 route du Vin (88 85 50 58). Popular half-timbered hotel in pretty Wine Road village; quiet and attractive rooms in several buildings, most with balconies and lovely views over vines and mountains; garden, terrace, little

shop selling food and drink made on premises; restaurant (FF–FFF, cl. Mon) serves good regional dishes in converted wine cellar, with décor to match; friendly family atmosphere throughout.

KAYSERSBERG 68240
Château (F) 38 rue du Général-de Gaulle (89 78 24 33), cl. mid-Jan to mid-Feb; modest hotel in centre; restaurant (F–FF, cl. Wed for dinner, Thur).
Remparts (F–FF) 4 rue de la Flieh (89 47 12 12, fax 89 47 37 24). Modern and not particularly attractive, but friendly welcome and quiet rooms overlooking forest near Schweitzer Museum; no restaurant.
Restaurants
Chambard (FF–FFFF) 9–13 rue du Général-de-Gaulle (89 47 10 17), cl. Mon, for lunch Tues, Christmas, most of Mar. Excellent cuisine, with both classical and *nouvelle* dishes, elegant atmosphere; very comfortable rooms in quiet modern annexe (FF).
Lion d'Or (FF–FFF) 66 rue du Général-de-Gaulle (89 47 11 16), cl. Tues for dinner (in winter), Wed, Jan. Traditional Alsace cuisine in charming 16thC building.

KIENTZHEIM 68240 Kaysersberg
L'Abbaye d'Alspach (F–FF) 2–4 rue Foch (89 47 16 00), cl. Jan, Feb. Attractive hotel in peaceful wine village; *winstub* (F–FF, evenings only, cl. Wed, Thur).
Irrmann'stub (FF) 68 Grand-Rue, cl. Mon, for lunch Tues. Lively *winstub* in Château de Reichenstein; good regional specialities.

KIFFIS 68480 Ferrette
Auberge du Jura (F–FF) 45 rue Principale (89 40 33 33), cl. Mon, mid-Feb to mid-Mar, mid-Aug to mid-Sept. Friendly Sundgau inn near Swiss border; fried carp and other regional dishes; a few spotless rooms (F).

KINTZHEIM 67600 Sélestat
Auberge Saint-Martin (FF) 80 rue de la Liberté, cl. Wed, for lunch Thur, most of Feb. Regional cuisine, convenient for Kintzheim's wildlife attractions.

LABAROCHE 68910
Auberge de la Rochette (F) (89 49 80 40), cl. Jan. Family hotel in heart of 'Pays Welche', run by same family for generations; traditional dining room (F–FFF, cl. Wed, Sun for dinner), with local china, antique furniture; garden.

LANDERSHEIM 67700 Saverne
Auberge du Kochersberg (FFF–FFFF) route de Saessolsheim (88 69 91 58, fax 88 69 97 25), cl. most of Feb, mid-July to mid-Aug, Sun for dinner, Mon. Adidas factory's canteen undergoes daily transformation into one of Alsace's best-known restaurants; panelled dining room, inventive cuisine, famous wine list.

LAPOUTROIE 68650
Les Alisiers (F) 5 rue Faude (89 47 52 82), cl. second half June, Dec. Peaceful and delightful mountain hotel; pretty rooms, unpretentious regional cuisine served in cosy dining room in *winstub* style (FF, cl. Mon for dinner, Tues); garden and magnificent views.

Faude (F) 28 rue du Général-Dufieux (89 47 50 35), cl. most of Mar, mid-Nov to mid-Dec. Pleasant hotel with garden, indoor pool, sauna; good-value *menus* in restaurant (F–FFF).

LEMBACH 67510
Le Relais du Heimbach (F) 15 rue de Wissembourg (88 94 43 46). Pretty rooms furnished in Alsace style in former private house opposite famous *Cheval blanc* restaurant.
Vosges du Nord (F) 59 route de Bitche (88 94 43 41), cl. Second half Aug. Small hotel with modest but attractive rooms; no restaurant.
10km/6 miles N at **Gimbelhof**:
Gimbelhof (F) (88 94 43 58), cl. second half Nov, Dec. Farm-inn converted into modest hotel, conveniently near Fleckenstein Castle; unpretentious regional dishes (F–FF, cl. Mon, Tues).
Restaurant
Le Cheval blanc (FF–FFFF) 4 route de Wissembourg (88 94 41 86, fax 88 94 20 74), cl. Mon, Tues, most of Feb, most of July. A former coaching inn, its large courtyard looking like a prosperous farmyard, is the setting for a well-known family-run restaurant with rather grand cuisine, excellent-value *menus*.

LIÈPVRE 68660
Auberge Vieille Forge (FF–FFFF) 13 route de Sainte-Marie-aux-Mines, on outskirts at Bois-l'Abbesse (89 58 92 54), cl. Mon for dinner, Tues, second half June, second half Nov. Smithy converted into friendly inn, serving light, modern cuisine in spite of traditional setting.

LUCELLE 68480 Ferrette
Le Petit Kohlberg (F) (89 40 85 30), cl. second half Feb. Well-known farm-inn near Swiss border is now small hotel, with pleasant restaurant (F–FF, cl. Fri).

MARLENHEIM 67520
Le Cerf (FFF–FFFF) 30 rue du Général-de-Gaulle (88 87 73 73, fax 88 87 68 08), cl. Tues, Wed. Former coaching inn near Strasbourg at beginning of Wine Road boasts one of France's finest restaurants, serving inventive cuisine in warm and elegant ambiance; family-run for generations; delightful bedrooms too (FF).

MASEVAUX 68290
Hostellerie alsacienne (F–FFF) rue Foch (89 82 45 25), cl. Sun for dinner, Mon, mid-June to mid-July. Emile Jung, chef-owner of *Le Crocodile* in Strasbourg, started his career in his family's little inn in Masevaux.

METZERAL 68380
Kastelberg (F) (89 77 62 25), cl. mid-Oct to mid-May. Well-known farm-inn at 1200m/4000ft.

MITTELHAUSEN 67170 Brumath
A l'Etoile (F) 12 rue de la Hey (88 51 28 44), cl. second half July. Charming country inn in Kochersberg with attractive rooms and popular restaurant (F–FF, cl. Sun for dinner, Mon).

MOERNACH 68480 Ferrette
Au Raisin (F–FF) 85 rue des Tilleuls (89 40 80 73), cl. Wed, first half Mar, first half Oct. Sundgau inn serving fried carp and other local dishes.

MOLSHEIM 67120
Centre (F) 1 rue Saint-Martin (88 38 54 50). Modest hotel in side street off central square; restaurant closed mid-Oct to May, but *winstub* in same courtyard run by same family.
Diana (FF) Pont de la Bruche (88 38 51 59). Comfortable modern hotel, with good restaurant (FF–FFFF) and *winstub* (F); indoor pool, sauna.
Restaurant
Auberge du Cheval blanc (F–FF) 5 pl. de l'Hôtel-de-Ville (88 38 16 87), cl. Tues for dinner, Wed. Friendly family-run inn, imaginative cuisine and a few modest rooms.

LE MONT SAINTE-ODILE 67530 Ottrott
Hostellerie du Mont Sainte-Odile (F) (88 95 80 65), cl. second half Nov. Over 100 rooms available in convent's guesthouse; reserve well in advance if you plan to stay longer than a night; restaurant.

MULHOUSE 68100
La Bourse (FF) 14 rue de la Bourse (89 56 18 44), cl. second half July. Traditional hotel in city centre, near station and Fabric-Printing Museum; quiet (double-glazed) modern rooms.
Du Parc (FFF) 26 rue de la Sinne (89 66 12 22, fax 89 66 42 44). Once grand residence of Schlumpf brothers whose vintage car collection is one of Mulhouse's main sights; now luxury hotel redecorated in art déco style; goodish restaurant (FF–FFF, cl. Sun for dinner).
Wir (F) 1 porte de Bâle (89 56 13 22), cl. July. Old-established city-centre hotel, with well-known restaurant (FF–FFFF, cl. Fri).
Restaurants
La Bûcherie (FF–FFFF) 2 av. Kennedy (89 42 12 51), cl. Sat for lunch, Sun, Feb. Lively bistrot in city centre; mainly regional cuisine.
Au Canon d'or (F–FF) 40 rue de Belfort, Mulhouse-Dornach (89 43 50 63). Popular with locals; good choice of *menus*; convenient when visiting museums on outskirts.
Gambrinus (F) 5 rue des Franciscains, cl. Sun for lunch. Inexpensive regional cuisine.
Au Quai de la Cloche (FF–FFFF) 5 quai de la Cloche (89 43 07 81), cl. Sun for dinner, Mon, first half Aug. A bit away from sights (by covered market), but worth booking for inventive cuisine mostly based on regional products.
Le Relais de la Tour (F–FFF) 3 blvd de L'Europe (89 45 12 14). Wonderful views and adequate cuisine in revolving restaurant atop modern Tour de l'Europe.
Winstub Henriette (F) 9 rue Henriette, cl. Sat for dinner, Sun. Lively *winstub* in city centre.
Zum Sauwadala (F) 13 rue de l'Arsenal, evenings only. Cosy *winstub* festooned with hams and salamis, open late.

8km/5 miles SW at **Froeningen**:
Auberge de Froeningen (FF) 2 route d'Illfurth (89 25 48 48), Sun for dinner, Mon, most of Jan, most of Aug. Small and charming family-run village inn; rooms decorated with painted furniture; excellent restaurant, offering modern variants on traditional recipes.
2km/1 mile E at **Riedisheim**:
Auberge de la Tonnelle (FFFF) 61 rue du Maréchal-Joffre (89 54 25 77), cl. Sat for lunch, Sun, part of Feb, second half Aug. Subtle cuisine in elegant modern dining room on outskirts.
8km/5 miles S at **Steinbrunn-le-Bas**:
Le Moulin du Kaegy (FFF–FFFF) (89 81 30 34), cl. Sun for dinner, Mon, Jan. Best restaurant in area, in beautifully converted water mill.

MUNSTER 68140
Au Val Saint-Grégoire (F–FF) 5 rue Saint-Grégoire (89 77 36 22), cl. Dec, Jan (but open Christmas and New Year). Late 19thC town house, with little garden, in town centre; plain but pleasant hotel; restaurant like private dining room (F–FF, cl. Wed, for lunch Thur) and *crêperie* (F); particularly helpful proprietors.
Restaurants
A l'Alsacienne (F–FF) 1 rue du Dôme (89 77 43 49), cl. Tues for dinner, Wed, Jan. Busy local restaurant.
6km/4 miles S on road to Le Petit Ballon at 1150m/3750ft:
Kahlenwasen (F) (89 77 32 49 or 89 77 64 26), cl. mid-Nov to mid-Apr. Well-known farm-inn.

MURBACH 68530 Buhl
Domaine Langmatt (FF–FFF) (89 76 21 12, fax 89 74 88 77). Peaceful setting in forest at 750m/2500ft, with indoor pool; self-catering chalets close to hotel; rich cuisine (FF–FFFF), helpful service.
Hostellerie Saint-Barnabé (FF) (89 76 92 15, fax 89 76 67 80). Elegant rooms, elaborate cuisine (FFF); paying tennis courts and miniature golf.

NEUF-BRISACH 68600
La Petite Palette (F–FFFF) 16 route de Bâle (89 72 73 50), cl. Mon, for dinner Tues. Mixture of classical and *nouvelle* cuisine; good range of *menus*.

NIEDERBRONN-LES-BAINS 67110
Cully (F) 35 rue de la République (88 09 01 42). Well-run traditional hotel with pleasant terrace; restaurant (F–FFF, cl. Sun for dinner, Mon).
Grand Hôtel (FF) 14 av. Foch (88 09 02 60). Charmingly old-fashioned, spacious and very comfortable rooms; restful atmosphere; good restaurant under same management in casino (**Le Parc**, FF–FFFF); tennis courts, garden.
Restaurants
Les Acacias (FF–FFFF) 35 rue des Acacias (88 09 00 47), cl. Fri for lunch, Sat, first half Feb, first half Sept. On edge of forest, with terrace beneath pine trees; classical cuisine with some *nouvelle* touches.
Bristol (F–FFFF) 4 pl. de l'Hôtel-de-Ville (88 09 61 44), cl. Wed, Jan. Good, mainly classical cuisine, excellent wine list, elegant dining room in old-established family-run hotel, with small but attractive bedrooms (F).

6km/4 miles S at **Gundershoffen**:
Chez Gérard (F–FFF) 13 rue de la Gare (88 72 91 20), cl. Tues for dinner, Wed, late July, early Aug. Spacious inn offering wide range of *menus* and types of cuisine, from classical to *nouvelle*/regional.

NIEDERSHASLACH 67280
La Pomme d'Or (F) 36 rue Principale (88 50 90 21), cl. Feb. Friendly family hotel in heart of little town; modest but pleasant rooms, good-value restaurant serving mostly regional cuisine (cl. Mon for dinner, Tues).

NIEDERMORSCHWIHR 68230 Turckheim
Caveau Morakopf (F–FF) 7 rue des Trois-Epis (89 27 05 10), evenings only, cl. Sun, second half Mar, late June, early July. Typical wine village *caveau* popular with people of Colmar for its warm ambiance, good regional dishes and local wines.

NIEDERSTEINBACH 67510 Lembach
Le Cheval blanc (F) 27 route de Bitche (88 09 25 31). Large, bustling inn with good restaurant and well-planned rooms, nicest with forest views.

OBENHEIM 67230 Benfeld
La Matelote (FF–FFF) 4 rue de Sand (88 98 31 53), cl. Mon, for dinner Tues. Good fish restaurant specializing in local freshwater species, in geranium-covered inn.

OBERNAI 67210
A la Cour d'Alsace (FFF) 3 rue De Gail (88 95 07 00). Beautiful, quiet rooms in delightful hotel recently converted from tithe buildings grouped round courtyard in centre of village; little garden beneath ramparts; pale restful colours; good restaurant (FF, cl. Sun, first half Aug).
A l'Etoile (F) 6 pl. de l'Etoile (88 95 50 57), cl. Jan, Feb, Mar. Modest apricot half-timbered building with busy pavement terrace; restaurant (FF, cl. Mon).
Grand Hôtel (FF) rue Dietrich (88 95 51 28), cl. most of Feb. Central, comfortable, traditional; classical cuisine (FF, cl. Sun for dinner, Mon).
La Maison du Vin (F) 1 rue de la Paille (88 95 55 80). Modest rooms above *winstub*.
Parc (FF–FFF) 169 rue du Général-Gourand (88 95 50 08, fax 88 95 37 29), cl. Dec. Family inn, expanded and modernized, with sauna and jacuzzi; well known for Sunday lunch buffet.
Restaurants
Crêperie Suzette (F) 13 rue Dietrich, cl. Mon. Handy for quick lunch.
La Cigogne (F) 49 rue du Général-Gourand, cl. Thur, for lunch Fri. Also a few rooms.
La Dîme (F) 5 rue des Pèlerins. Busy *winstub*.
Roland Fritz (F–FF) 24 pl. de la Mairie (88 95 55 69), cl. Wed. In *Diligence* hotel, adequate cuisine and busy terrace on central market square.
La Halle aux Blés (F–FF) pl. du Marché (88 95 57 09). Old cornmarket on main square, converted into cheerful brasserie with range of *menus*; touristy but fun.

OBERSTEINBACH 67510 Lembach
Anthon (F) 40 rue Principale (88 09 55 01). Peaceful inn with good restaurant (FF–FFF, cl. Tues, Wed), famous wine list and attractive rooms.

ORBEY 68370
Au Bois le Sire (F–FF) 20 rue Charles-de-Gaulle (89 71 25 25, fax 89 71 30 75), cl. Jan. Family-run hotel with motel annexe, pool, sauna; classical cuisine in comfortable dining room (F–FF, cl. Mon, for lunch Tues); very friendly.
At **Lac Blanc**:
Le Lac Blanc (F–FF) (89 71 21 97), cl. mid-Nov to mid-Dec. Hotel-restaurant (cl. Thur) with health club.
At **Lac Noir**:
Auberge du Lac Noir (F–FF) (89 71 21 80). Restaurant right beside lake; several *menus*.

OTTROTT 67530
Hostellerie des Châteaux (FF) 11 rue des Châteaux (88 95 81 54, fax 88 95 95 20), cl. mid-Jan to mid-Feb. Large and welcoming inn run by charming young couple; comfortable and quiet rooms, excellent, rather elegant restaurant (FF–FFFF, cl. Tues) serving inventive cuisine based on regional products, some of which can be bought in little shop in foyer.
Le Moulin (F–FF) 32 route de Klingenthal (88 95 87 33, fax 88 95 98 03), cl. mid-Dec to mid-Jan. Just outside village, in converted mill by river; *winstub* next door; pretty rooms, tennis court.
Restaurants
L'Ami Fritz (F–FFF) 8 rue des Châteaux (88 95 81 54), cl. Wed, Jan. *Winstub*-restaurant serving large portions of local specialities; rooms (F–FF) in annexe.
Beau Site (FF–FFFF) 1 rue du Général de-Gaulle (88 95 80 61), cl. Nov and first half Dec, mid-Feb to mid-Mar. Two restaurants in comfortable inn: *Le Spindler*, with warm Alsace décor, for mostly traditional cuisine, excellent wine list and game specialities, and *Les Quatre Saisons*, with stylish conservatory feel, for more modest regional dishes at any time of day; hotel cl. Nov–Mar.

LA PETITE-PIERRE 67290 Wingen-sur-Moder
Le Lion d'Or (F) 15 rue Principale (88 70 45 06), cl. Jan. Family hotel with quite large rooms, indoor pool, sauna; kitsch décor in dining room (F–FFFF, cl. Wed for dinner, Thur) cannot detract from lovely forest views.
Les Trois Roses (F–FF) 19 rue Principale (88 70 45 02), cl. Jan. Comfortable hotel with elegant little lounges (a rarity in France), attractive rooms, nicest with forest views, panoramic dining room (F–FFFF, cl. Sun for dinner, Mon); pool, tennis court.
Des Vosges (F–FF) 30 rue Principale (88 70 45 05), cl. part of Nov. Spacious rooms, some with private balcony overlooking garden and forest, antique furniture, good traditional restaurant (F–FFF, cl. Tues for dinner, Wed) plus *winstub*, sunny terrace and sauna.
3.5km/2 miles S:
Auberge d'Imsthal (F) (88 70 45 21, fax 88 70 40 26). Cosy inn, opened 1757 (and run by same family since 1858), beside meadow-surrounded mountain pool

popular with anglers; modern annexe with health complex; busy restaurant (F–FFF, cl. Mon for dinner, Tues, mid-Nov to mid-Dec) serving regional dishes; family atmosphere.

PFAFFENHOFFEN 67350
A l'Agneau (F–FFF) 3 rue de Saverne (88 07 72 38), cl. Sun for dinner, Mon, mid-July to mid-Aug). Friendly inn, just right for lunch before visiting folk art museum.

PFETTERHOUSE 68480 Ferrette
Au Raisin (F–FF) 2 rue de la Libération (89 25 61 02), closed Wed. Large Sundgau dining room near Swiss border, popular for fried carp and convivial atmosphere.

RIBEAUVILLÉ 68150
Le Clos Saint-Vincent (FF–FFF) route de Bergheim (89 73 67 65, fax 89 73 32 20), cl. mid-Nov to mid-Mar. Peaceful, attractive rooms overlooking vines, indoor pool, good classical cuisine (FFFF, cl. Tues, Wed).
Hostellerie des Seigneurs de Ribeaupierre (FF) 11 rue du Château (89 73 70 31), cl. Feb, first half Mar. 17thC building at far end of village turned into quiet hotel; attractive rooms with country-style antique furniture; no restaurant.
Des Vosges (F–FF) 2 Grand-Rue (89 73 61 39), cl. Jan, Mar. Well-modernized rooms and very good restaurant, marrying traditional and more inventive cuisine (FF–FFFF, cl. Mon, for lunch Tues).
Restaurants
Le Haut Ribeaupierre (FF–FFF), 1 route de Bergheim (89 73 62 64), cl. Tues for dinner, Wed, Feb, Mar. Apricot-coloured building on main street, popular for its *menus* (good game in season) and open-air terrace.
Au Lion (F–FF) 6 pl. de la Sinne. Modest *winstub*/restaurant in picturesque square; regional dishes.
Poste (F) Grand-Rue. Modest café-restaurant on high street, for quick meal.
Au Relais des Ménétriers (F–FFF) 10 av. du Général-de-Gaulle (89 73 64 52), cl. Sun for dinner, Mon, first half Feb, first half July, second half Nov. Cosy panelled dining room, mainly traditional cuisine.
Saint-Ulrich (F) 3 pl. de la République, cl. Wed, Sun (in winter), first half June, most of Nov. Tearoom at far end of village, handy for snack or light meal.
Aux Trois Châteaux (F) 2 route de Sainte-Marie-aux-Mines, cl. Feb. Modest meals for hungry walkers, at foot of path leading up to châteaux.
Zum Pfifferhüs (FF) 14 Grand-Rue (89 73 62 28), cl. Wed, Thur, mid-Feb to mid-Mar. Well-known *winstub* frequented by Alsace's top chefs for its genuine regional cuisine and good wine list; very attractive medieval building.

RIQUEWIHR 68340
Au Cerf (F) 57 rue du Général-de-Gaulle (89 47 92 18), cl. Jan, first half Feb. Small hotel on main street, with restaurant popular for its range of regional cuisine *menus* (cl. Mon for dinner, (in winter) Tues).
La Couronne (F) 5 rue de la Couronne (89 49 03 03), cl. mid-Nov to mid-Mar. Modest but very pleasant hotel in medieval building; no restaurant.

Le Sarment d'Or (F–FF) 4 rue du Cerf (89 47 92 85), cl. second half Dec, Jan. Charming, friendly little hotel in 17thC house; each room is called after a flower (Buttercup, Periwinkle etc.); cosy restaurant (F–FFF) serving local specialities.
Le Schoenenbourg (FF) rue du Schoenenbourg (89 49 01 11), cl. mid-Jan to mid-Feb. Comfortable hotel built recently at foot of vine-clad hill as annexe to well-known restaurant of same name.

Restaurants
A l'Arbalétrier (F–FF) 12 rue du Général-de-Gaulle (89 49 01 21), cl. Tues for dinner, Wed, Jan. Early 17thC building (by same architect as exuberant Maison des Têtes in Colmar); good regional dishes.
A l'Ecurie (F–FFF) 15 cour des Cigognes (89 47 92 48), cl. Sun for dinner, Mon, mid-Nov to mid-Mar. Restaurant and *winstub* (stays open Mon in summer) converted from 18thC stables in delightful cobbled courtyard, perfect for summer meals; very popular but not a tourist trap – good cuisine, beautifully served.
Au Petit Gourmet (FF–FFF) 5 rue de la 1ère-Armée (89 47 98 77), cl. Tues, second half Jan, Feb. Charming atmosphere in inn-like, low-ceilinged dining room in Renaissance house; blend of classical and more modern cuisine, range of *menus*.
Au Tire-Bouchon (F) 29 rue du Général-du-Gaulle, cl. Tues for dinner, Wed (but daily in high summer), mid-Nov to mid-Dec. Lively *winstub* in sky-blue half-timbered house with courtyard/garden for summer meals.
Auberge du Schoenenbourg (FF–FFFF, see hotel above), cl. Wed for dinner, Thur. Well-known for mainly classical cuisine, with some lighter touches.

ROSHEIM 67560
La Petite Auberge (F–FF) 41 rue du Général-du-Gaulle (88 50 40 60), cl. Wed, mid-Jan to mid-Feb. Pretty apricot half-timbered house close to church; a few tables outside, straightforward regional cuisine.

ROUFFACH 68250
Château d'Isenbourg (FFF) (89 49 63 53, fax 89 78 53 70), cl. Jan to mid-Mar. Delightfully elegant but not stuffy hotel in château rebuilt in 19thC; spacious rooms furnished with antiques, lawn for summer drinks, open-air pool, new sauna and health centre, tennis court, excellent cuisine (FFF–FFFF) in very pretty dining room with terrace overlooking vines; ideal for special short break, with helpful staff ready to plan excursions, organize riding or bike hire.

SARRE-UNION 67260
9km/5½ miles away at **Hinsingen**:
La Grange du Paysan (F–FF) 8 rue Principale (88 00 91 83), cl. Mon. Barn close to Lorraine border converted into modest restaurant serving straightforward country dishes.

SAINT-HIPPOLYTE 68590
Munsch/Aux Ducs de Lorraine (FF–FFF) 16 route du Vin (89 73 00 09), cl. second half Jan, Feb, first half Dec. Very comfortable and welcoming hotel; well-furnished rooms, some with balconies with views to Haut-Koenigsbourg Castle; good classical cuisine with some *nouvelle* dishes too, served in busy restaurant or in garden (FF–FFFF, cl. Mon); particularly friendly service.

SAVERNE 67700
Au Boeuf noir (F)22 Grand-Rue (88 91 10 53), cl. first half Mar, first half July. Modest hotel in attractive building; unpretentious restaurant (F–FF, cl. Sun for dinner, Tues).
Taverne Katz (FF) 80 Grand-Rue (88 71 16 56), cl. Tues for dinner, Wed for lunch. Delightful early 17thC building in pedestrian street houses one of Alsace's best *winstubs*; plenty of local colour, good regional cuisine.

SCHIRMECK 67130
Château de Barembach (F–FF) 5 rue du Maréchal-de-Lattre (88 97 97 50, fax 88 47 17 19), cl. first half Mar, second half Nov. Family home in 19thC turreted château converted into pleasant hotel with garden and quite good restaurant (FF–FFFF, cl. Thur) with river views; pool.

SÉLESTAT 67600
Auberge des Alliés (F–FF) 39 rue des Chevaliers (88 92 09 34), cl. second half Jan, most of Feb. Modest little restaurant near churches and library, for straightforward local cuisine.
Jean-Frédéric Edel (FFF–FFFF) 7 rue des Serruriers (88 92 86 55), cl. Tues for dinner, Wed and (in summer) Sun for dinner. Well-known restaurant in heart of Old Town; inventive cuisine, warm atmosphere.
La Vieille Tour (F–FFF) 8 rue de la Jauge, cl. Sun for dinner, Mon, first half July. Alsace ambiance with waitresses in regional costume, mixture of Alsace dishes and more modern cuisine; some good-value *menus*.

SESSENHEIM 67770
Auberge Au Boeuf (F–FF) 1 rue de l'Eglise (88 86 97 14), cl. Mon, Tues. Spacious inn furnished in traditional style with series of cosy dining rooms; run for several generations by same family, whose little Goethe Museum you can visit; good-value regional cuisine.

STRASBOURG 67000
La Cathédrale (FF) 12 pl. de la Cathédrale (88 22 12 12, fax 88 23 51 88). Being woken by cathedral bells and shutters going up on Maison Kammerzell seems small price to pay for bird's-eye view of spire and incomparable façade of former, lively musicians on latter; some rooms on two levels, with old beams but comfortable modern fittings; friendly service, stylish bar, only drawback a steep entrance staircase (could cause problems for elderly or unfit people).
Le Dragon (FF) 2 rue de l'Ecarlate (88 35 79 80, fax 88 25 78 95). Chic and stylish hotel with tiny garden, close to La Petite France (views of cathedral from some top-floor rooms); converted from 17thC townhouse of Margraves of Baden, later annexe of Dragen family's residence (hence name) where Louis XIV stayed in 1681. You will learn all this, along with wealth of practical information, from particularly helpful proprietor.
Hannong (FF) 15 rue du 22-novembre (88 32 16 22, fax 88 22 63 87), cl. Christmas period. Well-run hotel in busy street quite near station, decorated with faïence ware produced in 18thC by famous Hannong family's works on same site. Traditional rooms, small art gallery and popular *Wyn'Bar* for light meals.
Maison Kammerzell/Hôtel Baumann (FF) 16 pl. de la Cathédrale (88 32 13 02,

fax 88 23 03 92). Nine sleek modern rooms opened in 1989 in oldest and loveliest house in Strasbourg, right beside cathedral (see Restaurants below); tiny terrace for summer breakfasts.

Monopole Métropole (FF) 16 rue Kuhn (88 32 13 02, fax 88 32 82 55), cl. Christmas and New Year period. Large traditional hotel near station; spacious rooms, some furnished in Alsace style, with panelling and stained glass, others modern; large breakfast room feels like country inn.

Le Régent Contades (FFF) 8 av. de la Liberté (88 36 26 26, fax 88 37 13 70), cl. Christmas and New Year period. Elegant 19thC townhouse beside Ill, in unfrenetic area in walking distance of cathedral; attractive rooms, enchanting breakfast room with moulded cornice and tall windows, particularly helpful staff.

Des Rohan (FF) 17-19 rue du Maroquin (88 32 85 11, fax 88 75 65 37). Quiet and attractive rooms a few steps from cathedral and Château des Rohan; old-established, well run.

Suisse (FF) 2-4 rue de la Rape (88 35 22 11), cl. mid-Dec to mid-Jan. Friendly family hotel next to Château des Rohan, with busy restaurant, *L'Horloge Astronomique*.

Terminus-Gruber (FF) 10 pl. de la Gare (88 22 87 00). Large traditional hotel conveniently opposite station; comfortable rooms, restaurant and brasserie.

Vendôme (F) 9 pl. de la Gare (88 32 45 23). Modest but well-run; small but adequate rooms; opposite station.

Villa d'Est (FF) 12 rue Jacques-Kablé (88 36 69 02, fax 88 37 13 71), cl. Christmas and New Year period. A bit away from centre but convenient for motorists (parking easy and just by motorway exit); friendly service and comfortable rooms, some in Alsace style, others modern; restaurant.

Restaurants

L'Alsace à table (F-FF) 8 rue des Francs-Bourgeois (88 32 50 62). Appropriately salmon-pink décor for busy fish and shellfish restaurant a short walk from cathedral and La Petite France; open late every day, with some non-fish regional specialities too.

A l'Ancienne Douane (F-FF) 6 rue de la Douane (88 32 42 19, fax 88 22 45 64), cl. most of Jan. One of few brasseries left in Strasbourg and good for getting a feel of Alsace: bustling, noisy and fun, with cheerfully professional waiters, *kougelhopf* moulds adorning walls, rustic chairs with heart-shaped cut outs, Ribeauvillé Paisley tablecloths and painted ceiling; mainly regional food in large portions for serious eaters; terrace overlooking Ill.

L'Arsenal (FF) 11 rue de l'Abreuvoir (88 35 03 69), cl. Sat lunch, Sun, part of Aug. Lively little restaurant in Krutenau district, still *the* place to go for media and showbiz folk and for fashionable politicians, Euro- and otherwise; short menu of local dishes, carefully cooked, traditional décor enlivened with drawings (some erotic) by Tomi Ungerer.

Le Bec doré (F-FF) 8 quai des Pêcheurs (88 35 39 57), cl. Mon, Tues, Aug. Delightful little place specializing, as name ('golden beak') suggests, in poultry and game birds; soothing atmosphere, elegant décor, remarkable lunch *menu*.

Au Boeuf mode (FF) 2 pl. Saint-Thomas (88 32 39 03), cl. Sun. The name is again a pointer here – speciality is top-quality beef, though you can also order fish. Little garden behind, on edge of La Petite France.

Le Buerehiesel (FFFF) 4 parc de l'Orangerie (88 61 62 24), cl. Tues for dinner, Wed, most of Feb, most of Aug. One of Strasbourg's top two restaurants – so one of best in France – with bonus of enchanting setting in lovely Orangerie Gardens, in half-timbered farmhouse from nearby Molsheim lovingly reconstructed; cosy little rooms now complemented by elegant conservatory-style dining room; totally delicious, inventive variants on regional dishes; good-value weekday lunch and weekend dinner *menus*.

La Cambuse (FF) 1 rue des Dentelles (88 22 10 22), cl. Sun, Mon, Aug. Fish restaurant in heart of La Petite France, decked out like boat with mahogany tables, brass lamps, sea-blue mats and curtains, porthole-type windows; same attention to detail in food as in décor, and some interesting spicy touches (Vietnamese chef successfully wraps French fish in banana leaves or marries ginger with more traditional flavours).

Le Crocodile (FFFF) 10 rue de l'Outre (88 32 13 02, fax 88 75 72 01), cl. Sun, Mon, most of July, Christmas and New Year period. Perfection near the cathedral – Strasbourg's other top restaurant, presided over by chef-owner whose brilliant skills have achieved a blissfully happy marriage between the best that Alsace has to offer and classical cuisine *à la française*; sober, elegant décor, deft but unfussy service.

Au Gourmet sans chiqué (FFF–FFFF) 15 rue Sainte-Barbe (88 32 04 09), cl. Sun, for lunch Mon, part of Jan. Discreet little restaurant not far from cathedral or La Petite France. Restful apricot and black décor and furnishings, elegant ambiance combined with smiling service. *Nouvelle*-type cuisine, with some regional touches; good-value *menu*.

Chez Julien (FF–FFFF) 22 quai des Bateliers (88 36 01 54), cl. Sat for lunch, Sun, part of Feb, most of Aug. Away from tourist hordes, yet just the other side of the Ill from Palais des Rohan and beside lively rue Sainte-Madeleine; delicious cuisine, often with local flavour, pretty art nouveau décor.

Maison Kammerzell (FF–FFFF) 16 pl. de la Cathédrale (88 32 42 14, fax 88 23 03 92). Superb 15thC and 16thC house beside cathedral (see box, p. 000) rather surprisingly houses elegant yet lively restaurant on several floors, specializing in regional cuisine; friendly service, unbeatable view of cathedral from first floor.

Le Maison des Tanneurs (FFF–FFFF) 42 rue du Bain-aux-Plantes (88 32 79 70), cl. Sun, Mon. Archetypal Alsace half-timbered building, awash with geraniums, built over Ill in heart of La Petite France; popular for professional and friendly service, good regional cuisine (superb *foie gras*) and perfect setting.

Au Romain (F–FFF) 6 pl. du Vieux-Marché-aux-Grains (88 32 08 54), cl. Sun for dinner, Mon. Cheerful brasserie in city centre; regular daily specials, busy atmosphere, inlaid panels with Alsace scenes; half-timbered building on one side, sunburst windows on other to match thirties-style décor with globe lamps.

Zimmer-Sengel (FF–FFF) 8 rue du Temple-Neuf (88 32 35 01), cl. Sat for lunch, Sun, most of Aug. Elegant restaurant near cathedral; generally reliable cuisine, part-classical, part-*nouvelle*.

Some suggestions for a relaxed lunch or dinner when you are in the area:
Au Canon (F–FF) pl. du Corbeau, cl. Mon for dinner, Tues. Convenient for Musée alsacien and near Palais des Rohan and La Petite France; tiny sunny ter-

race, spacious dining room with glass roof; straightforward cuisine.
Les Halles du Pont (F) 14 rue des Moulins, cl. Sat for lunch. Friendly restaurant in La Petite France with famous help-yourself *hors-d'oeuvre* selection.
D'r Munsterspatz (F) rue du Maroquin. Right opposite cathedral, specializing in Alsace recipes; vegetarian dishes too.
Le Petit Bois Vert (F) 3 quai de la Bruche. Food's nothing special but attractive setting beside Ill in La Petite France for unpretentious meal, especially in summer, when you can eat outside beneath a spreading tree.
La Petite Faim (F) 13 pl. Saint-Etienne. Tiny place in attractive square; classical music and Lautrec posters make a change from *gemütlich* atmosphere of *winstubs*.
Le Renard Prêchant (F–FF) 34 rue de Zürich, cl. Sun. A restaurant since 1760, in former chapel in Krutenau district; generous portions; country inn décor.
Au Rocher du Sapin (F) 6 rue du Noyer, cl. Sun, for dinner Mon. Strasbourg institution near place Kléber: huge dining room, low prices and unpretentious home-style cooking – a place for seeing ordinary Strasbourgeois *à table*.
Le Saladier (F) 12 rue des Ecrivains, cl. Sun. Lacy café curtains and mainly vegetarian salads, in quiet street behind cathedral.

Tearooms
Christian (F) 10 rue Mercière, cl. Sun. First-floor tearoom in old house a few paces from cathedral.
Patachou 9 pl. du Marché-aux-Cochon-de-Lait, cl. Mon. Near cathedral, with large sunny terrace overlooking picturesque square.
Suzel (F) Corner rue du Moulin and rue du Bain-aux-Plantes, cl. Mon, also Sun in winter. Enchanting painted façade in La Petite France, doll's-house interior with lacy curtains, walls crammed with pictures and samplers, tasty hot lunch dishes as well as salads and vegetable flans, good range of teas and cakes.
Winter (F) 25 rue du 22-novembre, cl. Sun. Attractive façade picks out this busy *pâtisserie* in shopping street near place Kléber.

Winstubs
L'Ami Schutz (FF) 1 rue des Ponts-Couverts (88 32 76 98, fax 88 60 30 25), cl. Sun for dinner, Mon. More *bierstub* than *winstub*, with 'beer menu' (beer, soup, *schiffala rôti à la bière*, kidneys braised in beer), and unusual local specialities (snail soup and snail *choucroute*); old panelling, stained glass and plenty of ambiance; ideal spot by Ponts Couverts; even non-smoking dining room.
D'Choucrouterie 20 rue Saint-Louis (88 36 52 87), evenings only, cl. Sun, Mon, part of Aug. Lively place with tiny theatre where you can hear local singers' regional repertoire before or after tucking into *choucroute*; other side of Ill from Eglise Saint-Thomas.
Au Clou (FF) 3 rue du Chaudron (88 32 11 67), evenings only, cl. Sun. Picturesque building in heart of Old Town close to cathedral; lively atmosphere (popular with theatre crowd), good *winstub* dishes – even air-conditioning.
La Coccinelle (F) 22 rue Ste-Madeleine (88 36 19 27), cl. Sat for lunch. Friendly service and local dishes in little street opposite Palais des Rohan lined with fashion boutiques.
Le Pigeon (F) 23 rue des Tonneliers (88 32 31 20), cl. Mon, for dinner Tues. Early 16thC building covered with carvings near Musée historique; good regional menu.

Au Pont Corbeau (F) 21 quai Saint-Nicolas (88 35 60 68), cl. Sat, for lunch Sun. Traditional décor of coffered ceiling and panelling, bottle-glass windows, red-and-white-checked tablecloths, flowery china; for trying some tasty local dishes before or after visiting the Musée alsacien.
Le Saint Sépulcre (F) 15 rue des Orfèvres (88 32 39 97), cl. Sun, Mon, mid-July to mid-Aug. Family-run *winstub* in picturesque street near cathedral; also known by dialect name *Hailich Graab*.
Zum Strissel (F) 5 pl. de la Grande-Boucherie (88 32 14 73), cl. Sun, Mon, most of July. Centuries of atmosphere – built in 1385, then rebuilt after fire in 1565 – and unpretentious regional cuisine, near cathedral.
Le Tire-Bouchon (F) 5 rue des Tailleurs-de-Pierre (88 32 47 86), cl. Sat, for lunch Mon, mid-July to mid-Aug. Reliable cuisine and authentic ambiance, again near cathedral.
Chez Yvonne (F–FF) 10 rue du Sanglier (88 32 84 15), cl. Sun for dinner, Mon, mid-July to mid-Aug. Technically known as *'s'Burjerstuewel'*, but *patronne* Yvonne is famous for her warm welcome in this most attractive of *winstubs*, with tall vases of fresh flowers adorning cosy décor of wooden panelling, carved chairbacks, pretty tablecloths and china in regional style; mixture of celebrities and ordinary locals – and excellent Alsace specialities.

THANNENKIRCH   68590 Saint-Hippolyte
La Meunière (F) 38 rue Sainte-Anne (89 73 10 47), cl. Dec. to mid-Mar. Pleasant small hotel in village famous for its cherry trees; pretty rooms, regional cuisine (F–FF, cl. Wed), terrace with views of Haut-Koenigsbourg Castle.

LES TROIS-EPIS   68410
Grand Hôtel (FF–FFF) pl. de l'Eglise (89 49 80 65). Luxury hotel with traditional painted furniture, lovely views from private balconies, indoor pool, sauna; two restaurants: *Le Hohlandsbourg* (FFFF) offering grand cuisine and even grander views; and *L'Auberge* (F–FF), *winstub* with good regional specialities.
Marchal (F–FF) (89 49 81 61), cl. mid-Dec. to mid-Jan. Lower prices and more modest, but still comfortable, and same superb views; restaurant (FF–FFF).

TURCKHEIM   68230
Le Deux Clefs (F–FF) 3 rue du Conseil (89 27 06 01), cl. Jan. A bit shabby, but attractive 17thC building on main square; some rooms in modern annexe; restaurant (FF, cl. Mon).
Caveau Le Chemin de Ronde (F) porte de Munster, evenings only (except Sun), cl. Tues, mid-Dec to mid-Jan. Picturesque *winstub* built into old walls.
Berceau du Vigneron (F) 10 pl. Turenne (89 27 23 55), cl. Nov to Mar. Modest rooms in charming old building; *caveau* but no restaurant.
A l'Homme sauvage (FF–FFF) 19 Grand-Rue (89 27 32 11), cl. mid-Dec to mid-Jan. Attractive restaurant in 18thC house on narrow high street; good, mainly fish cuisine.

VILLÉ   67220
A la Bonne Franquette (F) 6 pl. du Marché (88 57 14 25), cl. Feb. Modest, pretty family hotel in mountain village; regional dishes (F–FF, cl. Wed for dinner, Thur).

WANGENBOURG-ENGENTHAL 67710
Des Vosges (F) 5 rue de Steigenbach (88 87 34 11). Peaceful little family hotel, with garden and restaurant (F–FF, cl. Tues for dinner, Wed).

LA WANTZENAU 67610
Le Moulin (F–FF) 27 route de Strasbourg (88 96 27 83, fax 88 96 68 32). Charming rooms in converted mill, with long-standing restaurant opposite of same name, separate but run by same family (FF–FFF, cl. Wed, Sun for dinner).
Relais de la Poste (F–FF) 21 rue du Général-du-Gaulle (tel 88 96 20 64, fax 88 96 36 84), cl. Feb. Another charming hotel in pretty village only 12km/7½ miles from Strasbourg; comfortable rooms, well modernized, with good restaurant (FF–FFFF, cl. Sun for dinner, Mon) serving judicious mixture of classical and more modern cuisine.

WASSELONNE 67310
Auberge du Marché (F–FF) 17 pl. du Marché, cl. Wed. Conveniently central for unpretentious meal.
Au Saumon (F–FF) 69 rue du Général-de-Gaulle, cl. Sun for dinner, Mon, most of Feb. Family-run restaurant in village high street; also has rooms.

WESTHALTEN 68250 Rouffach
Auberge du Cheval blanc (FF–FFFF) 20 rue de Rouffach (89 47 01 16), cl. Sun for dinner, Mon, Jan. Delicious and reliable cuisine and home-produced wines served in spacious dining room; charming service; also a few comfortable rooms.

WISSEMBOURG 67160
Hostellerie du Cygne (F) 3 rue du Sel (88 94 00 16), cl. Feb, first half July. Delightful 16thC half-timbered building set back from street beside town hall, with some rooms in separate house 'At the Sign of the Falcon' with grey-blue shutters painted with falcons; good restaurant (FF–FFF, cl. Wed, for lunch Thur).
Restaurant
L'Ange (FF–FFF) 2 rue de la République (88 94 12 11), cl. Sun for dinner, Mon, most of June. Medieval inn offering delicious local fish and game; also a few rooms (F).

ZELLENBERG 68340 Riquewihr
Au Riesling (F) 93 route du Vin (89 47 85 85), cl. Jan. Lovely views over vines from comfortable modern rooms; adequate restaurant (FF–FFF, cl. Sun for dinner, (except in high summer) Mon).
Au Schlossberg (F) 59 rue de la Fontaine (89 47 93 85). Small hotel with *caveau*-restaurant (FF–FFF, cl. Wed).

Index

Albé 146
Alfeld, Lac d' 139
Alsace bossue, L' 8, 94, 99
Altkirch 13, 151, 156, 160, 161
Ammerschwihr 122
Andlau 37, 128, 133
Arp, Jean/Hans 15, 77, 85, 168
Arzwiller 98
Avolsheim 129

Baden-Baden 94, 106, 164–7, 170
Baldung, Hans ('Grien') 15, 171
Ballersdorf 157
Bartholdi, Frédéric-Auguste 15, 117, 118
Barr, 24, 71, 128, 133
Basel 81, 126, 151, 157, 160, 164, 167–70
Benfeld 24
Bennwihr 124
Betschdorf 13, 100, 106
Bismarck, Prince Otto von 46, 46–7
Bischwiller 24
Blaesheim 88
Bonhomme, Le 143, 145, 148
Bouxwiller 96–7, 106
Brant, Sebastian 15, 41, 78, 81, 167
Breisach-am-Rhein 120, 121, 170
Bruche, Vallée de la 138, 146
Brumath 86, 89
Buhl 141

Cernay 48, 113, 138
Champ du Feu 146
Charlemagne 35, 36, 50, 97, 141, 142, 150
Charles the Bald 36, 50
Charles the Bold 40, 96, 175
Châtenois 128
Cleebourg 104, 132
Colmar 6, 8, 9, 12, 13, 15, 22, 24, 27, 29, 30, 38, 44, 49, 71, 112, 116–21, 124, 133, 145; *14, 39, 111, 119*
Cronenbourg 86

Dambach-la-Ville 24, 128, 133

Dannemarie 157, 160
Decapolis 38, 126, 151
Doller Valley 113, 139
Dreyfus, Alfred 153
Dürer, Albrecht 15, 81, 120, 167
Durmenach 24

Ebersmunster 88, 89
Eco-Museum 12, 13, 26, 150, 156, 158; *159*
Eguisheim 110, 113, 116, 133; *3, 35, 115*
Erasmus, Desiderius 40, 72, 126, 167, 169, 170, 171
Erstein 88, 89
Erwin von Steinbach 73, 74, 101, 146, 166
Eschau 88, 89–90

Falkenstein Castle 105, 107
Feldbach 151, 160, 161
Ferrette 150–1, 160, 161
Fischboedle, Lac de 143
Fleckenstein Castle 93, 105
Florival 113, 141
Four à Chaux 49, 93, 105, 107
Frankenbourg Castle 145
Freibourg-im-Breisgau 164, 170–2
Fréland 143, 148
Freppel, Charles-Emile 46, 127, 129
Fried Carp Roads 8, 56, 150, 151

Geiler, Johann ('of Kaysersberg') 41, 77, 81, 126
Geisberg 93, 104, 109
Geispolsheim 24, 88, 90
Gérardmer 143, 164, 172–3
Géroldseck Castle 96
Girsberg Castle 125
Goethe, Johann Wolfgang von 10, 44, 76, 100, 101
Gommersdorf 157
Gottfried von Strassburg 15, 16, 37
Gougenheim 86
Grand Ballon, Le 138, 141

Index

Graufthal 99
Grentzingen 160
Guebwiller 37, 113, 133–4, 142; Valley 141
Gunsbach 143, 144, 148
Gutenberg, Johann 40, 42, 81; *82*

Hachimette 143
Haguenau 13, 24, 37, 38, 89, 99, 106; Forêt de 8, 46
'Hansi' 9, 15, 26, 45, 47
Harth, Forest 9, 156
Hartmannswillerkopf 141
Haut-Andlau Castle 128
Haut-Barr Castle 96
Haut-Koenigsbourg Castle 47, 125, 134, 136, 145
Haut-Ribeaupierre Castle 125
Hoerdt 86
Hohlandsbourg Castle 116
Hohneck, Le 142, 143
Hohrodberg 143
Hohwald, Le 146
Hunawihr 24, 26, 124, 134; *frontispiece*
Huningue 157, 161
Hunspach 104, 107
Husseren-les-Châteaux 113

Illkirch-Graffenstaden 87
Imsthal 99
Ingwiller 97

Joffre, Joseph 48; Route 138, 139, 147

Kaiser, The (Wilhelm II) 46, 47, 48, 125, 127
Kaysersberg 24, 37, 38, 41, 122, 134, 143, 144; *6, 43, 123*
Kientzheim 71, 122–4, 134
Kintzheim 26, 111, 125, 134
Kleber, Jean-Baptiste 15, 44, 81; *14*
Kochersberg, The 8, 12–13, 86–7, 89, 94, 106

Lac Blanc 143
Lac Noir 143
Lac Vert 143; *147*
Landskron Castle 151, 157, 161
Lapoutroie 143, 148
Lautenbach 37, 141
Lembach 105, 107
Leo IX, Pope 36, 116, 130, 159
Leszcynski, Stanislas 102, 104; *175*
Lichtenberg Castle 97, 107
Lièpvre 145
Linge, Le 48, 143, 149; *142*
Lothaire 36
Louis XIV 6, 41, 43, 46, 102, 121, 170

Louis the German 36, 50
Lucelle 157
Luther, Martin 16, 40, 41
Lutter 157, 158
Lutzelhardt Castle 105, 107

Maginot Line 48, 49, 93, 100, 105, 112, 121, 134
Marckolsheim 49, 112, 121, 134
Mariastein 157
Markstein, Le 141, 148
Marlenheim 24, 87, 89, 90, 110, 132
Marmoutier 35–6, 37, 87, 96, 106
Masevaux 24, 138, 139, 148
Meisenthal 94, 97
Merkwiller-Pechelbronn 104, 107
Metz 164, 173–4
Mittlewihr 124
Molsheim 24, 30, 129, 132, 135
Mont Sainte-Odile 34, 129, 135
Moosbronn 46, 104
Mooslargue 157, 160
Morimont Castle *163*
Mossig Valley 87, 138
Mountain Road 6–8, 17–18, 48, 113, 121, 122, 138, 140–5, 147, 172
Muhlbach 143, 148
Mulhouse 2, 8, 29, 30, 38, 41, 44, 46, 48, 48–9, 49, 52, 150, 151–6, 160, 161–2
Munster 24, 38, 143, 148; Valley 8, 11, 32, 57, 140, 142–3, 144, 147
Murbach 37, 113, 141–2, 148, 157
Mutzig 132, 134

Nancy 102, 164, 174–6
Neuf-Brisach 24, 46, 112, 121, 135
Neuwiller-lès-Saverne 96
Nideck 146
Niederbronn-les-Bains 34, 44, 92, 93, 104–5, 106, 107
Niederhaslach 146, 148–9
Niedermorschwihr 122; *cover, 123*
Northern Vosges 8, 14, 22, 32, 52, 57, 89, 92–109, 138, 147, 150; *91*; Nature Park 8, 10, 32, 92, 93, 97
Nouveau Windstein Castle 105

Oberhaslach 24, 146
Oberhausbergen 86
Oberlin, Jean-Frédéric 15, 146
Obernai 38, 88, 110, 127, 128–9, 130, 135
Obersteigen 146
Obersteinbach 93, 105, 107
Odile, St 35, 37, 113, 116, 128, 130, 139
Offwiller 13, 93, 105, 107–8
Oltingue 13, 30, 151, 157, 162
Orbey 14, 24, 143–5, 149; Val d' 145, 147

Index

Ortenbourg Castle 145
Osenbach 24
Osthouse 88
Ottmarsheim 156, 163
Ottrott 129
Outre-Forêt, L' 8, 89, 99–100

Pairis 143, 145
Petit-Arnsberg Castle 105, 107
Petite-Pierre, La 13, 92, 93, 97–9, 106, 108
Petit Géroldseck Castle 96
Pfaffenhoffen 13, 93, 97, 108
Pfetterhouse 160
Pflixbourg Castle 116

Quatzenheim 86

Raedersdorf 26, 157
Ramstein Castle 145
Rastatt 94, 166
Rhenanus, Beatus 16, 40, 126, 167
Ribeauvillé 13, 24, 60, 70, 125, 127, 135
Ried, The 8, 56, 89
Riquewihr 24, 70, 110, 124, 125, 136
Rixheim 154, 163
Rosheim 24, 37, 38, 129, 136
Rothau 100, 146
Rouffach 44, 113, 136
Rouget de Lisle, Claude Joseph 44, 45
Route des Crêtes see Mountain Road
Route du Fromage 140
Route du Tabac 86, 87
Route du Vin see Wine Road

Sainte-Marie-aux-Mines 48, 138, 145, 149
Saint-Hippolyte 125, 136
Saint-Jean-Saverne 96
Saint-Louis-lès-Bitche 97
Saint-Ulrich Castle 125
Sarre-Union 94, 99, 108
Saverne 6, 40, 44, 47, 87, 89, 93–4, 94–6, 106, 108, 138; Forêt de 96, 146
Scherwiller 128
Schiessrothried, Lac de 143
Schirmeck 146
Schnepfenried 142
Schoenenbourg 49, 100
Schongauer, Martin 15, 30, 40, 118, 120, 121, 141, 170; *39*
Schweitzer, Albert 48, 80, 122, 143, 144
Schwendi, Lazarus von 116, 124
Seebach 24
Sélestat 24, 37, 38, 40, 88, 112, 125–6, 128, 136
Sessenheim 10, 44, 100, 101, 106, 109
Sewen, Lac de 139

Sigolsheim 124
Simserhof 49
Sondernach 143
Soucht 13, 94
Soufflenheim 13, 100, 106, 109
Steinbrunn-le-Bas 156
Strasbourg 4, 8, 10, 13, 14, 15, 20, 22, 24, 25, 26, 27, 29, 30, 35, 37, 38, 40, 41, 42, 43, 44, 45, 46, 47, 50, 72–85, 86, 87, 88, 89, 101, 102, 104, 144, 145, 146, 166, 171; *47, 50, 75, 79, 82, 83*
Struthof, Le 49, 138, 146, 149
Sundgau, The 8, 22–3, 33, 35, 52, 56, 150–1, 156–7, 160–3

Thann 24, 48, 110, 112–13, 136, 138; *114*
Thur Valley 139
Trois-Epis, Les 122, 143
Truchtersheim 87, 90
Turckheim 38, 43, 116, 121–2, 137, 143

Ungerer, Tomi 15, 82
Ungersheim 13, 24, 158, 163

Vauban, Sébastien le Prestre de 46, 97, 112, 121, 157, 170
Vieil-Armand 48, 140–1
Vieux-Thann 112
Vieux Windstein Castle 105
Villé 146, 149; Val de 138, 145–6

Waldersbach 146, 149
Wangen 87
Wangenbourg Castle 146
Wangenbourg-Engenthal 87, 138, 146, 149
Wantzenau, La 86
Wasenbourg Castle 105
Wasigenstein Castle 105, 107
Wasselonne 24, 87, 89, 90
Weiss Valley 143
Westhoffen 87
Weyersheim 86
Willgottheim 86
Wineck Castle 105
Wine Road 2, 4, 8, 13, 17, 22, 23, 24, 27, 30, 49, 70, 71, 87, 88, 89, 104, 110–37, 138, 143, 147, 150
Wingen-sur-Moder 97
Wingersheim 86
Winkel 157
Wissembourg 24, 38, 92–3, 102, 104, 106, 109, 132; *95, 103*
Woerth 93, 104, 109

Zellenberg 110, 124–5